T0269689

Whitework Embroidery

Designs and Accessories with a Modern Twist

SEIKO NAKANO

SCHIFFER
CRAFT
4880 Lower Valley Road • Atglen, PA 19310

Contents

My first encounter with whitework was at a bookstore. I can still clearly remember, as I paged through a book, the shock of being moved by the beauty of the white drawn threadwork on white cloth.

The theme of this book is Telling a story.

Why? Well, there are no colorful embellishments on whitework. That being said, it stimulates your imagination and evokes new embroidery worlds; whitework tells new stories. I hope you enjoy embroidering in this way while imagining your main character, and even its background, telling their parts, and that you enjoy becoming absorbed in the story conveyed by the design.

My hope is that this book will move someone as much as I was moved when encountering that whitework book so long ago.

May it inspire wonderful stories in each and every one of you.

Seiko Nakano

Preface

Schwalm Embroidery

Schwalm embroidery is a whitework technique that originated in the Schwalmstadt region of Germany. Using drawn and pulled threadwork, Schwalm embroidery makes various designs by creating gaps in the underlying medium. It is necessary to outline your chosen patterns with coral stitches and chain stitches prior to embroidering because the threads of your base fabric are pulled apart. You can embroider any design you wish; however, patterns that cover large areas highlight Schwalm's beauty. Some stitches create more appealing looks than others depending on the type of embroidery pattern. So, be sure to give different stitches a try.

a
b
c
d
e
f

Stitches 1

a Rose Stitch
b Weave Stitch (filling stitch)
c Flower Garden Stitch
d Mosquito Stitch
e Double Wrapping Stitch
f Double Small-Column Stitch

page 70

g
i
h
j
k
l

Stitches 2

g Three-Sided Stitch
h Star Rose Stitch
i Wrapping Stitch
j Waffle Stitch
k Basic Stitch (to tie weft/warp)
l Four-Sided Stitch

page 71

1. / design page 72

Filling stitches on the poodle body and cat body create their coats and markings. Loosely stitched French knots produce the raised, fluffy poodle coat.

2. / design page 74

Gorgeous filling stitches, which create a large-gapped fabric grid, highlight the clothes of a circus clown. Use gold or silver floss for a small number of elements in the pattern to produce an elegant look.

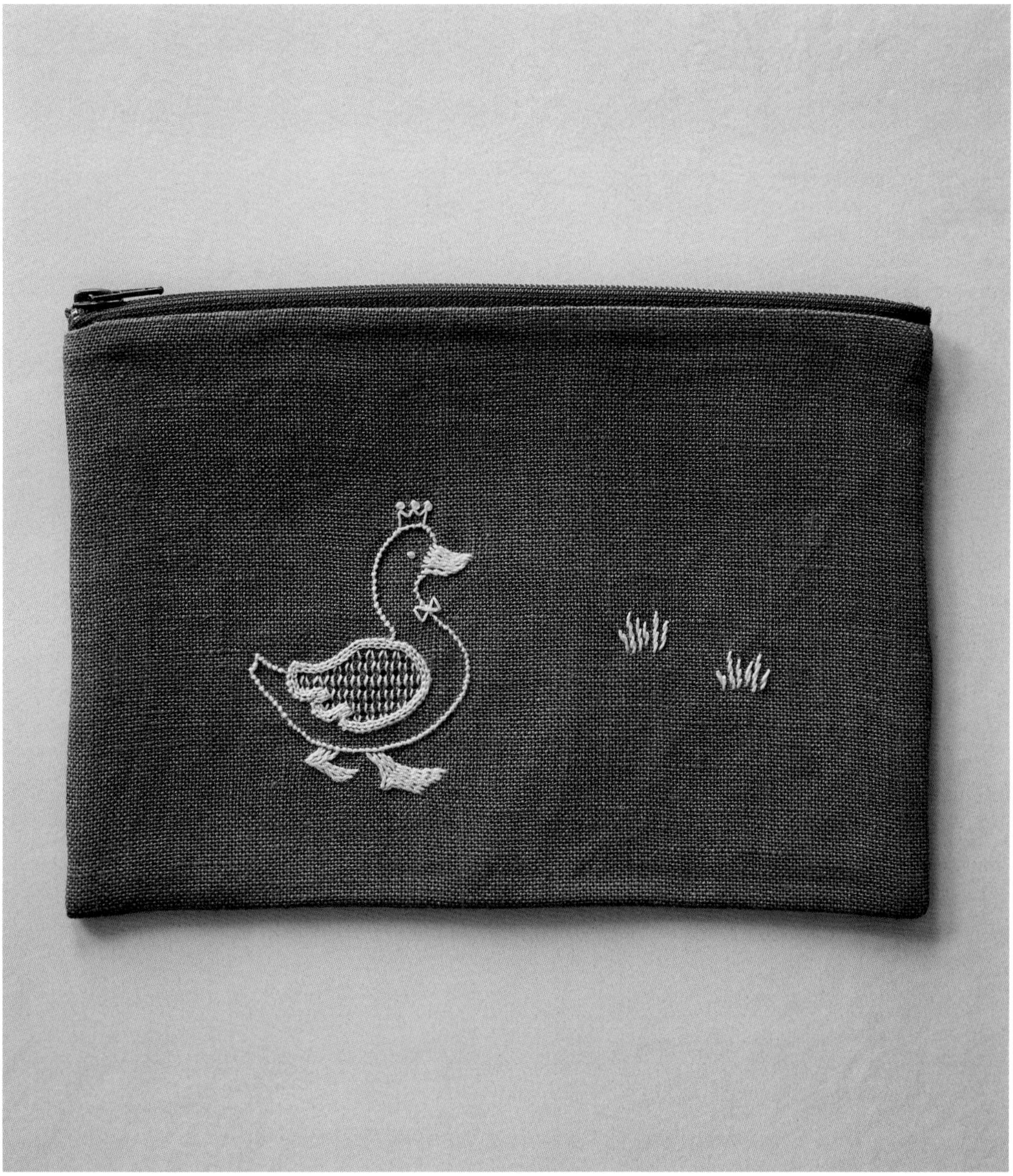

You can embroider the duck motif from page 10 on a zippered pouch. Using white floss on white fabric is a basic principle of whitework, but using chic, colored fabric as a background can make a great project too.

4. / How To page 76

3. / design page 73 Zippered Duck Pouch

The filling stitch pattern on the donkey is my original. It is also used on the duck and sheep. As you can see, depending on the pattern, my original stitch pattern may be used to fill either the entire motif (as with the donkey) or just a portion.

The same embroidery design can look quite different when shape and size are altered. The stitch pattern on the bird is my original. It is derived from a lazy daisy stitch.

Flowers and Bird

6. / How To pages 78, 79

The embroidery work on page 12 is mounted on a panel, as you see here. Wrapping an embroidery work around a wooden frame can easily turn any piece into beautiful wall decor. Using a thick wooden frame works best.

For the first step, use coral stitch and chain stitch to outline the pattern. For the second step, we need to snip threads at certain intervals within the outline and pull them to the edge of the outline, where they will be cut off (the term used for this is *withdrawing*). Then, begin stitching. Use a sharp-pointed needle to outline the pattern and a blunt-pointed needle to unweave snipped threads. Stitch diagrams are shown on pages 66–67.

1. Outline Pattern

1

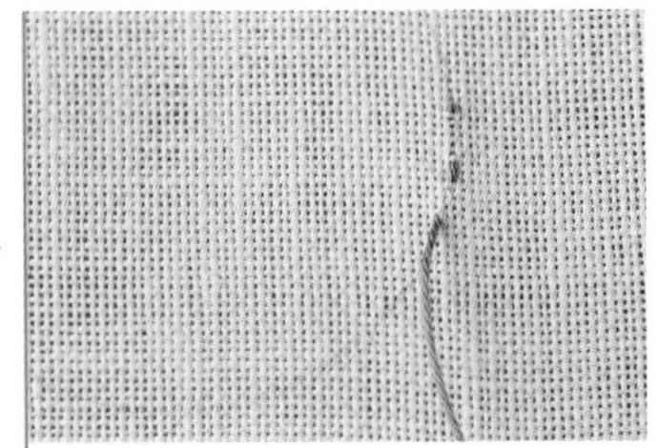

Transfer pattern onto fabric. Decide on the position where you want to begin stitching the outline. Make running stitches toward the starting position from a few stitch lengths away. Leave a very short floss tail. This is the best way to start stitching since the floss is anchored without actually making any knots.

2

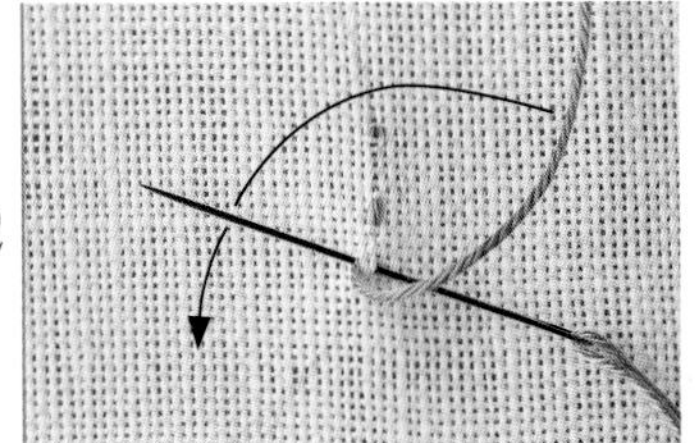

Once the starting position is reached, pass needle from right to left under the marked outline. Next, wrap loose floss loop under the needle tip.

3

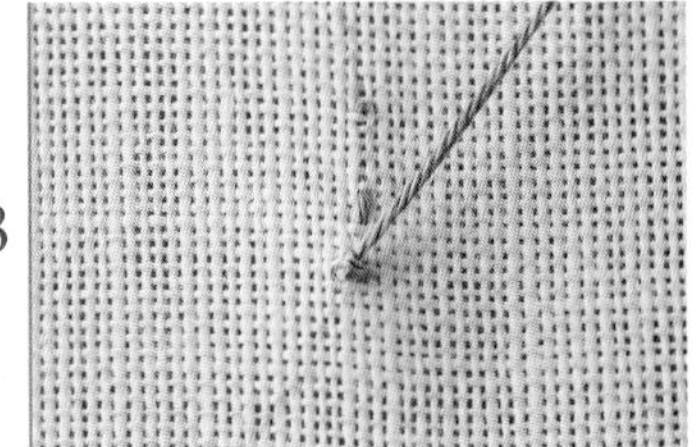

Pull both needle and loose floss through to tighten. The first coral stitch is complete.

4

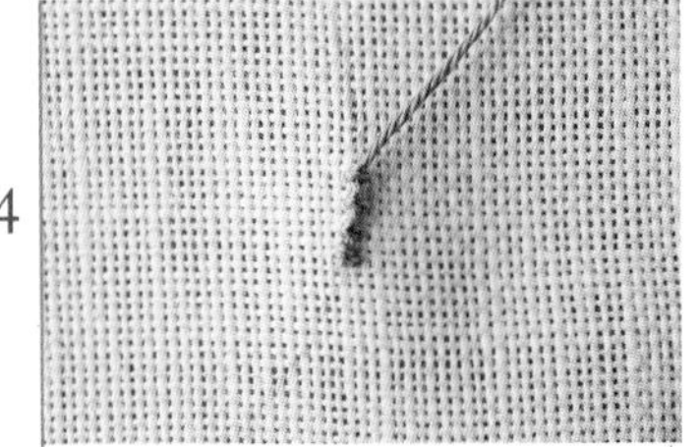

Make consecutive coral stitches along the marked outline in a counterclockwise direction.

5

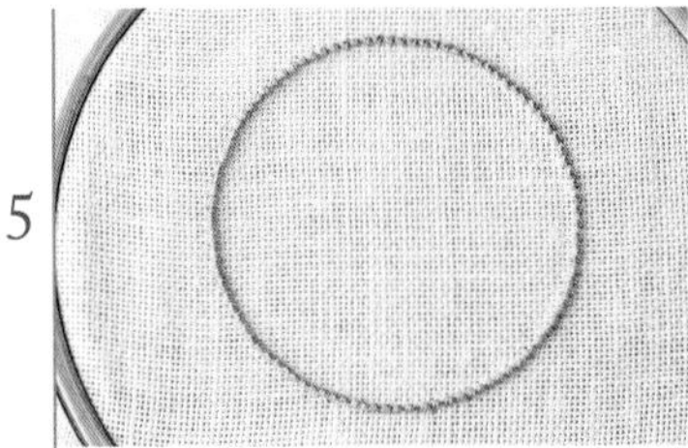

One round of coral stitches is complete.

6

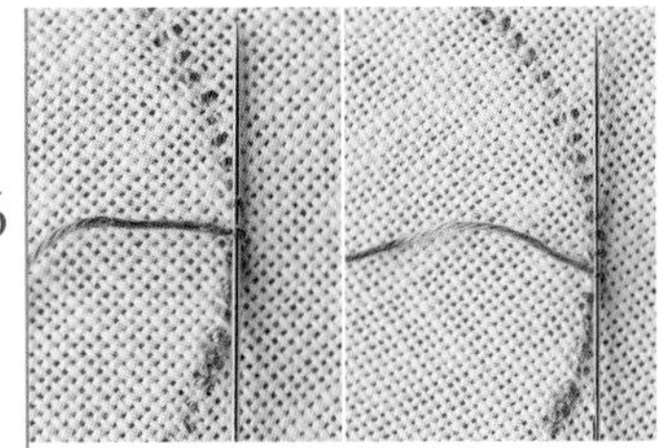

Secure the floss on backside of piece. Bring needle back through and slide it under one of the stitches. Pull floss taut. Repeat. Slide needle under a few stitches and pull floss through. Cut off excess.

7

Bring needle up just inside coral stitch. Similar to step 1, decide on a beginning position and start to make running stitches a few stitch lengths away.

8

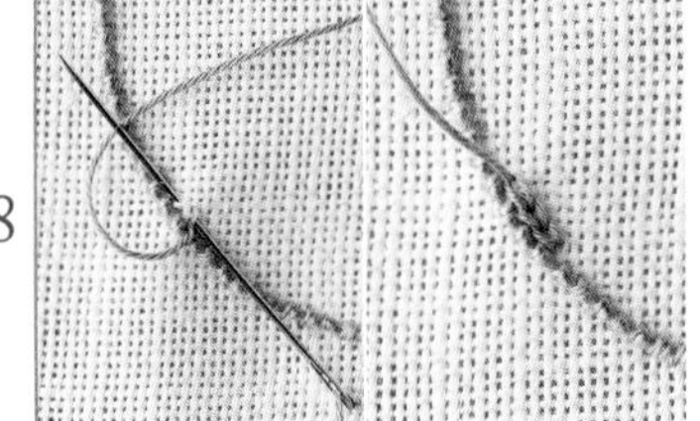

Once you have reached the beginning position, make a backstitch. Wrap floss under needle and pull all the way through. Then, make a chain stitch. Work chain stitches continuously along the coral stitches in a clockwise direction.

9

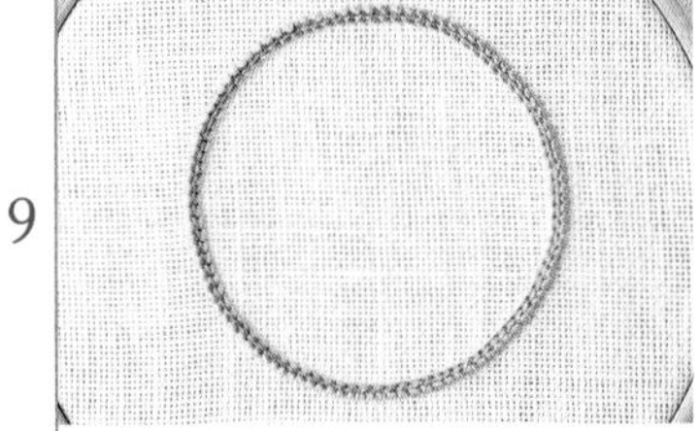

One round of chain stitches is complete. Bring needle to back and secure floss in the same manner as in step 6. Cut off excess. Now we are ready to snip threads inside the outlined area.

2. Pulling Threads

1

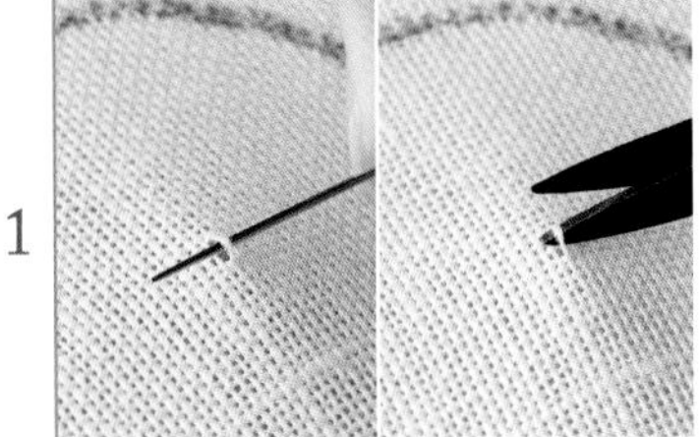

With fabric facing backside up, lift a warp thread from the center of the outlined area with a needle. Snip the warp thread while being careful not to cut any other threads.

2

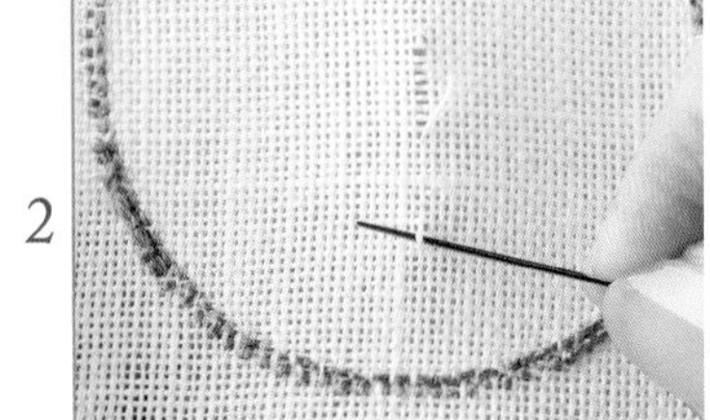

Unweave the snipped warp thread with a needle. Go slowly, unweave little by little. Do not forcefully unweave all at once from the outline edge.

3

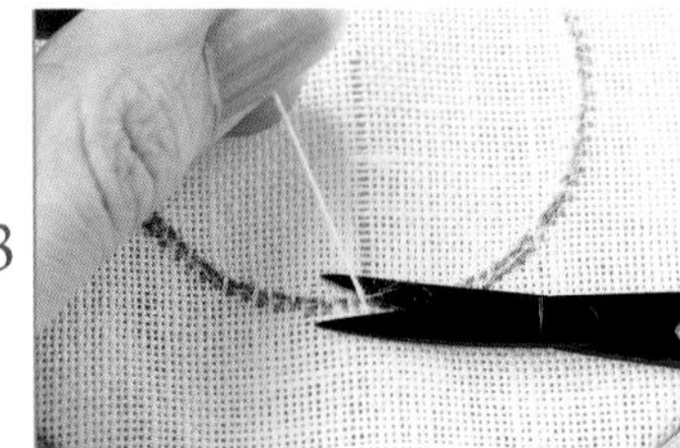

Once the warp thread has been unwoven all the way to outline edge, snip off at edge. Do the same for the other half of the thread. Then perform same operation for central weft thread.

4

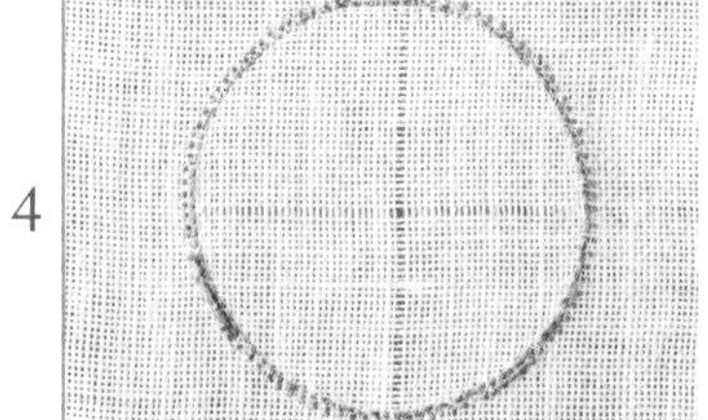

One warp thread and one weft thread have been pulled.

5

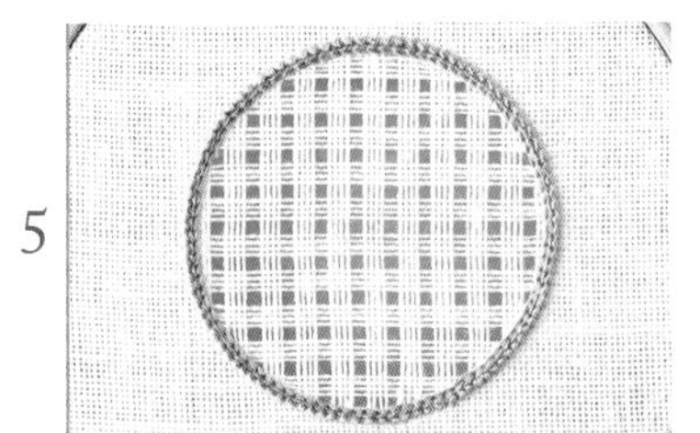

Using the previous technique, repeatedly withdraw threads at specified intervals. The foundation for your filling stitches is complete.

3. Filling Stitches

Double Small-Column Stitch

To form grid, pull two fabric threads while leaving four threads for both the warp and weft. The filling stitch is simple and binds two threads in each block.

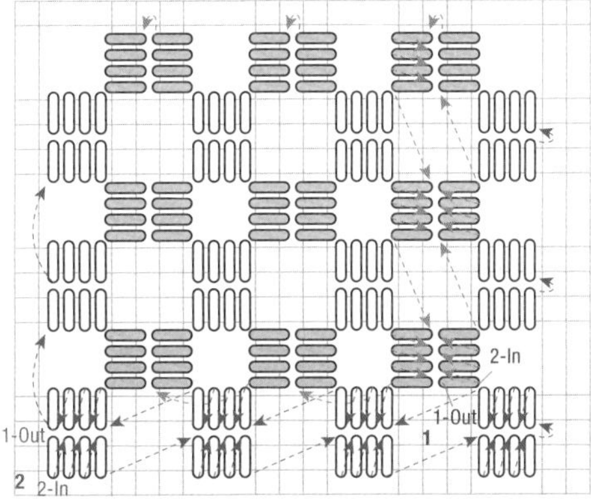
2-In
1-Out
1
1-Out
2
2-In

1

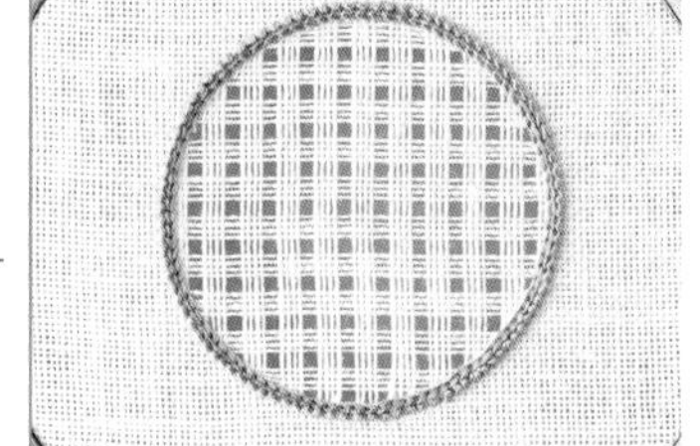

Inside outlined area, withdraw two threads and leave four threads for both warp and weft. Withdrawing two threads in both directions creates large gaps.

2

Secure floss tail at back (refer to page 63). Bring needle up through back, at edge of outline, two threads in, thus splitting the four warp threads. Slide needle right to left, as shown, under two rightmost warp threads. Needle should reemerge from middle of four warp threads. Repeat four times.

3

Pass needle under four weft threads so that it emerges from middle of four warp threads one block above.

4

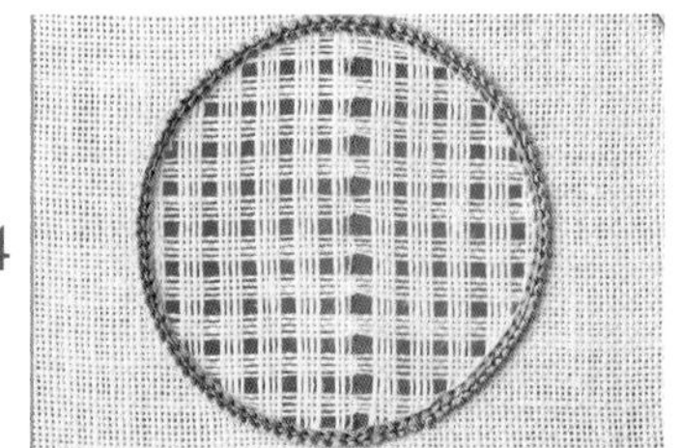

Repeat steps 2 and 3 for each block. Move upward.

5

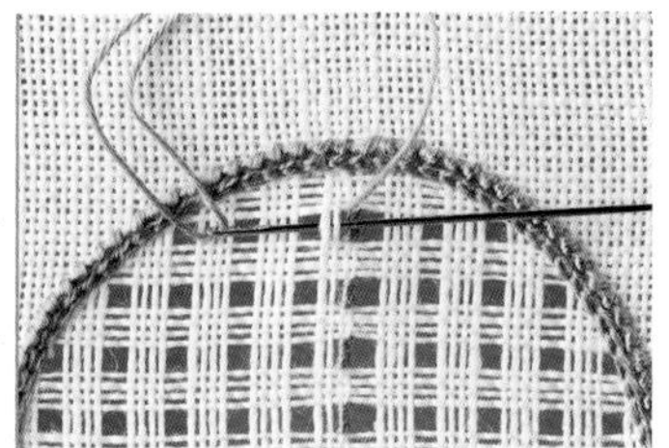

Move on to next two warp threads. Bring needle up from middle. Slide needle left to right under two leftmost warp threads so that it reemerges. To show stitching position clearly, this example leaves the fabric facing the same direction. When you actually stitch, rotate fabric for ease.

6

Repeat steps for all warp threads. Each column must use two bundled threads.

7

Next, begin stitching weft threads. Similar to with the warp threads, bring needle up from middle of four weft threads and then go under two bottom weft threads. Repeat four times. Slide needle under four warp threads to bring it up at next block.

8

Continue all the way to the other edge. Repeat steps to complete the row.

Three-Sided Stitch

To form this type of grid, withdraw every fifth weft thread. Withdrawing warp threads isn't required here. This stitch forms a triangular shape using up-and-down zigzags.

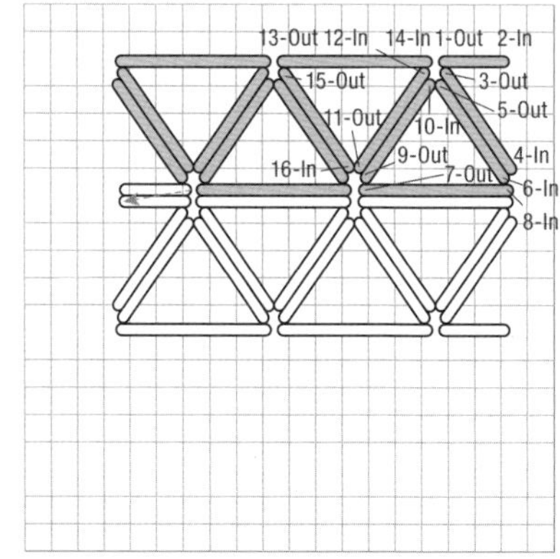
13-Out
12-In
14-In
1-Out
2-In
15-Out
3-Out
5-Out
11-Out
10-In
16-In
9-Out
4-In
7-Out
6-In
8-In

1

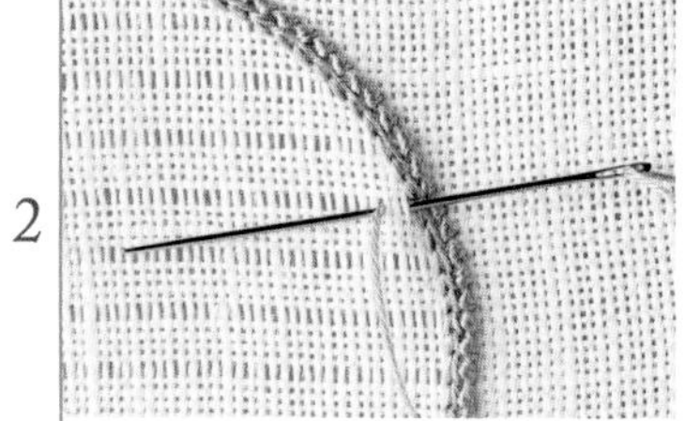

Inside outlined area, withdraw one out of every fifth weft thread. Since withdrawing warp threads isn't required, there is only the hint of a pattern at this stage.

2

Secure floss tail at back (refer to page 63). Bring needle up three warp threads away from outline edge where weft thread was withdrawn. Count back three warp threads and push needle through to back. Slide needle under the three warp threads and pull out again.

3

Push needle back through, four weft threads down and three warp threads back toward edge. Slide needle under four weft threads, moving upward at an angle, and reemerge at the same point as in step 2. Repeat twice.

4

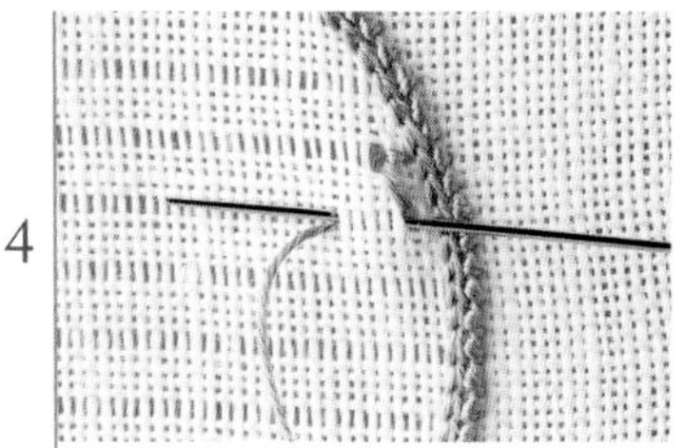

Slide needle, from right to left, under six warp threads from entry point in step 3. Reemerge from same position.

5

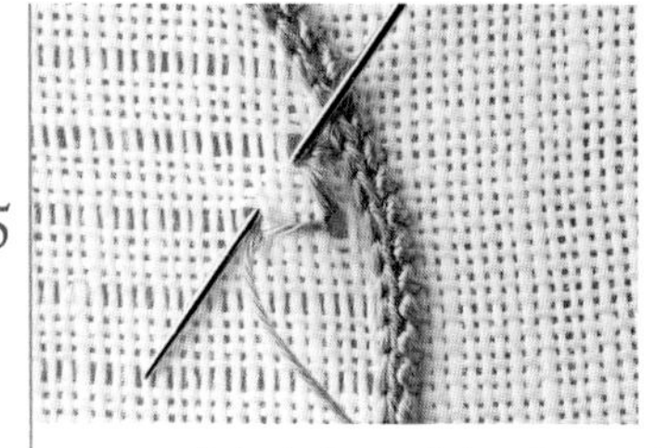

Bring needle back, four weft threads up and three warp threads right. Reemerge at where needle came out in step 4. Repeat twice.

6

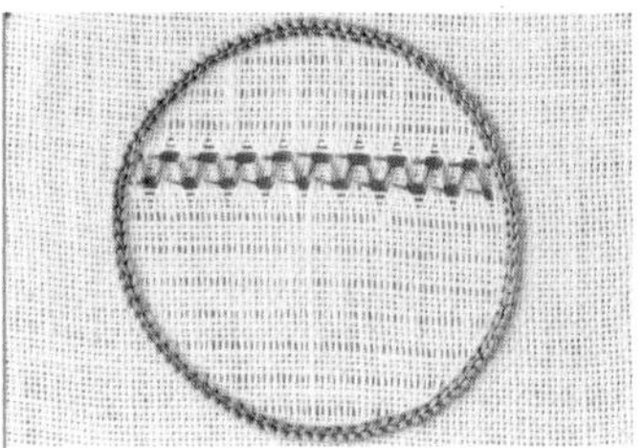

Repeat steps to make consecutive stitches all the way to the other side. Stitch once along weft threads and twice along warp threads.

7 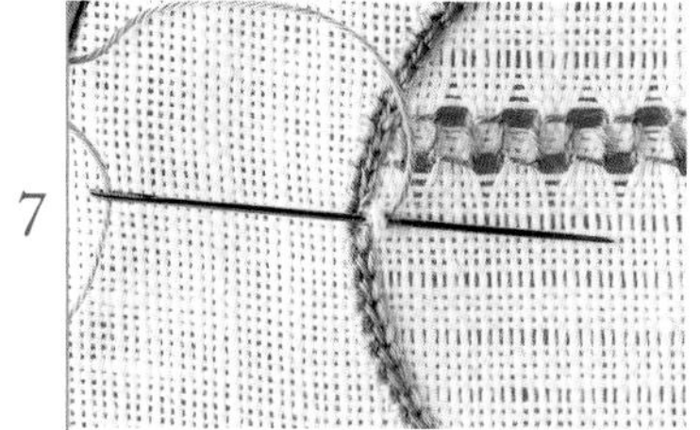

Along the back, slide needle under outline stitches and bring it up at next row—four weft threads down. Insert needle as shown near edge of outline. Go over four warp threads and exit at original exit point.

8 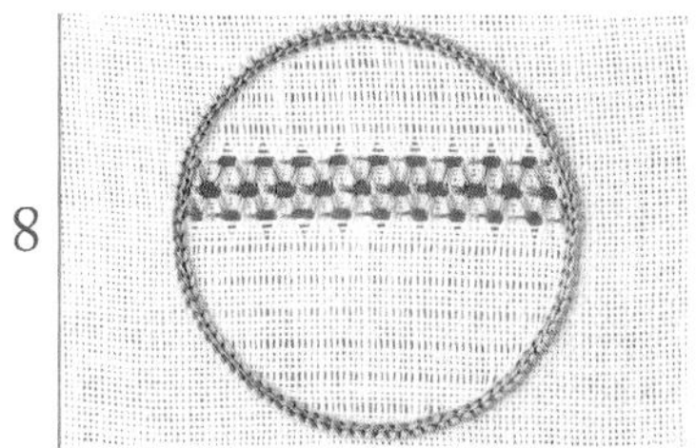

Repeat same sequence as for the block above and continue to other side. Repeat steps until entire area inside outline is filled with three-sided stitches.

Weave Stitch

Withdraw two fabric threads in each direction. Make sure to leave two fabric threads for both warp and weft. This stitch binds the two threads with fill blocks to make a cross pattern.

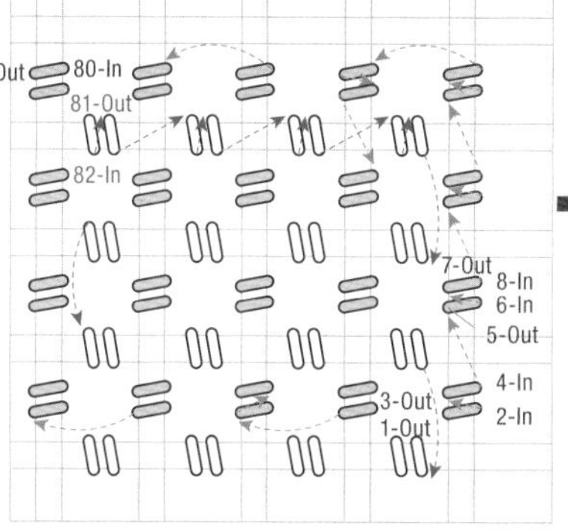
79-Out
80-In
81-Out
82-In
7-Out
8-In
6-In
5-Out
4-In
3-Out
2-In
1-Out

48-In
47-Out
45-Out
44-In 46-In
43-Out
41-Out
40-In 42-In
39-Out
37-Out
38-In
36-In
32-In 33-Out
35-Out
31-Out
34-In
30-In
23-Out 29-Out
28-In 24-In
25-Out 27-Out
22-In
26-In
15-Out 21-Out
20-In
19-Out
14-In
13-Out
16-In 17-Out
18-In
12-In
11-Out
9-Out
8-In 10-In
7-Out
5-Out
4-In 6-In
3-Out
1-Out
2-In

1 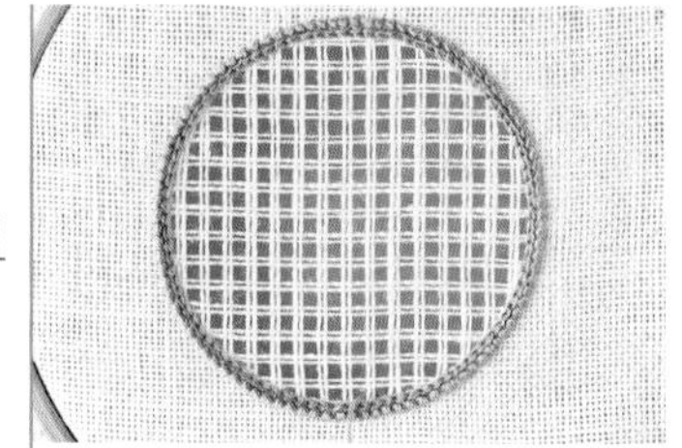

Alternating between withdrawing two warp threads and two weft threads creates large gaps.

2 

Secure floss tail at backside (refer to page 63). Bring needle up at edge of outline. Run needle right to left under two warp threads and pull. Repeat two times.

3 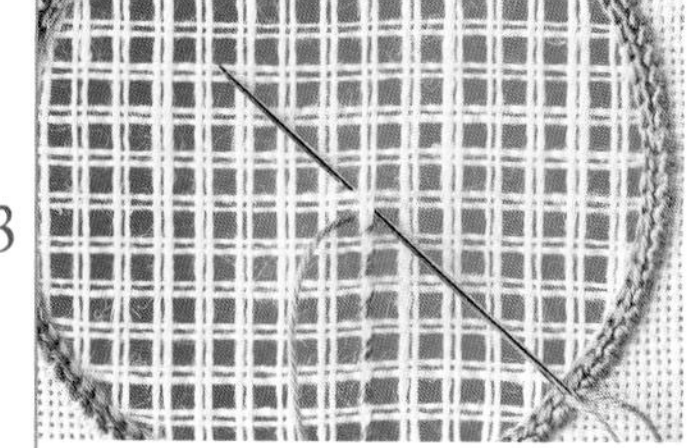

Slide needle right to left diagonally under two weft threads and up one block. Bind the warp threads twice.

4 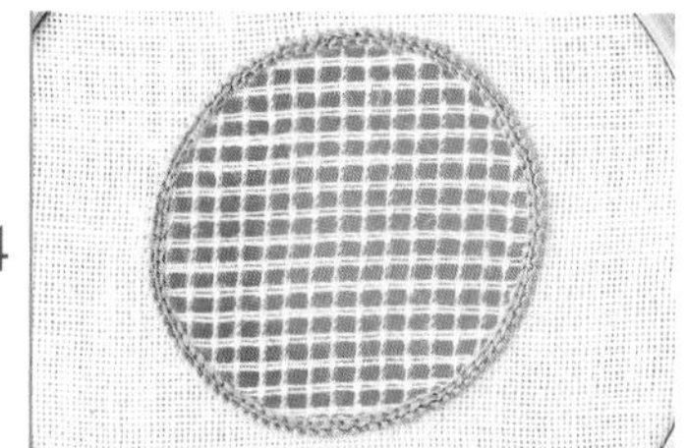

Repeat steps until all warp threads inside outline are bound.

5 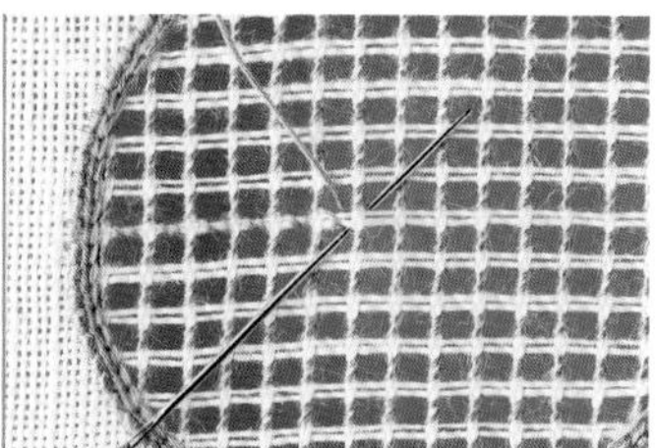

Next, bind weft threads. In the same manner as the warp threads, bring needle up from edge of outline and bind two weft threads. To show stitching position clearly, this example faces the same direction as previously. When actually stitching, rotate fabric to make working easier.

6 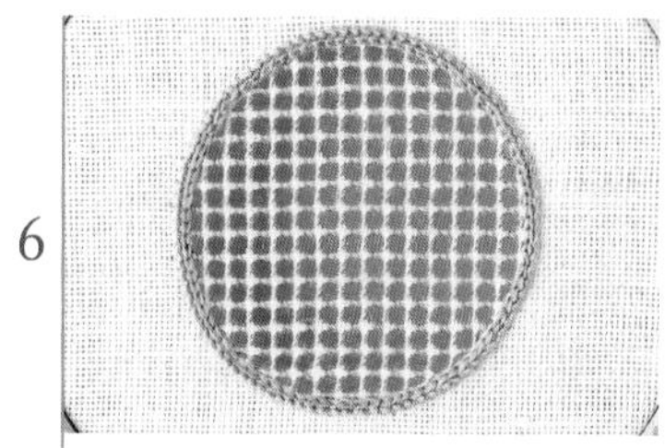

Repeat steps until all weft threads are bound.

7

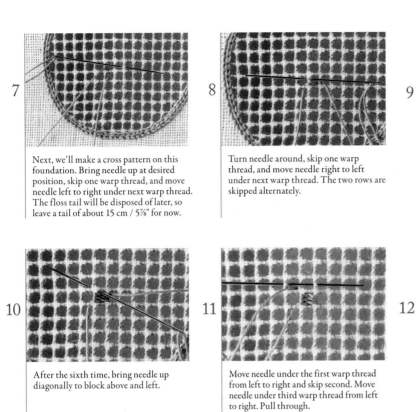

Next, we'll make a cross pattern on this foundation. Bring needle up at desired position, skip one warp thread, and move needle left to right under next warp thread. The floss tail will be disposed of later, so leave a tail of about 15 cm / 5⅞" for now.

8

Turn needle around, skip one warp thread, and move needle right to left under next warp thread. The two rows are skipped alternately.

9

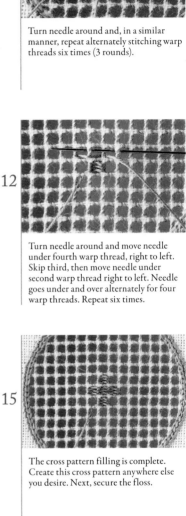

Turn needle around and, in a similar manner, repeat alternately stitching warp threads six times (3 rounds).

10

After the sixth time, bring needle up diagonally to block above and left.

11

Move needle under the first warp thread from left to right and skip second. Move needle under third warp thread from left to right. Pull through.

12

Turn needle around and move needle under fourth warp thread, right to left. Skip third, then move needle under second warp thread right to left. Needle goes under and over alternately for four warp threads. Repeat six times.

13

After sixth pass, bring needle up at second warp thread to block above.

14

Similar to steps 7 through 9, repeat alternately moving the needle under and over on two warp threads.

15

The cross pattern filling is complete. Create this cross pattern anywhere else you desire. Next, secure the floss.

16

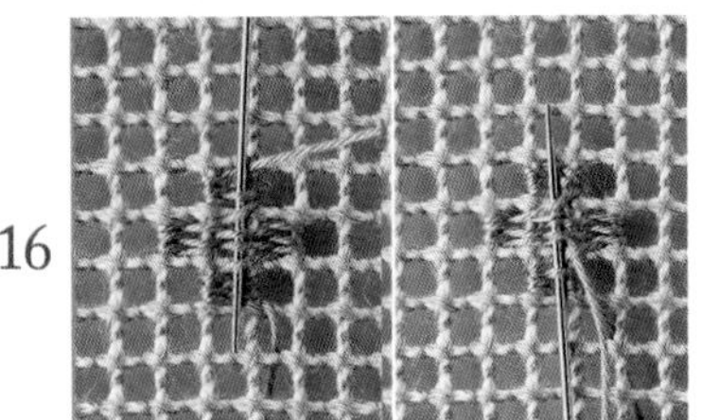

Bring needle back and insert upward under about four stitches. Pull floss tight. Do the same in a downward direction. Cut off excess. Bring untreated floss tail from the beginning to backside of work and secure it in the same manner.

Four-Sided Stitch

Withdraw one in every fifth weft thread. Withdrawing warp threads isn't required here. This stich is worked in a square shape over four fabric threads.

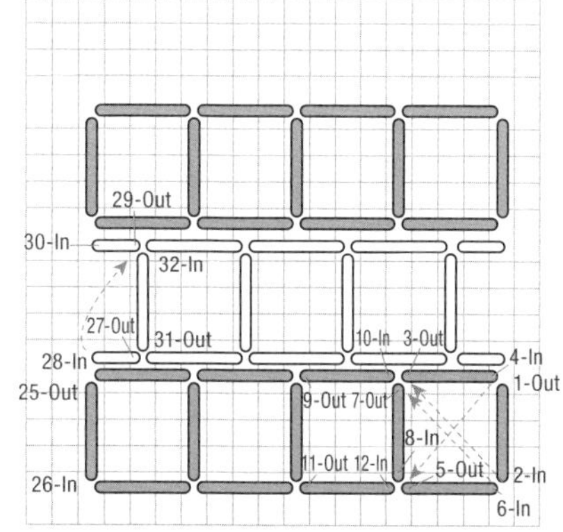

29-Out
30-In
32-In
27-Out
31-Out
10-In
3-Out
28-In
4-In
1-Out
25-Out
9-Out
7-Out
8-In
11-Out
12-In
5-Out
26-In
2-In
6-In

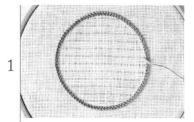

1 

Withdraw one in five weft threads inside the outlined area. Only weft threads have been withdrawn, so the area inside the outline appears to have a faint pattern.

2 

Secure floss tail at backside (refer to page 63). Bring needle up at edge of outline and then reinsert down four weft threads. Push back up four weft threads above and four warp threads to left of initial exit point.

3 

Insert needle back at initial extraction point from step 2. The needle reemerges four weft threads down and four warp threads left from entry point.

4 

Insert needle at entry point from step 2. Then pull it back out at same extraction position as in step 2.

5 

Push needle back through four weft threads down and then pull it back out four up and four to the left. The four-sided stitch is named such precisely because it uses four weft and four warp threads.

6 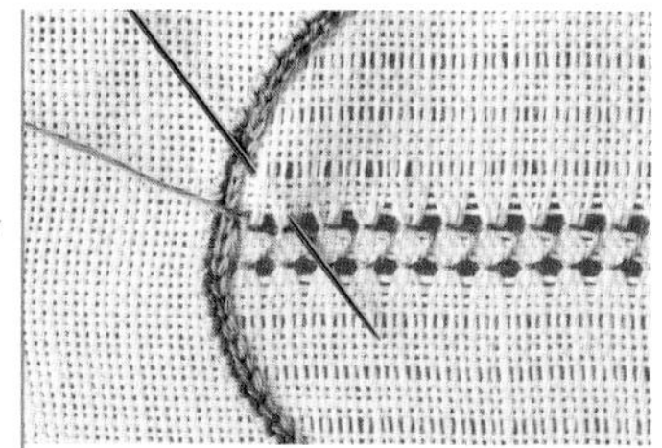

Repeat sequences all the way to the other side.

7 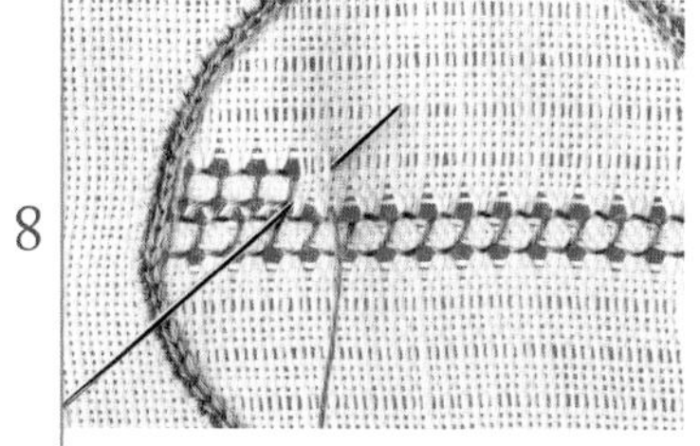

Move up a row. Bring needle up in the middle of four warp threads (second warp thread from left) and then reinsert four weft threads up. Reemerge from four weft threads down and four warp threads to right. Rotate your work to the easiest sewing position.

8 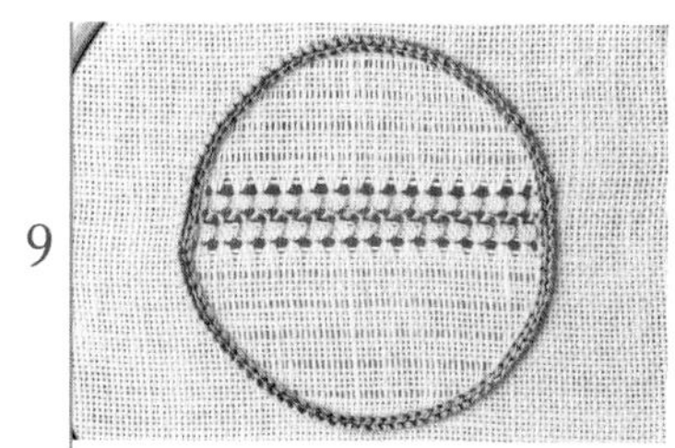

Repeat sequences from first row until you reach the other side, but remember that the second row stitches are all shifted two warp threads to the right of the first row.

9

Repeat these sequences to fill the entire outlined area. Note: for the third row the stitches shift back two warp threads to left. They should match up with the first row.

Flower Garden Stitch

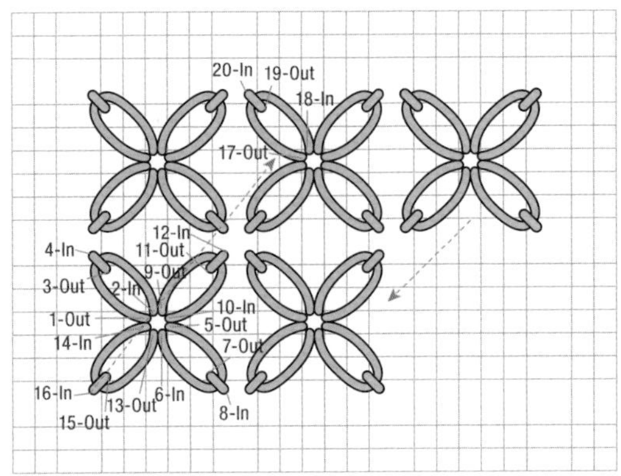
20-In
19-Out
18-In
17-Out
12-In
11-Out
4-In
9-Out
3-Out
2-In
10-In
1-Out
5-Out
14-In
7-Out
16-In
6-In
13-Out
8-In
15-Out

Withdraw one thread, leaving six threads for both warp and weft. Bring needle up at center of six warp and six weft block. Make lazy daisy stitch.

1

To form grid, withdraw one thread while leaving six threads from both warp and weft inside outlined area. Begin stitching at left bottom corner of outlined area. Bring needle up from center of a block.

2

Bring needle up diagonally left under two warp and weft threads and reemerge. Lay floss under needle and pull floss all the way through.

3

Bring needle back to gap one weft thread above and one warp thread to left. The first lazy daisy stitch is complete!

4

Again, bring needle up at center of block. Go diagonally down and right under two weft threads and two warp threads and reemerge. Make lazy daisy stitch. Next, bring needle up at center of block and make lazy daisy stitch in the right upper section of the block.

5

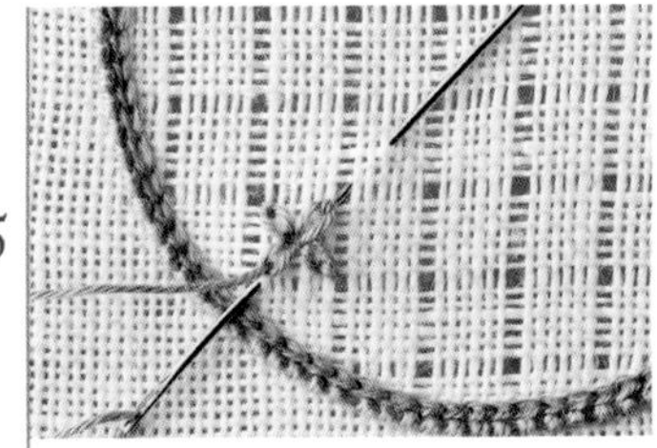

Last, bring needle up at center of block and make lazy daisy stitch toward bottom left of block. Now, one flower is complete. Next, bring needle up at center of block to next column on the row above.

6

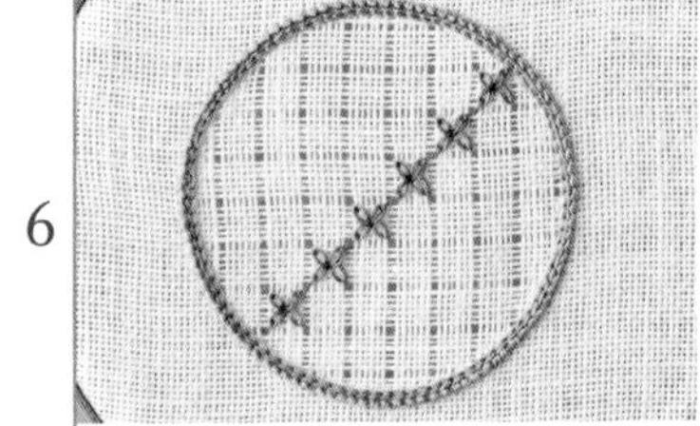

Work lazy daisy stitches, using the same steps. Proceed diagonally to the right.

7

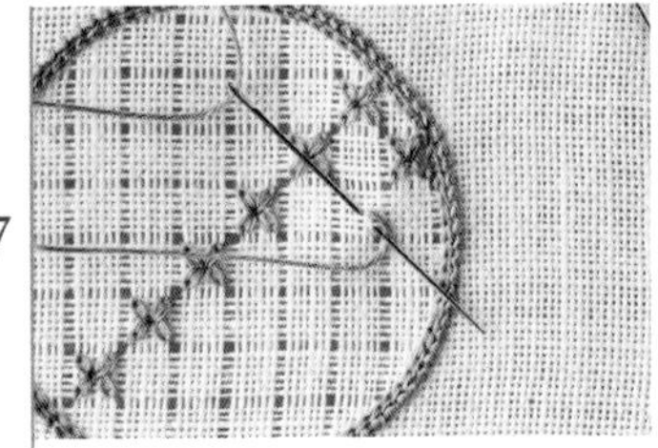

Once the other side is reached, slide needle under floss at backside and move on to next row. Bring needle up at center of block and make lazy daisy stitch.

Ajour Embroidery

Ajour embroidery is similar to Schwalm, but it uses pulled-thread techniques. Ajour embroidery uses coarse linen fabric because its threads are not withdrawn. Coarse fabric allows for threads to be easily pulled, and you can also get an accurate thread count before stitching. Similar to other forms of embroidery, but especially for Ajour embroidery, you must be careful to keep the floss tension even. In French, *ajour* means "made translucent."

a
b
c
d
e

Stitches 1

a Pebble Filling Stitch
b Eyelet Stitch
c Checker Filling Stitch
d Reverse Wave Stitch
e Faggot Stitch

page 80

f
g
h
i
j

Stitches 2

f Mosaic Filling Stitch
g Feston Stitch
h Wave Stitch
i Basket Filling Stitch
j Drawn Buttonhole Stitch

page 81

7. / design page 82

This is a pretty Scandinavian cityscape in which each motif could be a cute single-motif embroidery on its own. The chosen stitches work really well with the bicycle wheel and roof designs.

8. / design page 83

For the knitted cap and socks on this embroidery work, we combined stitches that produce both a snow and knitted-fabric feel. Use French knot stitch to produce the fluffy look of the pompom on the knitted hat and the cuffs of the mittens.

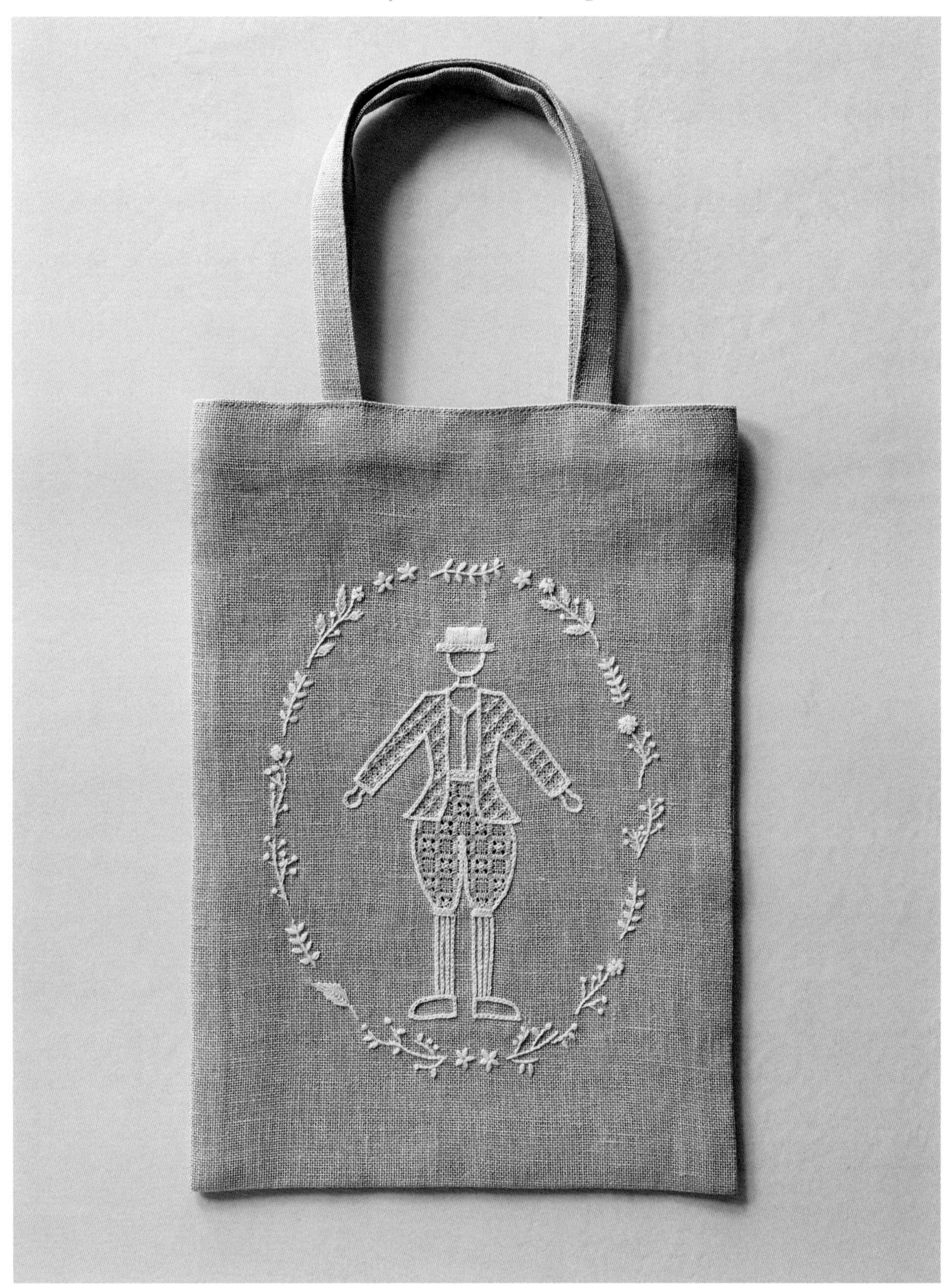

This bag features the boy motif from page 26. The white floss stitching on pale blue-gray linen creates an elegant look.

10. / How To page 86

9. / design page 84

Create this cute couple dressed in folk costume. Bring out different looks on the folk costume by varying the size of the stitching pattern and pulled-thread tightness.

11. / design page 88

Three rhythmically marching soldiers.
The design is the same for all three, but the stitching on the hats is different.

12. / How To page 89 Toy Soldier Bookmark

Make these soldier bookmarks as flat as possible. Add drawn threadwork hemstitching at the top and bottom.
Also, fray the bottom to create a fringed edge.

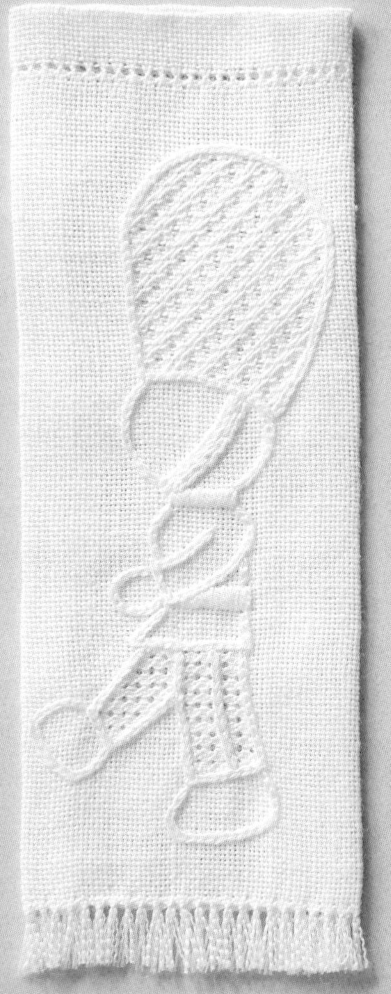

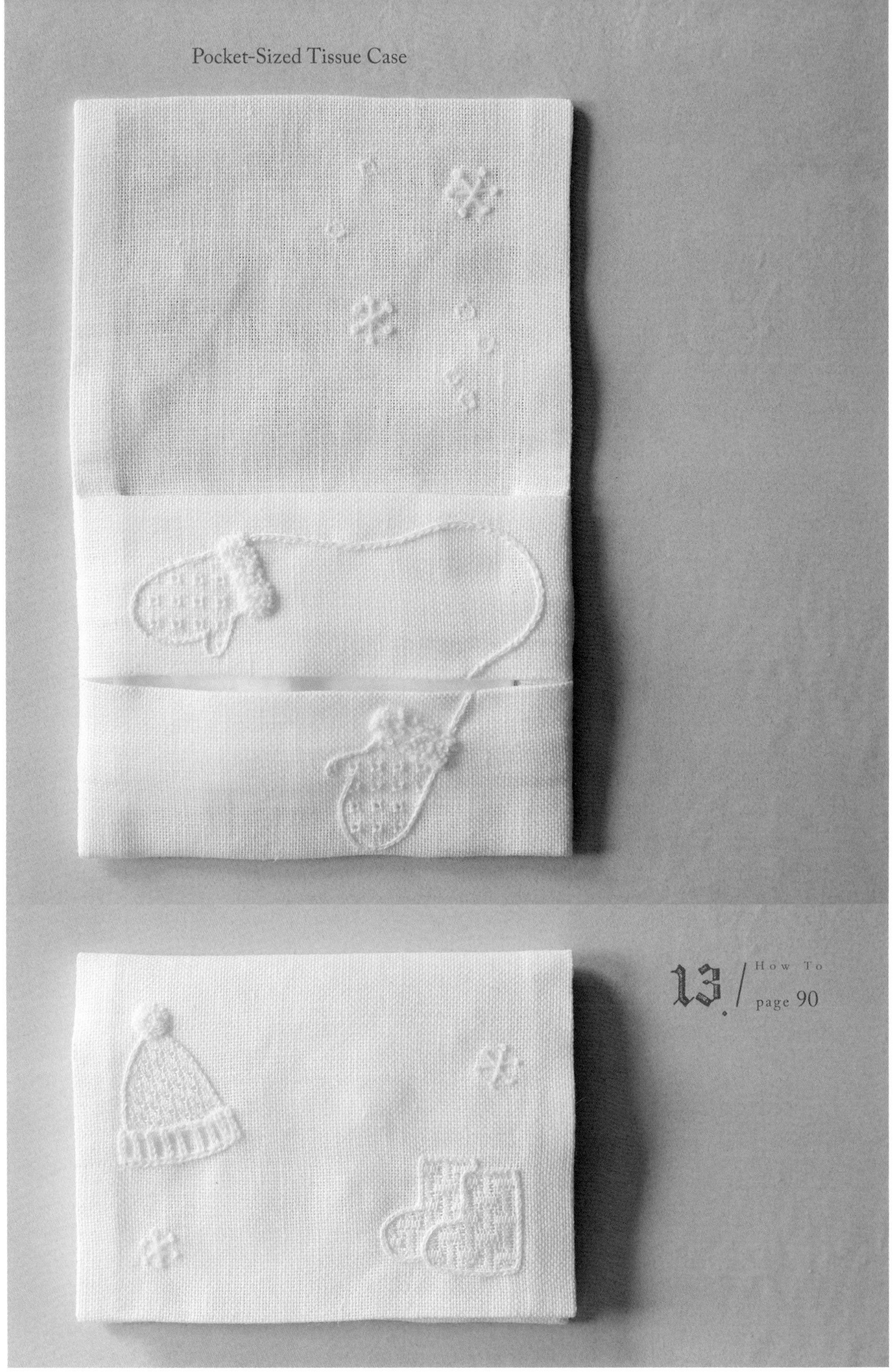
Pocket-Sized Tissue Case
13. / How To page 90

Designs from page 25, such as mittens and socks, are used on this pocket-sized tissue cover.
The delightful mitten design is fully visible once the flap is completely open.

First, use chain stitch for the outline. Then, begin to stitch–without withdrawing any fabric threads. Use a pointed needle for stitching the outline, and a round needle for the interior of the outlined area. Stitching diagrams are found on pages 66–67.

1. Outline the Pattern

1

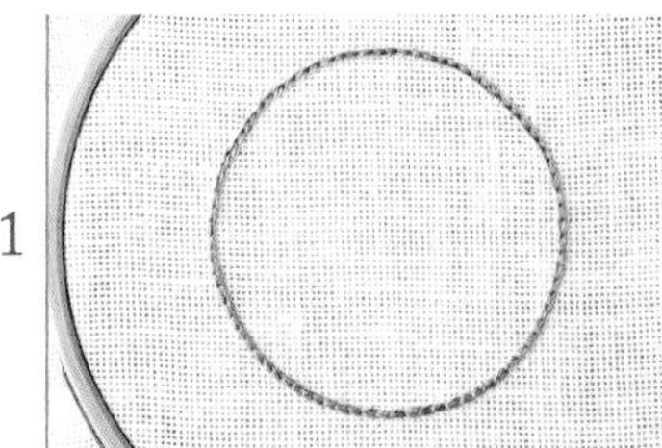

Transfer pattern to fabric. Chain-stitch along the pattern outline.

2. Work Filling Stitches

Basket Filling Stitch

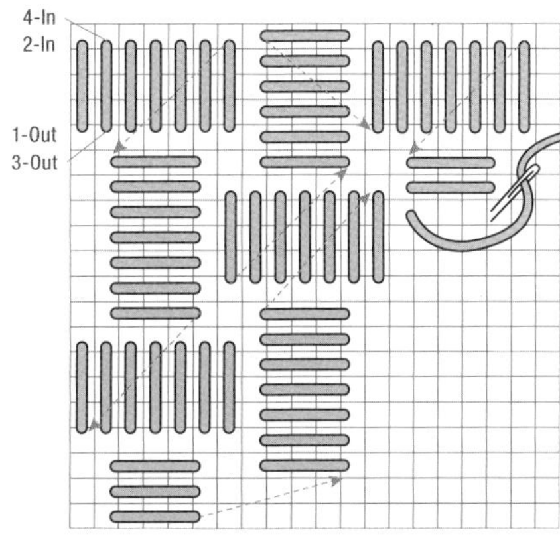
4-In
2-In
1-Out
3-Out

Make seven satin stitches. Each stitch is four fabric threads in length. After the seventh stitch, alternate horizontal and vertical blocks. This produces a basket weave pattern.

1

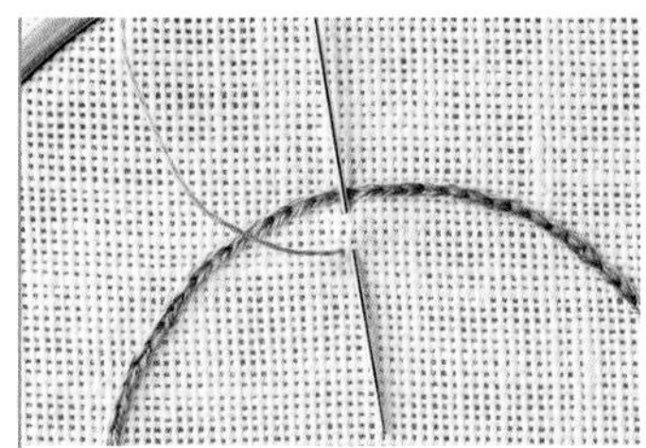

Secure floss tail at back (refer to page 63). Bring needle up four weft threads down from outline edge. Insert needle four weft threads above and then bring needle up four weft threads down and one warp thread to the right.

2

Insert needle four weft threads above and push it back out four weft threads down and one warp thread to the right. Repeat this sequence to make satin stitches, moving one warp thread to the right each time.

3

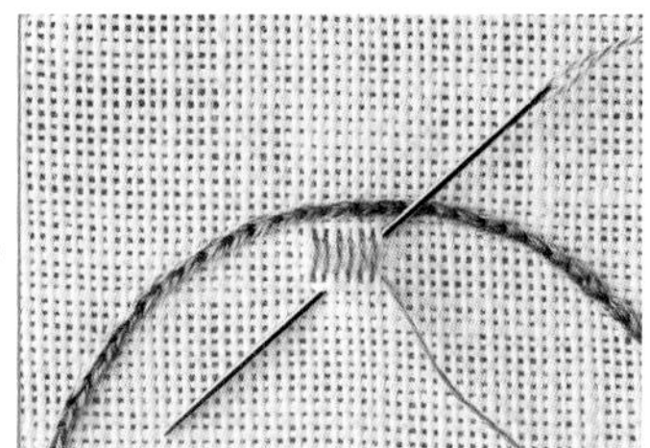

After making the seventh satin stitch, move down a block. Bring needle up one weft thread down. To find the midpoint of the horizontal satin stitches for the next block, align with middle of the seventh satin stitch block above.

4

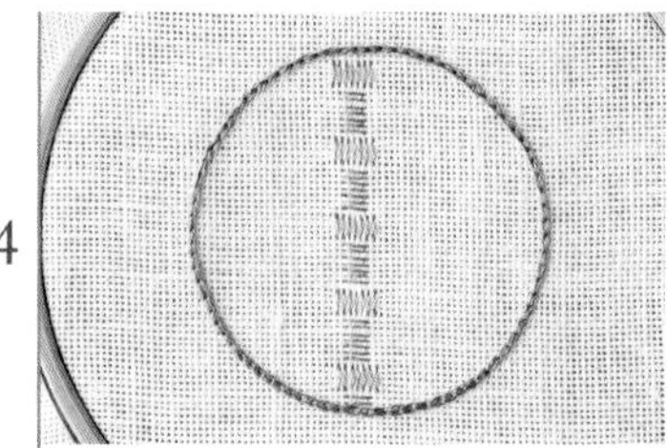

Repeat steps and stitch to the other side. Alternate vertical and horizontal blocks every seven satin stitches. Be sure to count the fabric threads as you stitch, and make sure that the center of each block lines up correctly.

5

Move to next column. At back, slide needle under outline stitches and bring it up at next position. Reverse satin stitch directions compared to first column. Start stitching one warp thread to right.

6

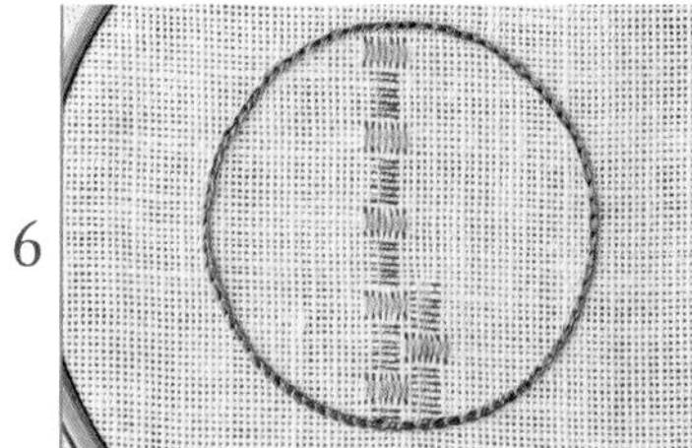

Repeat steps to fill the entire outlined area.

Wave Stitch

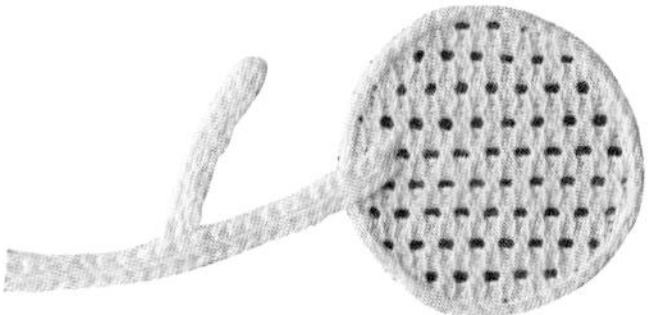

Make V-shaped stitches and inverted V-shaped stitches to fill area. The fabric gaps and stitches will make a zigzag pattern.

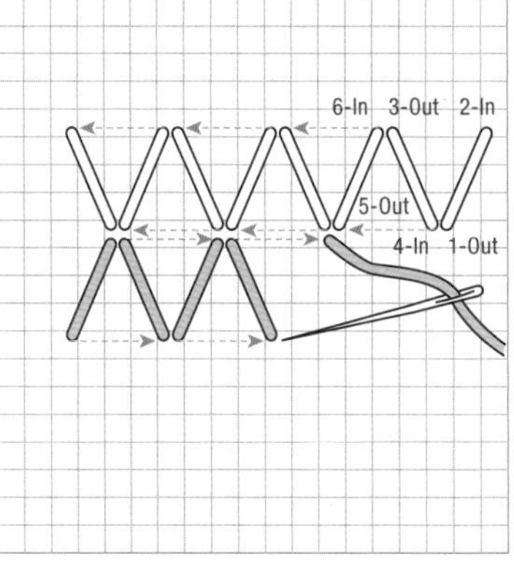

6-In
3-Out
2-In
5-Out
4-In
1-Out

1 Secure floss tail at back (refer to page 63). Bring needle up at second warp thread from outline edge. Insert needle four weft threads up and two warp threads to right. Pass needle under four warp threads and reemerge.

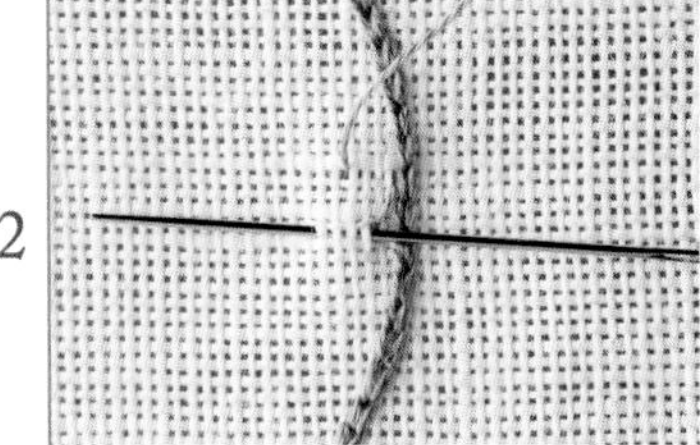

2 Next, bring needle back to where it initially came out, pass it under four warp threads, and reemerge.

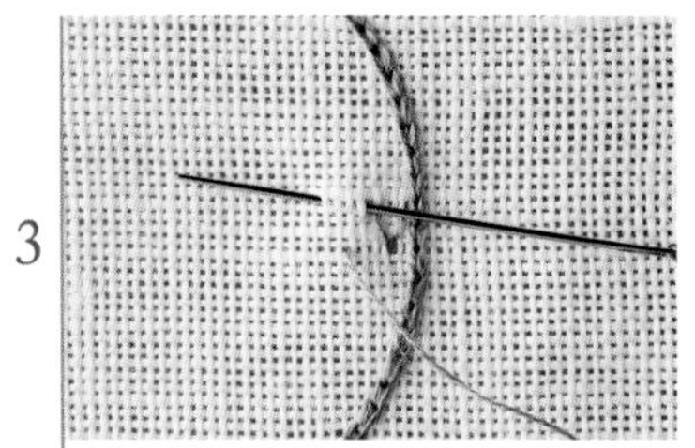

3 Bring needle back at a point where it reemerged in step 1. Pass it under four warp threads. Repeat diagonal stitching up and down, always four warp threads apart.

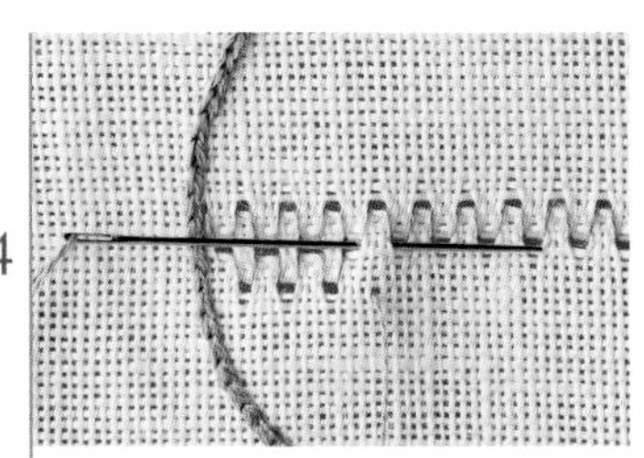

4 Stitch all the way to other side and begin to return. The entire next row should mirror the first. Repeat steps to fill outlined area entirely.

Eyelet Stitch

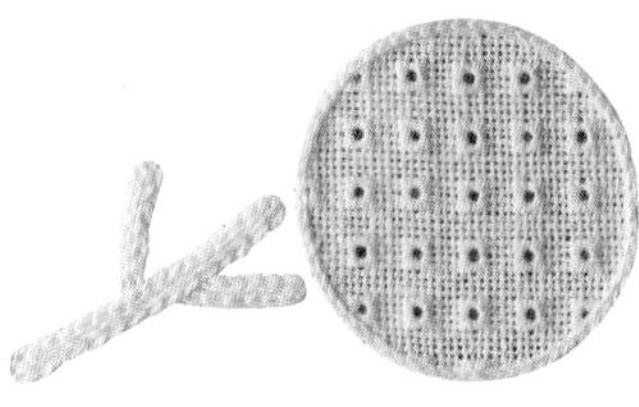

Stitches radiate from center of block. You can imagine there is a round eye in the center.

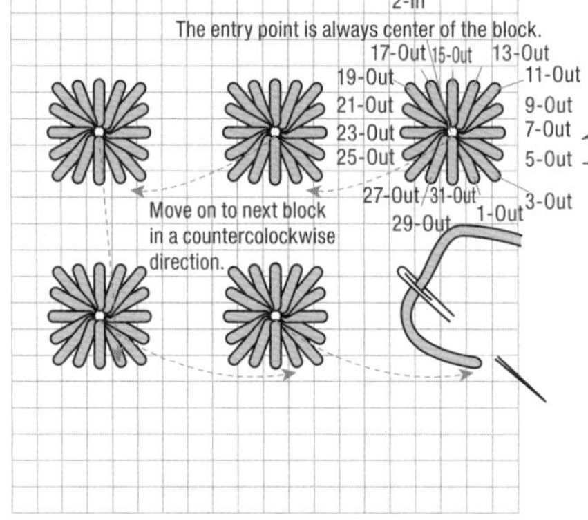

2-In
The entry point is always center of the block.
17-Out
15-Out
13-Out
19-Out
11-Out
21-Out
9-Out
23-Out
7-Out
25-Out
5-Out
27-Out
31-Out
3-Out
29-Out
1-Out
Move on to next block in a countercolockwise direction.

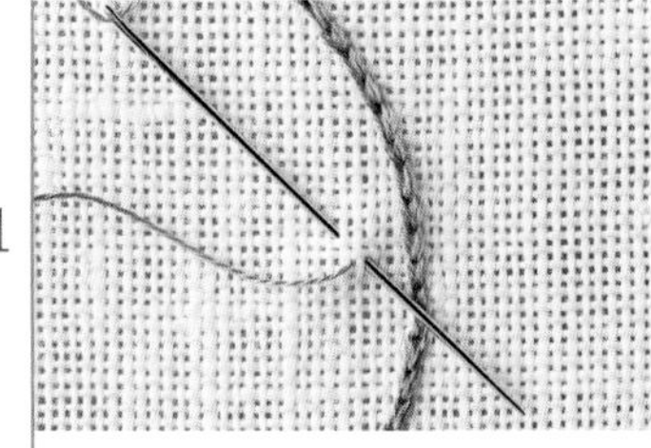

1 Secure floss tail at back (refer to page 63). Bring needle up at desired position. Push needle back through diagonally, two weft threads up and one warp thread to left. Reemerge one warp thread to right of where needle initially came up. This position, where the needle reemerges, will be the eyelet center.

2 From center, make a series of two thread-length stitches in a counterclockwise direction. This should make a square shape.

3 The last stitch is complete. The first eyelet is done.

4 Bring needle up at desired position and repeat the steps to fill outlined area entirely.

Feston Stitch

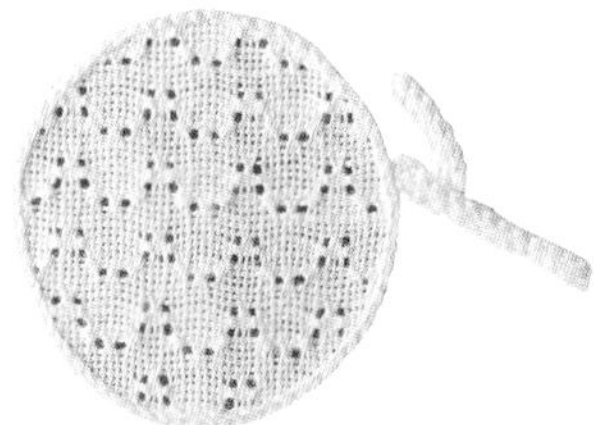

This design is something akin to the decorative garlands you see at festivals, with their lovely, drooped curves. Two stitches at the same position are required to achieve the proper effect.

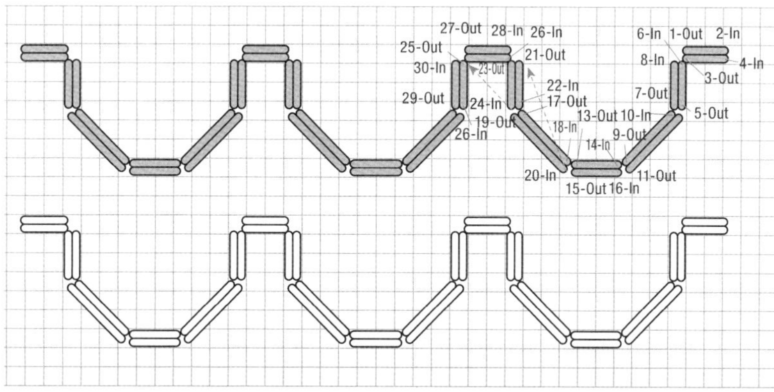
27-Out
28-In
26-In
6-In
1-Out
2-In
25-Out
21-Out
8-In
4-In
30-In
23-Out
3-Out
22-In
17-Out
7-Out
29-Out
24-In
13-Out
10-In
5-Out
19-Out
18-In
26-In
14-In
9-Out
20-In
11-Out
15-Out
16-In

1

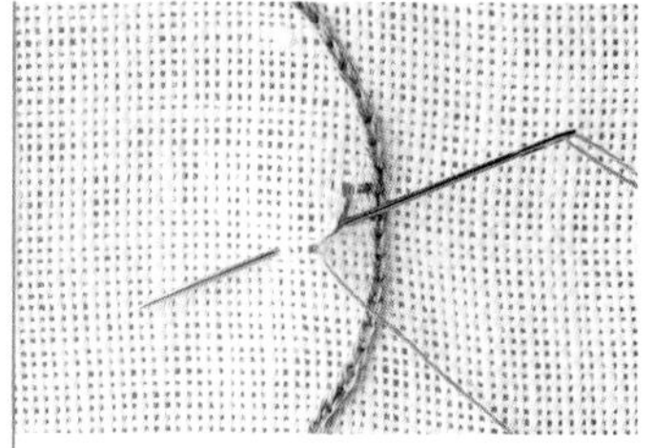

Secure tail of floss at back (refer to page 63). Bring needle up at third warp thread from outline edge. Count back three warp threads and push needle through. Pull back out at initial exit point. Stitch twice.

2

Push needle back in three weft threads down. Reemerge at initial exit point in step 1 (three weft threads up).

3

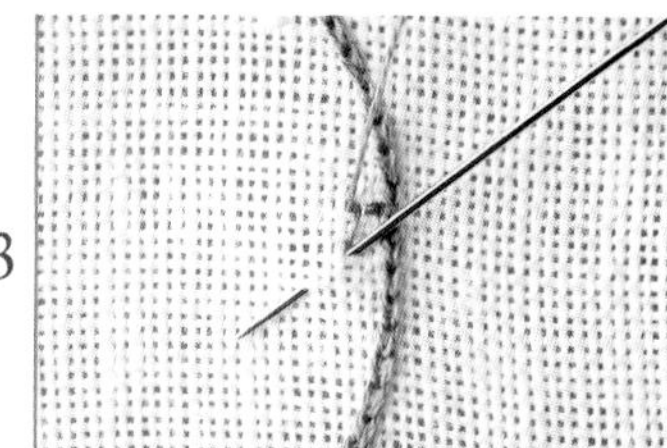

Push needle back through at same entry position as in step 2 (three weft threads down). Reemerge three weft threads down and three warp threads to left. Repeat once.

4

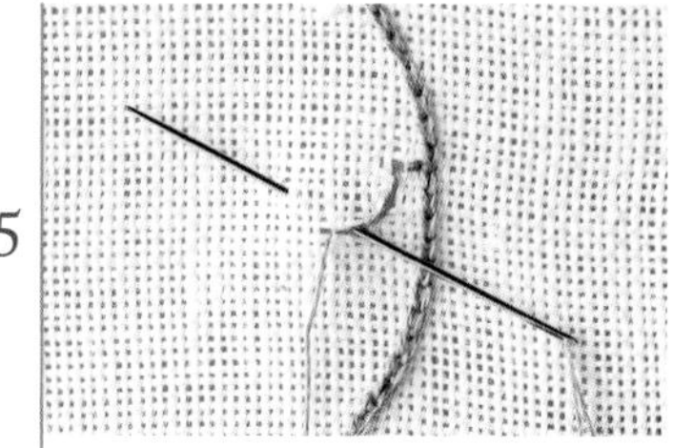

Push needle back in at same position as in step 3. Reemerge three weft threads down and six warp threads to left. Push needle back through where needle came out in step 3. Slide needle under three warp threads and reemerge.

5

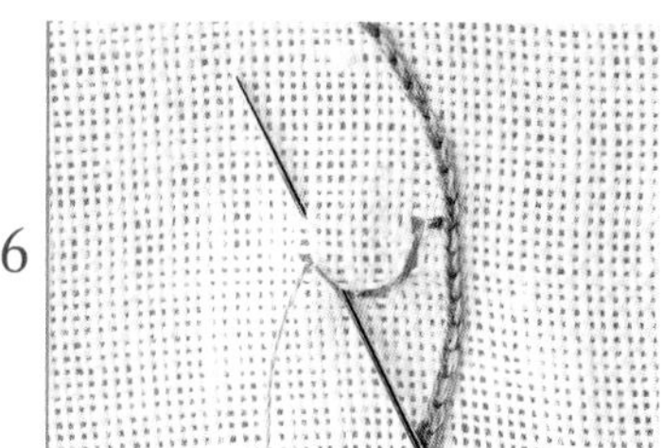

Count back three warp threads and insert needle. Pull back out three weft threads up and six warp threads to left. This stitch should be the mirror image of step 4.

6

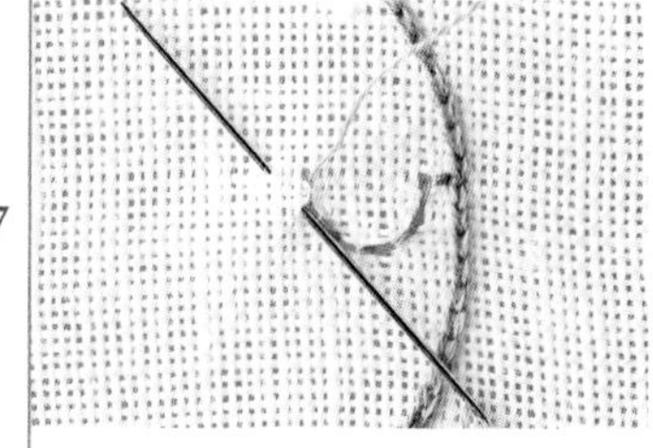

Insert needle again at same position as in step 5. Reemerge six weft threads up and three warp threads to left. Repeat once.

7

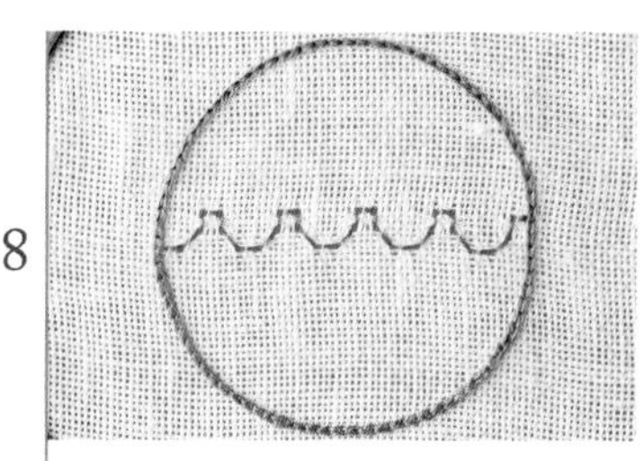

The pattern is complete. Repeat steps and continue to the other side.

8

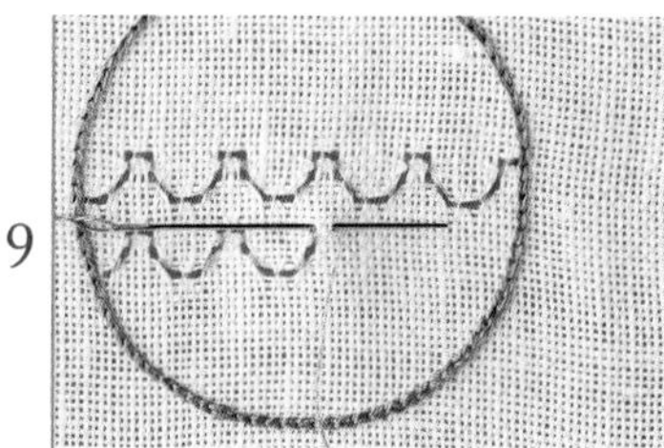

This is what the pattern should look like.

9

Move three weft threads down to begin second row. Repeat steps above to move across outline.

Ajour Embroidery

Faggot Stitch

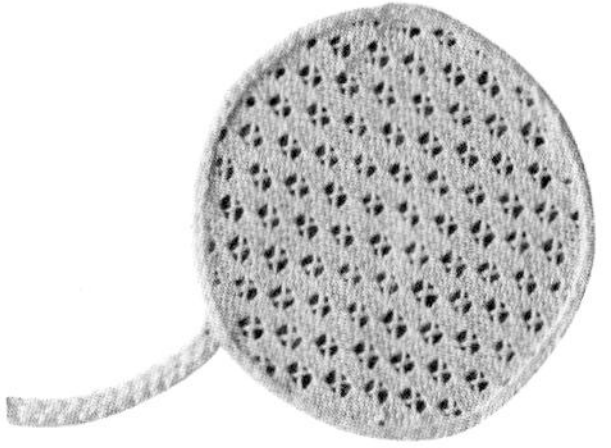

Stitch a staircase pattern diagonally. If two or more rows are stitched, a cross pattern will form between them.

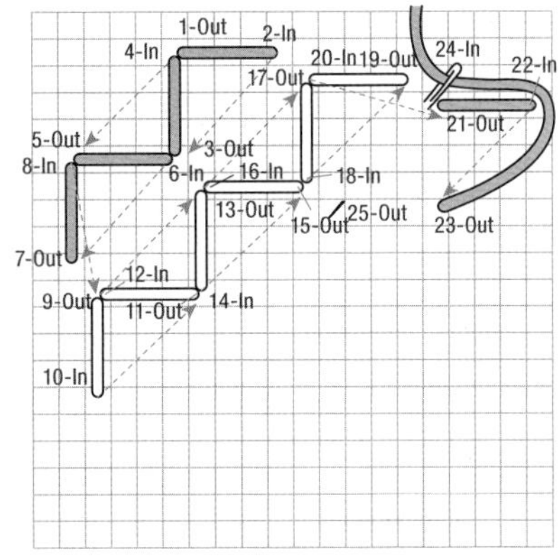

1-Out
2-In
4-In
17-Out
20-In
19-Out
24-In
22-In
21-Out
5-Out
8-In
3-Out
6-In
16-In
18-In
13-Out
15-Out
25-Out
23-Out
7-Out
12-In
9-Out
11-Out
14-In
10-In

1 

Secure floss tail at back (refer to page 63). Bring needle up at fourth warp thread in from outline edge. Count back four warp threads and insert needle. Reemerge four weft threads down and four warp threads left.

2 

Insert needle at initial exit point in step 1. Reemerge from four weft threads down and four warp threads left.

3 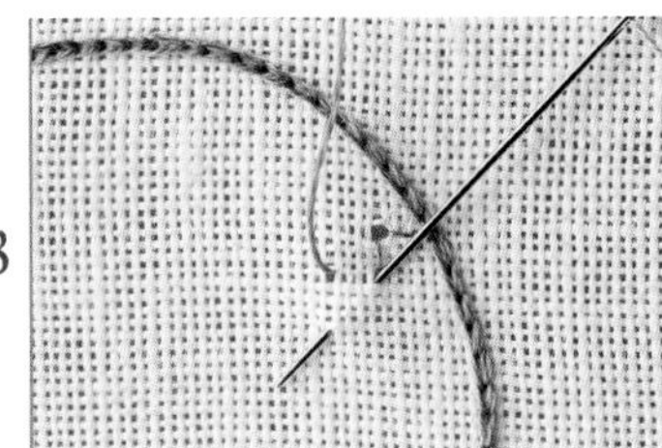

Insert needle at a point where it reemerged in step 1. Reemerge at four weft threads down and four warp threads left.

4 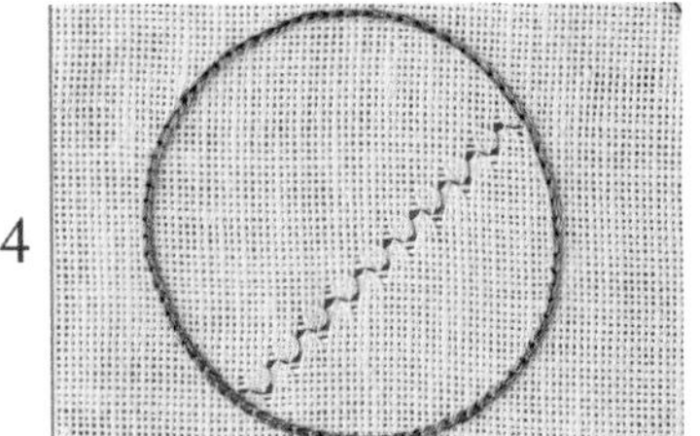

Repeat steps until you reach opposite outline edge.

5 

For the second row, stitch from bottom left to top right. On the backside, slide needle under outline stitches and then bring it up one weft thread below and one warp thread to right of first-row end stitch. Insert needle at four weft threads down (three in this example) and reemerge from four (three) weft threads up and four warp threads diagonally to the right.

6 

Continue by advancing four weft threads up and four warp threads to right. Repeat until you cross to the other side of the outline.

Hedebo Embroidery

Hedebo is a traditional form of whitework embroidery that originated in Denmark. Most stitches are based on the Hedebo buttonhole stitch. Shapes tend to be small circles and triangles, but many variations can be made by combining filling stitches. There are a variety of Hedebo techniques. This book uses mainly buttonhole stitched edging around cutouts and lacelike pattern filling. Originally, Hedebo embroidery used linen floss, but this book uses *coton à broder*, which is much easier to find.

a

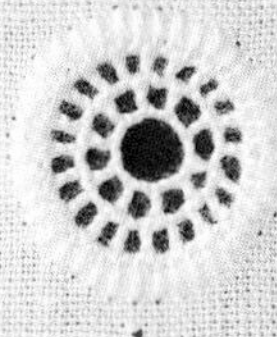

b

c

d

e

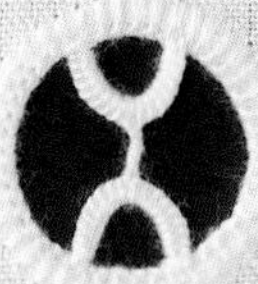

f

g

h

i

Stitches 1

a Hedebo Buttonhole Stitch, One Tier
b Hedebo Buttonhole Stitch, Two Tiers
c Buttonhole Scallops
d Buttonhole Scallop, Two Tiers + Bar
e Buttonhole Scallops + Bars
f Buttonhole Scallops + Bar Linking Scallops
g Bars
h Buttonhole Scallops + Bars Linking Scallops
i Hedebo Buttonhole Stitch, Four Tiers

page 92

j
k
l
m
n
o
p
q

Stitches 2

j Darning Stitch
k Pyramids
l Pyramid + Bar
m Pyramids + Buttonhole Scallop + Bars
n Bars + Coral Knot (Drawn Threadwork, page 57)
o Star (connected pyramid)
p Pyramids + Bars
q Hedebo Buttonhole Stitch, Three Tiers + Pyramids + Bars

page 93

Combining mosaic-like Hedebo rings produces a lovely bird. The filling stitches influence the bird's overall appearance. Feel free to experiment with various combinations until you achieve your desired effect.

15. / design page 95

14. / design page 94

Hedebo embroidery makes wonderful plants. In combination or by themselves, Hedebo rings can be used to create various shapes based on your ideas. You can make a flower with one Hedebo ring or combine them to make many flower petals. The pyramids in this example are raised to produce a three-dimensional feel.

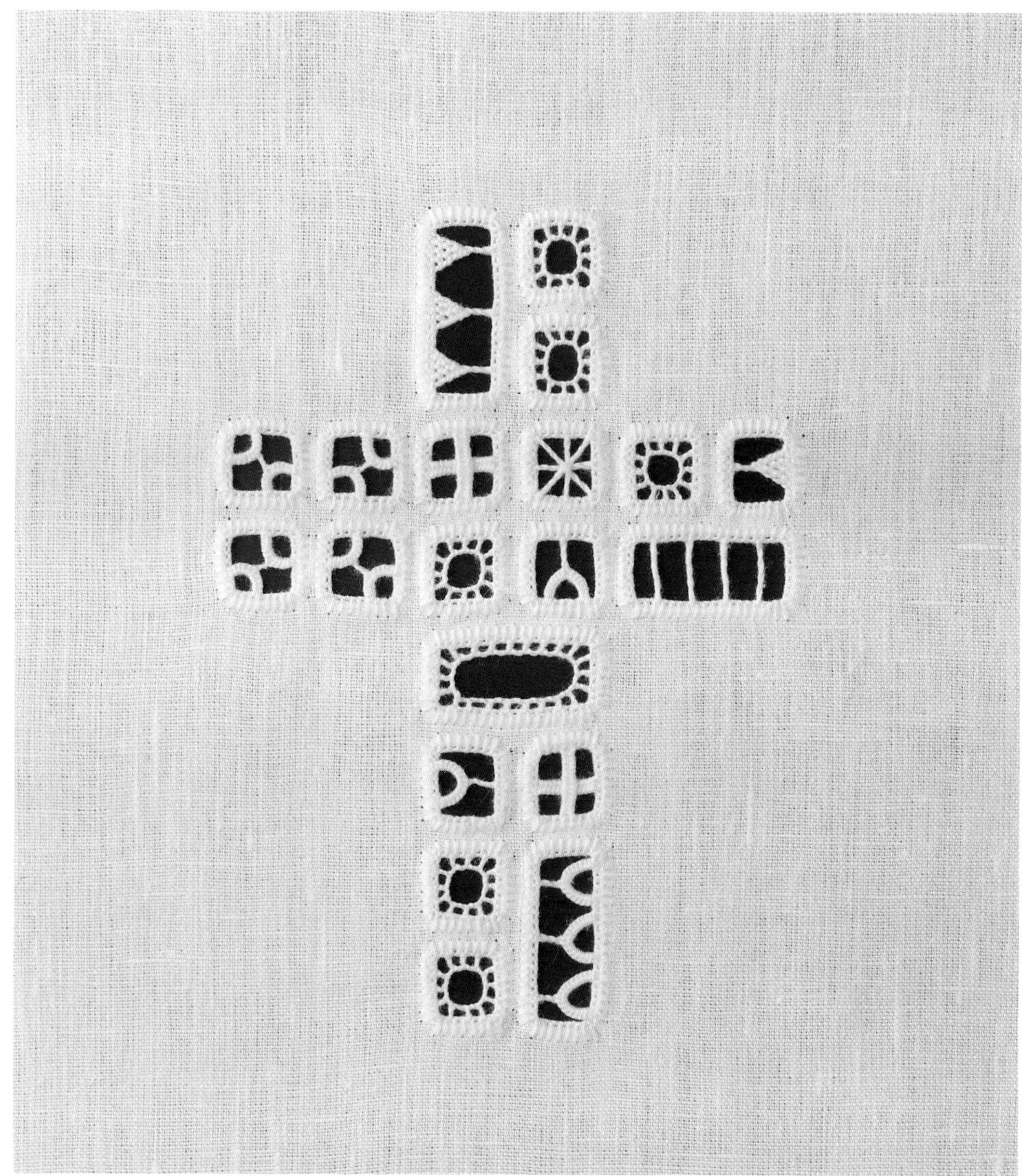

This design combines a number of four-sided figures to create a cross. You can make a cross with squares alone, but it's much more interesting to combine squares and rectangles to produce something unique.

17. / design page 97

16. / design page 96

This beautiful Hedebo embroidery night sky has a fairy-tale atmosphere. Only the tops of the stars are anchored to the fabric, so they appear to sway and shimmer like real stars.

Embroidery Hoop Case

18. / How To page 98

Your embroidery hoop is such a reliable friend that it deserves a case. Embroidering directly on the case would look wonderful, of course, but embroidering on another piece of fabric and layering it on the case allows the case fabric color to show through and stand out.

Cross Motif Drawstring Pouch

19. / How To page 100

This stylish pouch layers two different-colored fabrics and uses buttonhole scallops for threading.

Place Mats and Coasters

20. / How To page 102

These will allow you (or a lucky recipient) to eat in high style. All you need to do is embroider motifs in the desired positions.

First, make a running stitch to mark the position of the Hedebo ring. Next, cut fabric inside the ring, little by little, and work Hedebo buttonhole stitches along the cut edge. Once the ring is outlined with Hedebo buttonhole stitches, begin stitching inside the ring as desired by combining different stitches. Use sharp and blunt-pointed needles to outline, but only a blunt-pointed needle to stitch inside the outlined area.

1. Outline the Circle

1

Transfer pattern onto fabric. Outline pattern with running stitch.

2

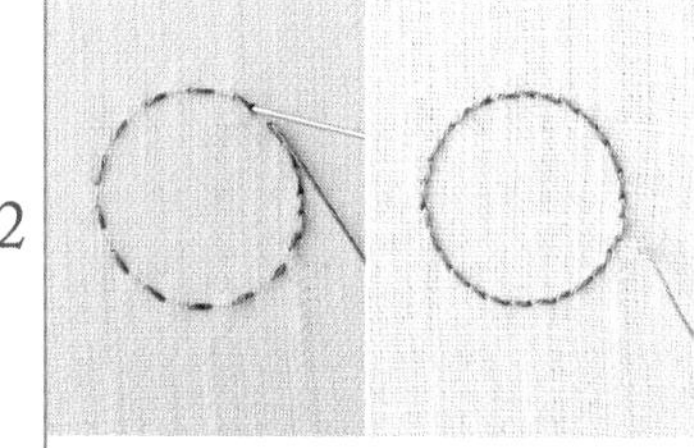

Work running stitches (double running stitches) to fill in empty spaces. Bring needle up about 2–3 mm / ⅛" outside outline.

3

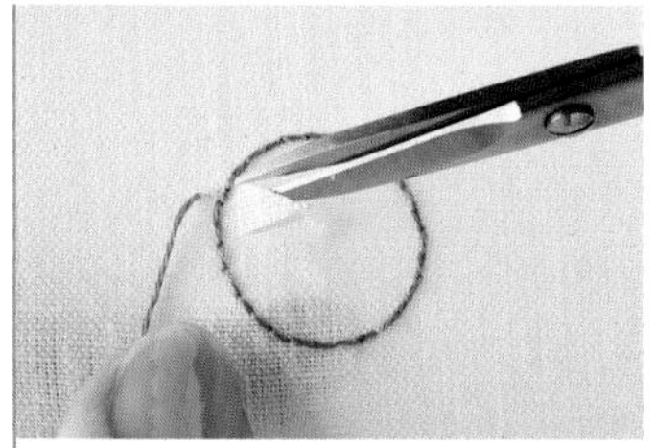

Cut fabric outward from center. Divide circle into ten to twelve equal parts—just eyeball it—and make an incision from center to where needle exited in step 2. Be careful not to cut running stitches.

4

Fold cut fabric toward backside. Slide needle under running stitches and bring needle up about 2 mm / ⅛" from where the needle emerged in step 2.

5

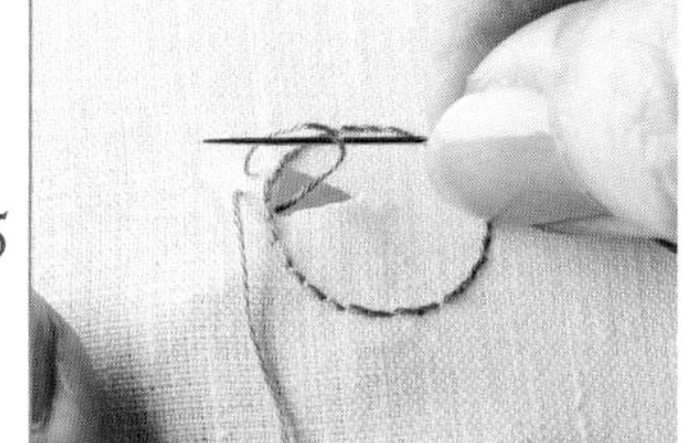

Pull needle through and start pulling floss slowly. Before pulling tight, pass needle through loop from back to front.

6

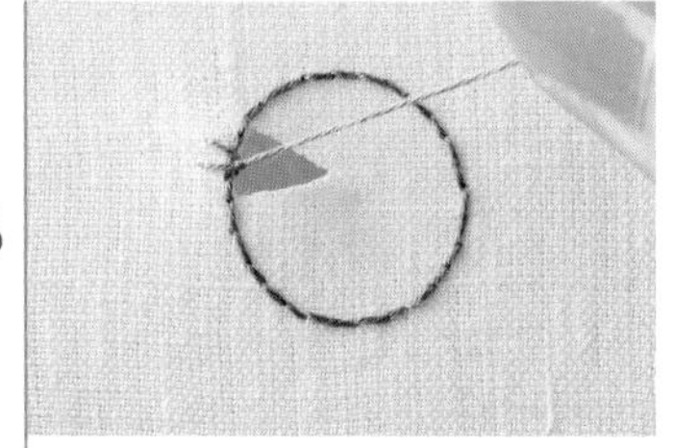

Tighten. This completes one Hedebo buttonhole stitch. Repeat steps counterclockwise along the circle up to cut fabric edge.

7

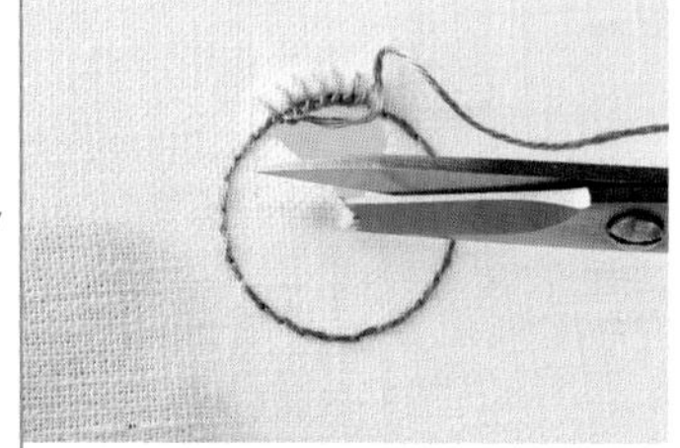

After the cut portion has been stitched, cut another section, adjacent to the first, in the same manner as before. Fold to the back and work buttonhole stitches. Repeat this process for the entire circle.

8

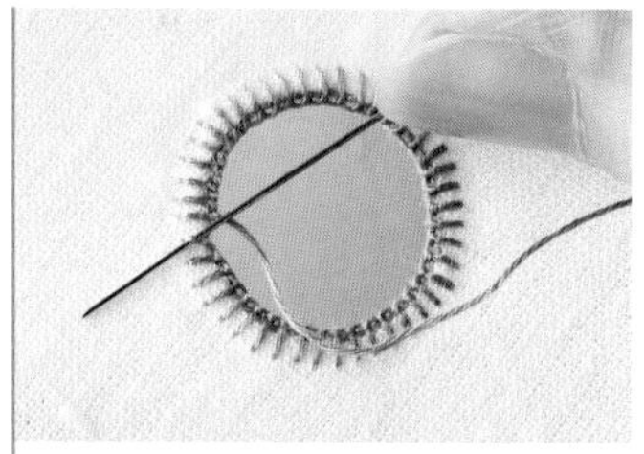

Outline is complete. Change to a blunt-pointed needle. Slide it under the thread from the first stitch. Pull floss taut.

9

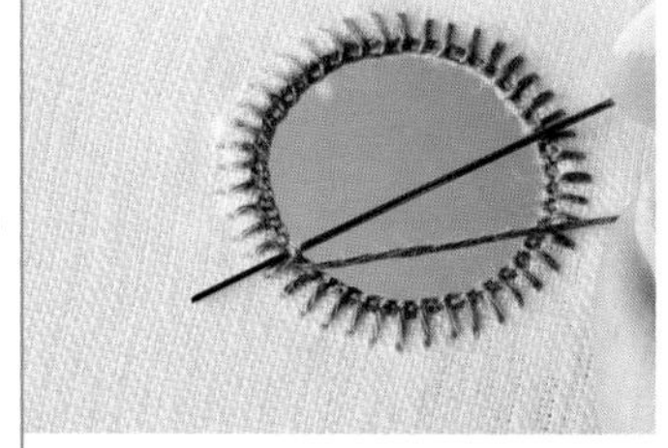

Next, slide needle under looped edge thread from back to front.

10

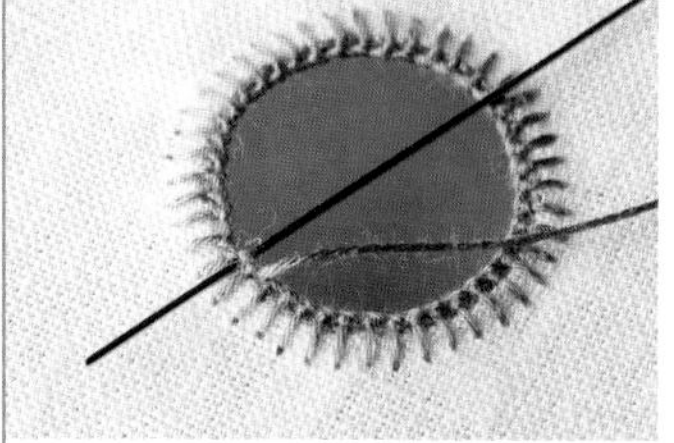

Repeat step 9 and stitch up the threads all around. Slide needle under the first stitch at end.

11

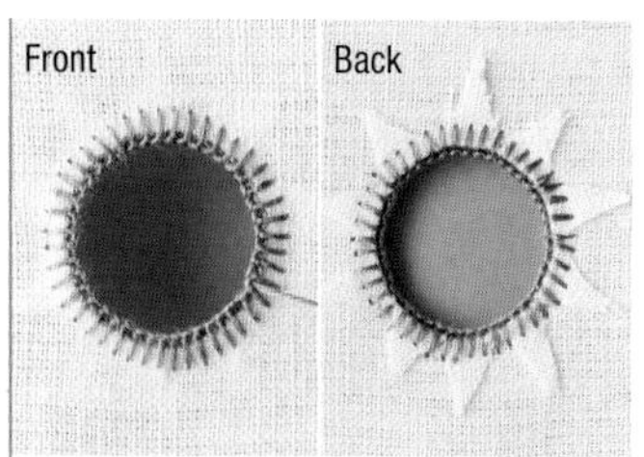
Front
Back

This completes the circle outline. The backside is shown in the photo above. If you don't fill the circle, secure floss at back (refer to page 63).

2. Work Filling Stitches

Hedebo Buttonhole Stitch

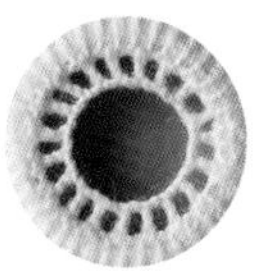
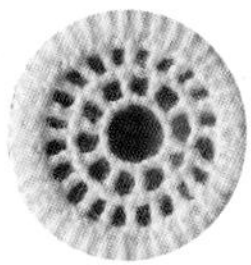

Making Hedebo buttonhole stitches inside a circle creates a ladderlike lace pattern. As the Hedebo buttonhole stitches increase, the pattern becomes more intricate.

*Tier 1

1

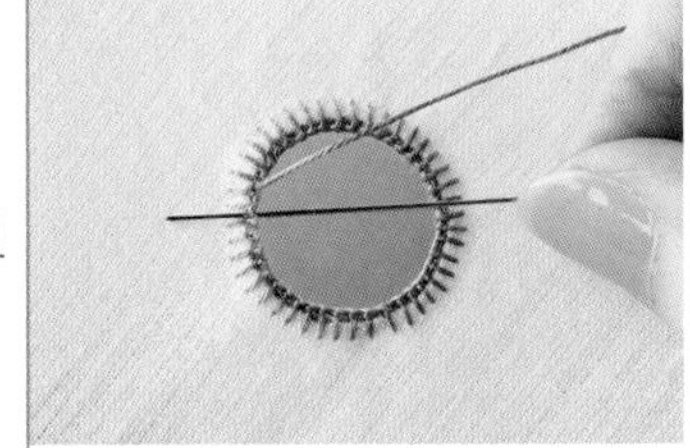

After outlining is complete, slide needle—from back to front—under looped edge two stitches away in a counterclockwise direction.

2

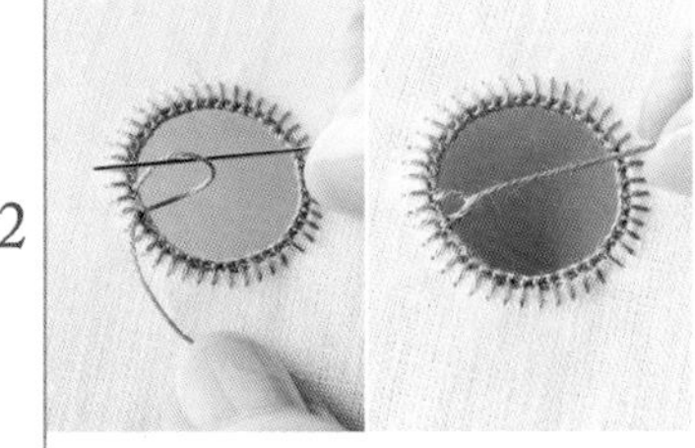

Before pulling floss all the way through, pass needle through loop from backside. Pull floss lightly and leave a loop (see photo above). This completes a single Hedebo buttonhole stitch.

3

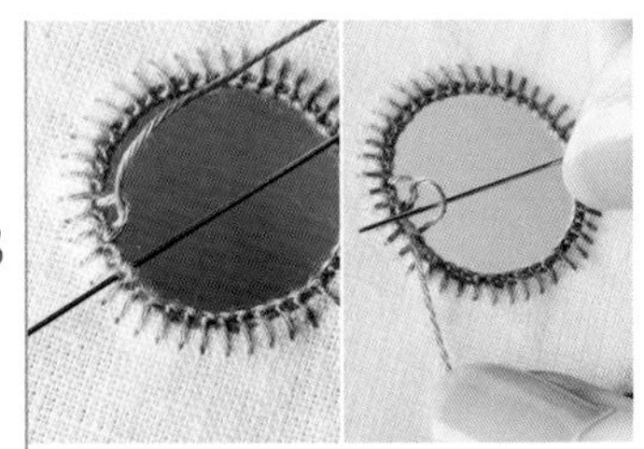

Repeat steps 1 and 2. Slide needle—back to front—under looped edge two stitches down. Pull floss lightly and pass needle through loop from back to front.

4

Repeat steps noted above to stitch perimeter of circle. For the last stitch, pass needle through the first stitch from back to front.

5

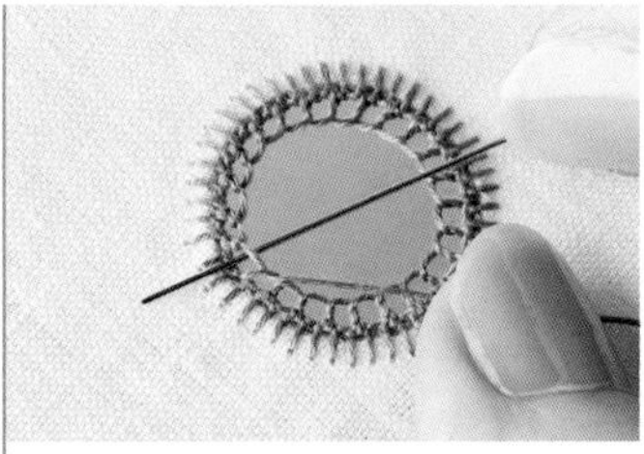

Next, pass needle through next loop from back to front, in a clockwise direction. Repeat stitching all the way around.

6

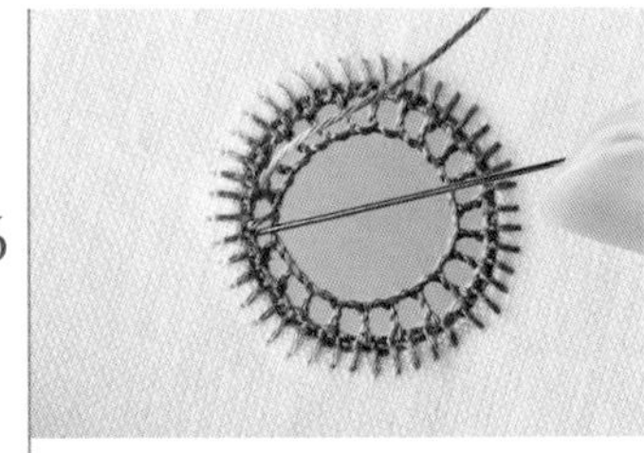

Once complete, slide needle under the first stitch and pass through to the back at initial stitch.

7

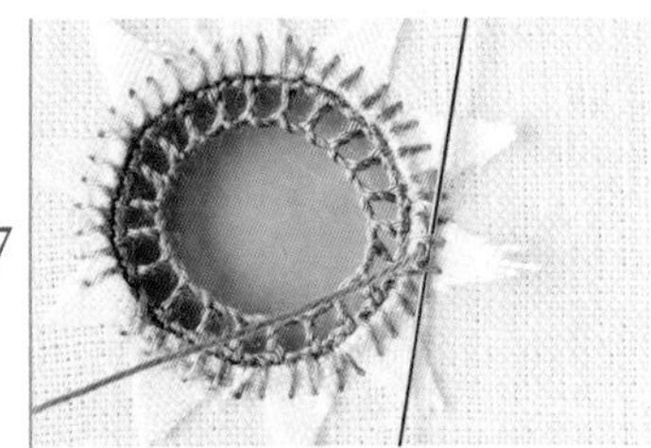

At rear, slide needle under stitches and secure the floss (refer to page 63).

8

Cut excess folded fabric on backside. Be careful not to cut the stitched floss. The first row is now complete.

*Tier 2

9

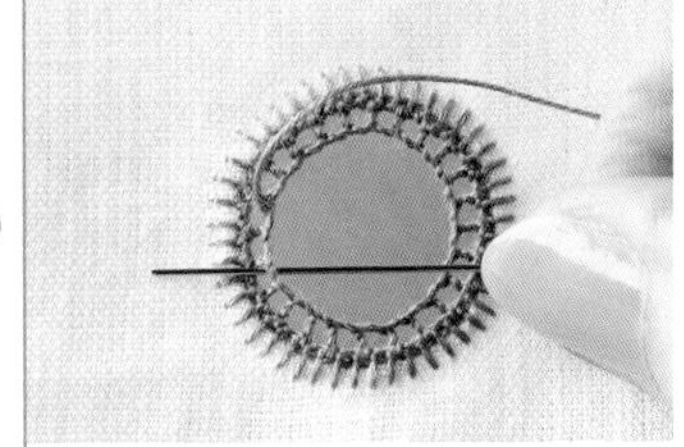

To continue with the second tier, pass needle in a counterclockwise direction—from back to front—through second stitch loop.

10

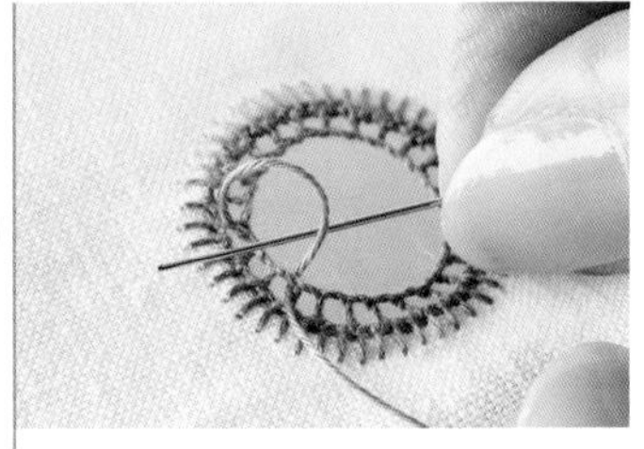

Before pulling floss all the way through, pass needle through loop from the backside. Pull floss lightly but leave a loop. The first stitch on the second tier is now complete.

11

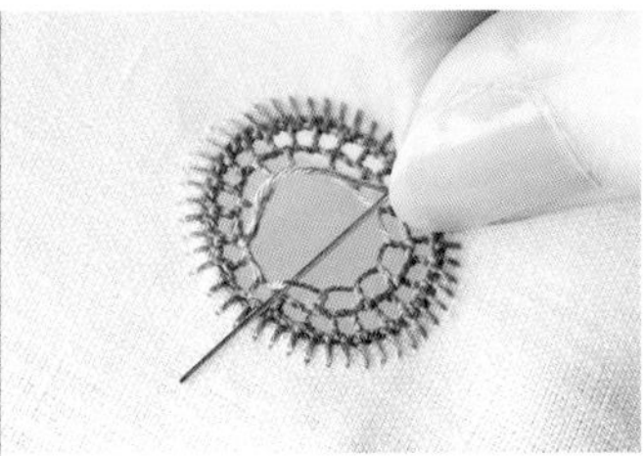

Repeat stitching counterclockwise. For last stitch on row, pass needle through first stitch—from back to front. The rest of the stitching is done in the same way as steps 5 through 7. Secure floss at backside once the tier is complete.

Buttonhole Scallop

Building up an arc with floss to make a base, and then using Hedebo buttonhole stitches, creates scallops. A second row can be made to span two buttonhole scallops.

*Tier 1

1

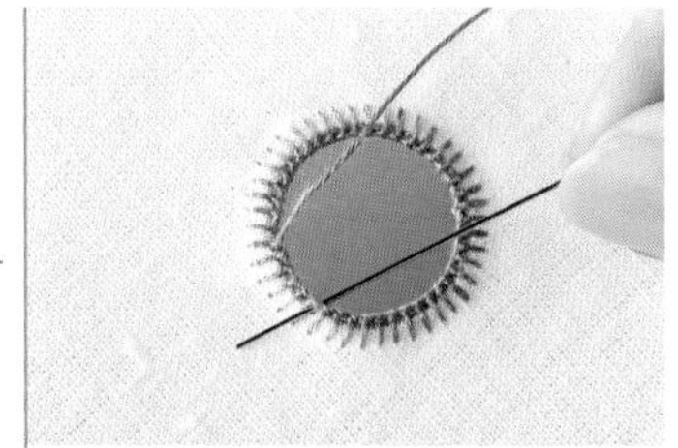

After outlining is complete, slide needle—back to front—under fifth looped edge stitch counterclockwise.

2

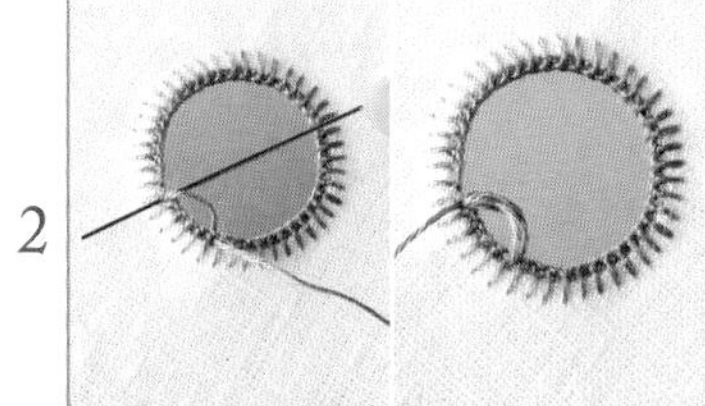

Make an arc to describe a semicircle without pulling floss all the way through. Repeat four times.

3

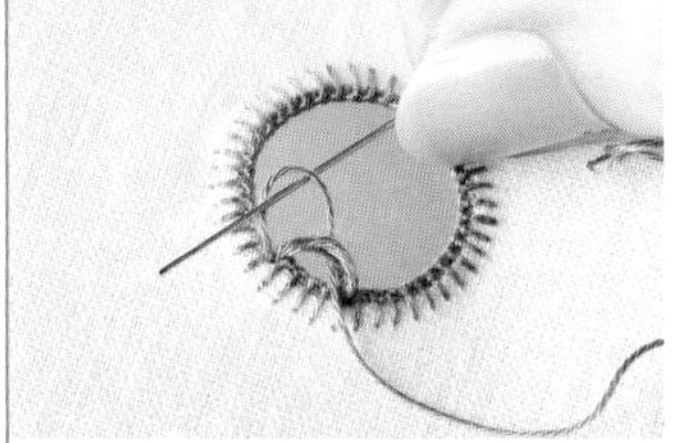

Insert needle through arc—back to front. Pull needle through while leaving a small loop. Insert needle through loop from back to front.

4

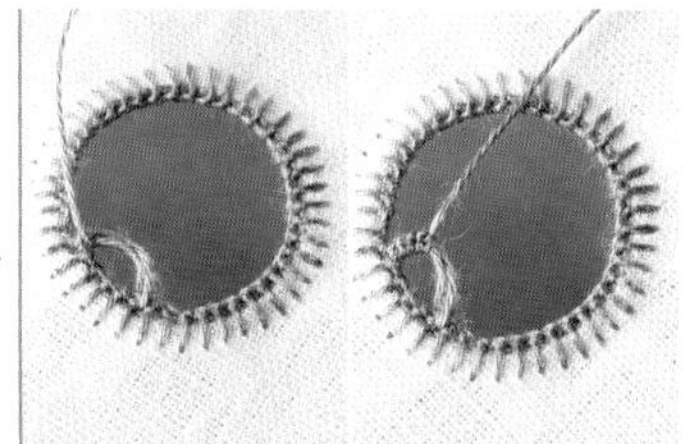

Pull floss taut to tighten loop. One Hedebo buttonhole on arc is complete. Repeat to wrap arc with buttonhole stitches.

5

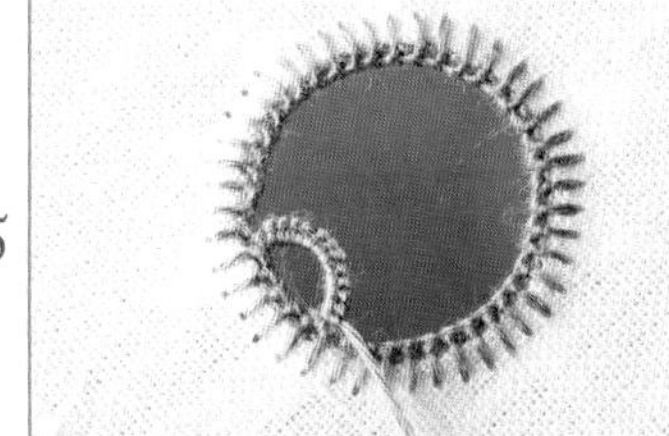

The arc is filled now. If you wish to finish at this point, slide needle under same stitch as in step 1 and secure the floss (refer to page 63).

*Tier 2

6

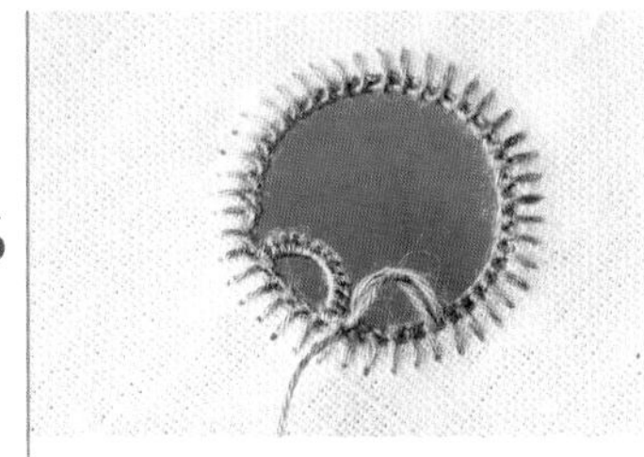

To make the second tier, slide needle under next looped edge stitch—back to front. Make arc in same manner as above.

7

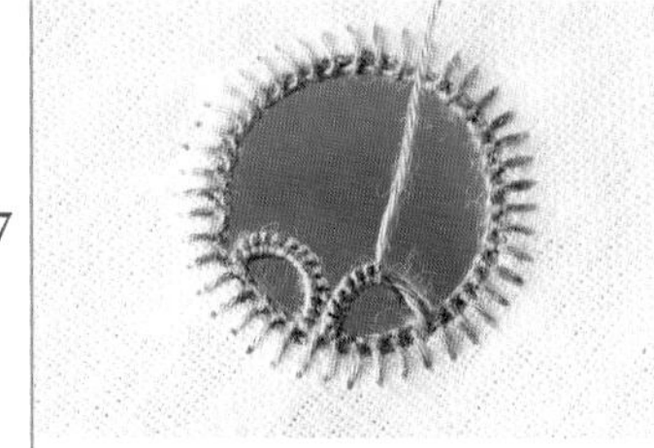

In a similar manner to steps 2 through 4, fill half of the arc with Hedebo buttonhole stitches.

8

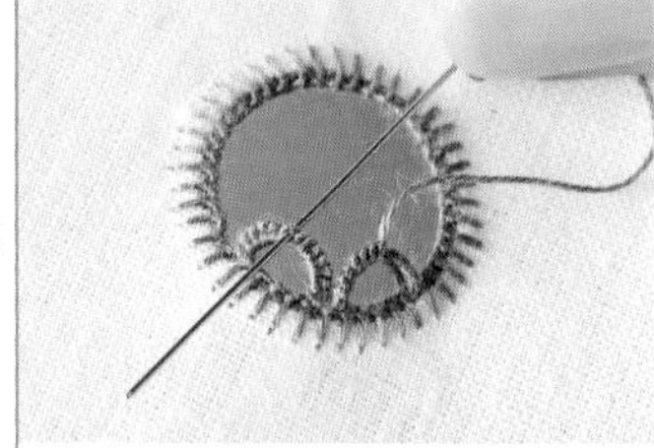

Next, insert needle at peak of first scallop—back to front.

9

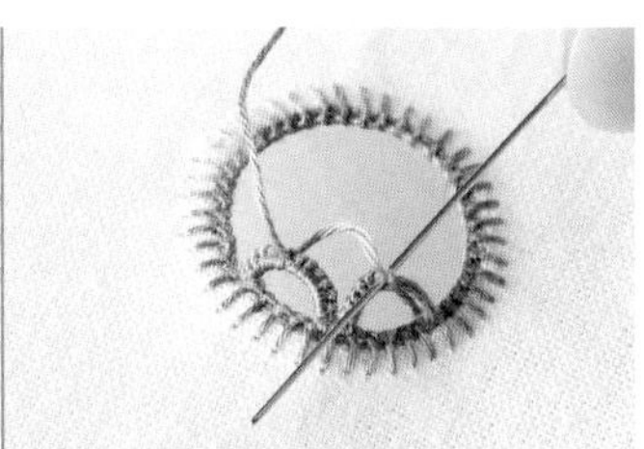

Go back to the second scallop and insert needle into the stitching. Repeat three times to build arc. Then, fill arc with Hedebo buttonhole stitches.

10

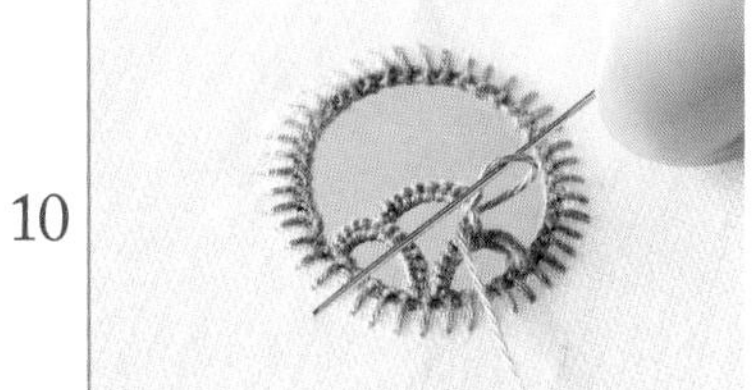

Once arc is filled, the second tier is complete.

11

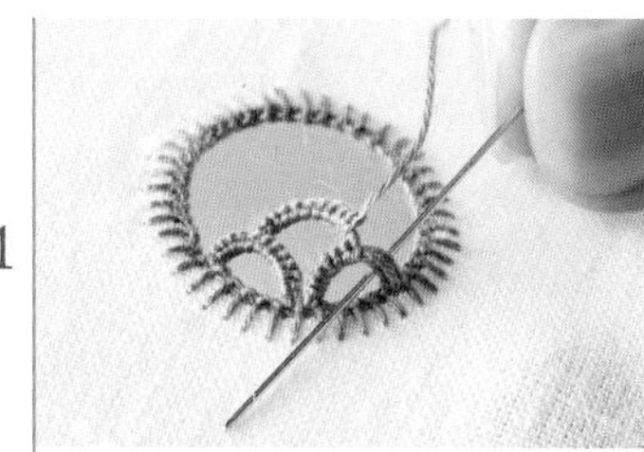

Insert needle into stitching on second scallop of first tier and then continue to fill arc.

Make Bar

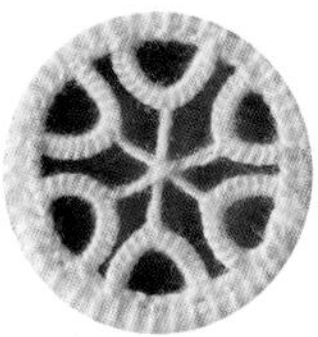

Bars are used to pass floss directly across the circle and to connect buttonhole scallops that face each other. This section explains how to pass the floss through all six buttonhole scallops.

1

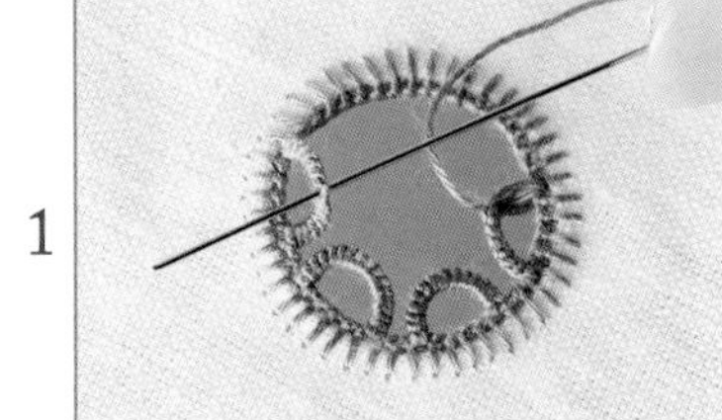

First, make three buttonhole scallops. Then, fill arc of fourth scallop with Hedebo buttonhole stitch to midpoint. Then, insert needle into peak of scallop across from the fourth scallop, going from back to front.

2

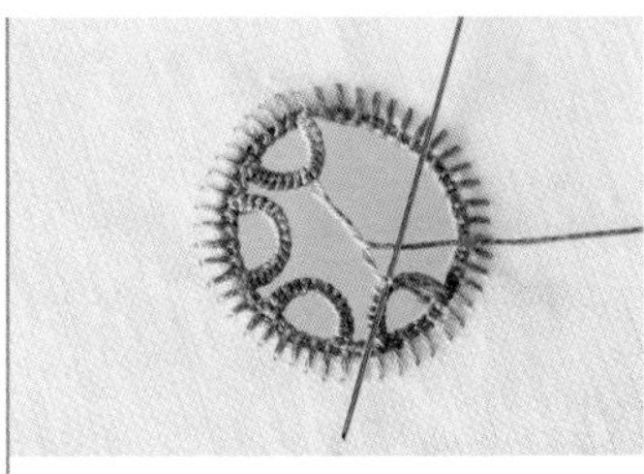

Wrap floss around piece that goes back to the fourth scallop. Insert needle into the stitching on fourth scallop from back to front.

3

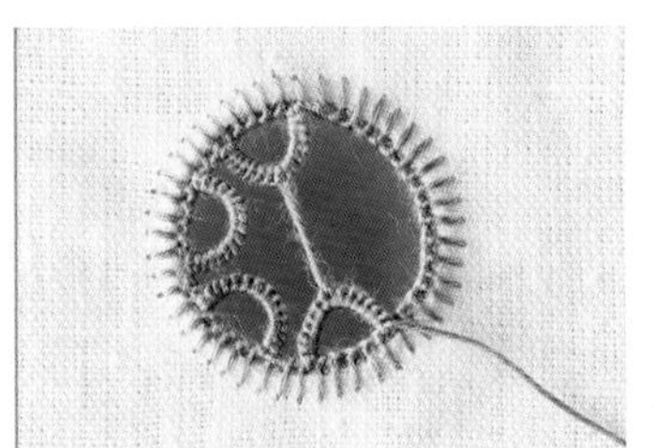

Fill remaining half of arc with Hedebo buttonhole stitches. One bar is finished.

4

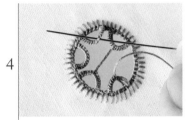

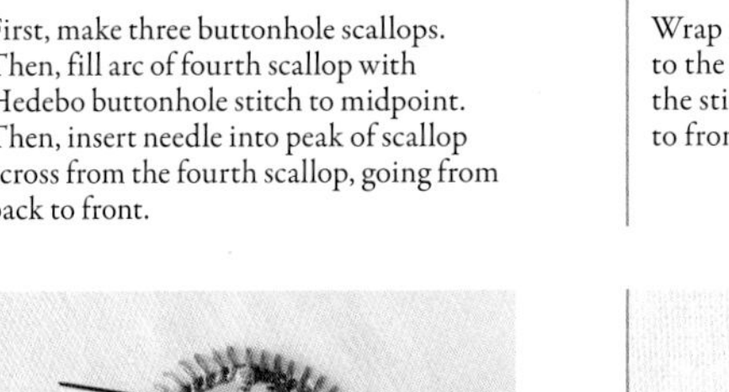

For remaining two scallops, pass floss back and forth in the same manner.

5

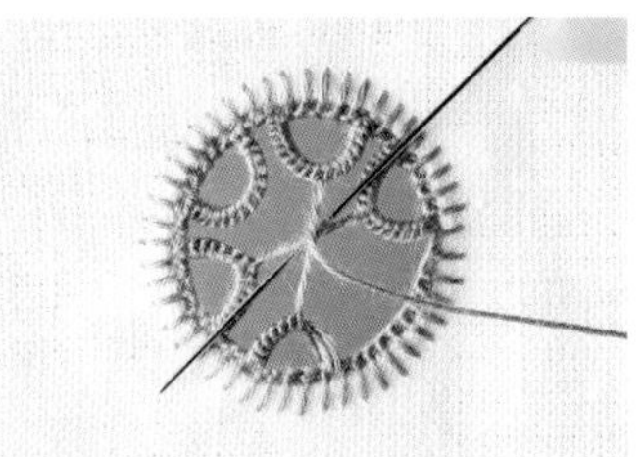

At bar intersections, insert needle into the bar and wrap.

Darning Stitch

Alternate passing needle over and under the two bars inside the circle. This is similar to the weave stitch that makes up the cross pattern presented in Schwalm embroidery (page 18).

1

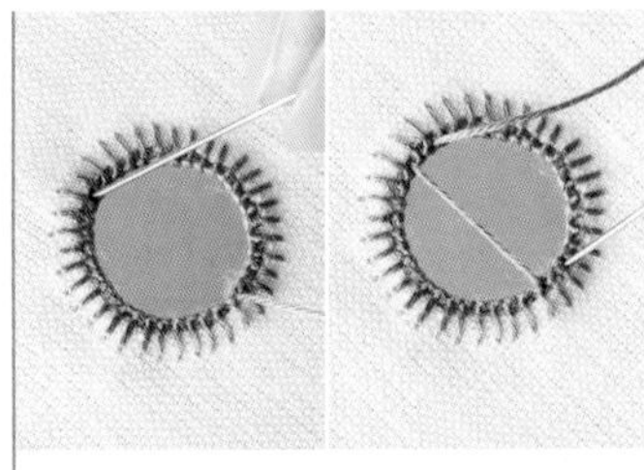

Once outlining is complete, pass needle from front to back across circle. Bring needle up two stitches to right and insert—from front to back—on opposite side. Two parallel bars are made.

2

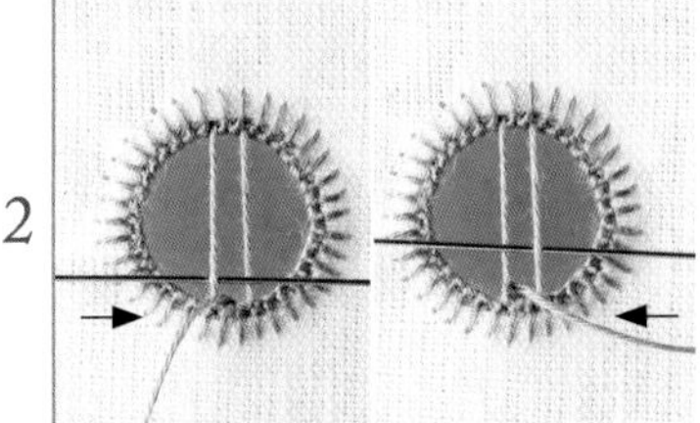

Bring needle up between bars and then pass it under the left and over the right. Next, pass needle under right bar and over left.

3

Repeat steps above and stitch all the way to the other side.

4

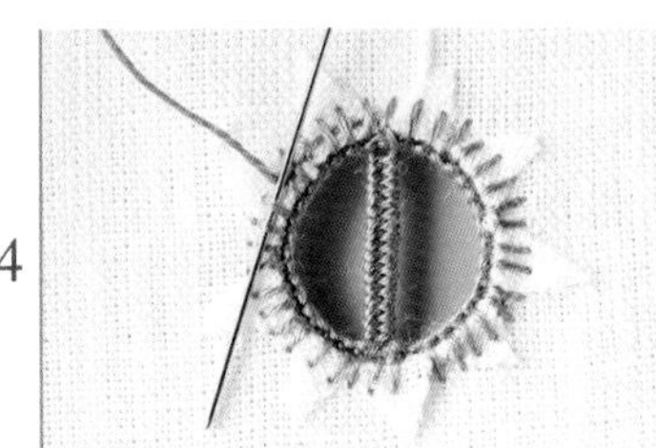

To make the cross, slide needle under stitches at backside and move around until you arrive at a position that is at right angles to the original bar.

5

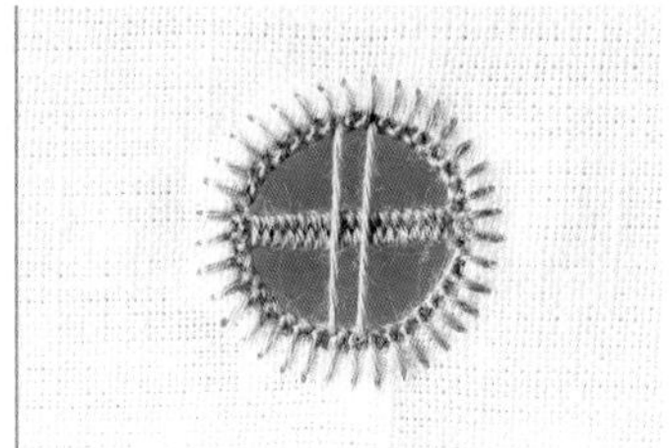

In a similar manner to before, make two parallel bars and work darning stitches to fill them.

Pyramid

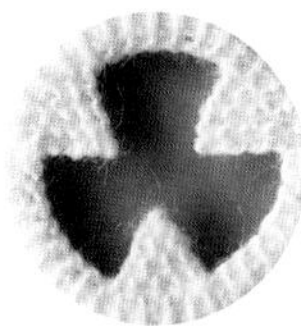

Make pyramid shapes inside the circle, using Hedebo buttonhole stitches. The size of the pyramid will vary depending on the length of the base. Be aware that the curved base may produce a crooked shape. Having said that, dividing the circle into eight to ten equal parts is the best way to make a beautiful pyramid or pyramids.

1

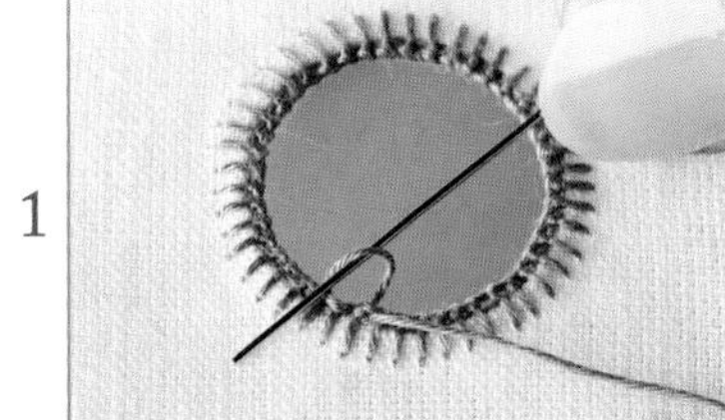

Once outlining is complete, slide needle, from back to front, under next looped edge stitch in a counterclockwise direction. Pull needle through while leaving a small loop. Insert needle through loop from back to front.

2

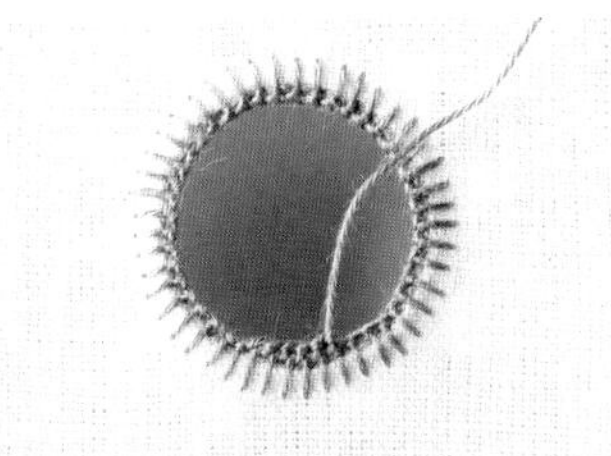

Repeat steps above and make five Hedebo buttonhole stitches.

3

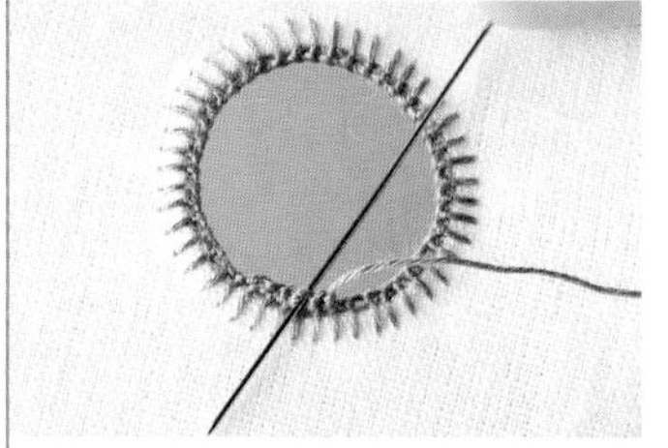

Next, insert needle into fifth looped edge stitch from back to front and go back to first Hedebo buttonhole stitch. This completes the first row.

4

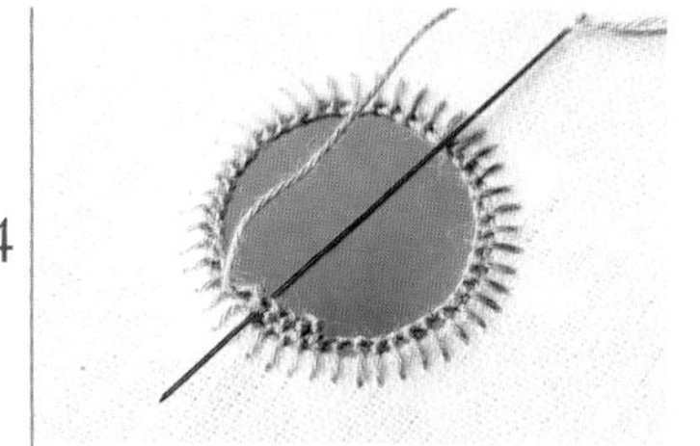

Move on to the second row. Insert needle into second looped edge stitch on the first row and make Hedebo buttonhole stitch. After making four Hedebo buttonhole stitches, go back as you insert needle into each looped edge stitch in the same manner as the first row.

5

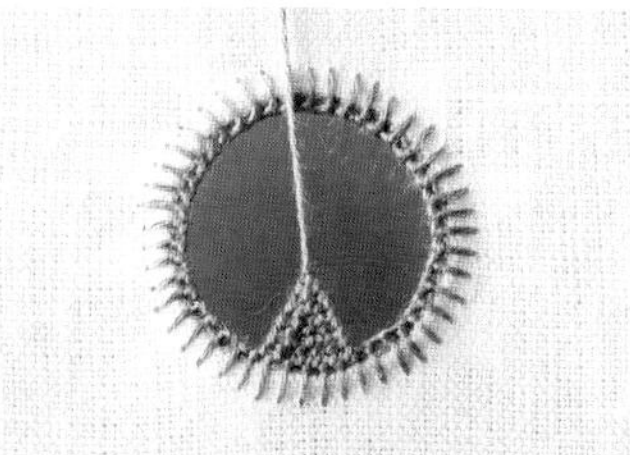

Repeat steps until you have a single stitch on the fifth row. That forms the pyramid peak.

6

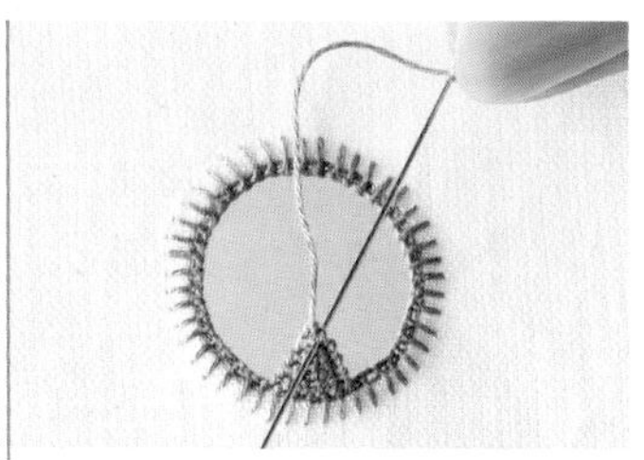

Insert needle at rightmost stitch on fourth row—moving from back to front. Reverse steps 3, 2, and 1 to create the descending row.

7

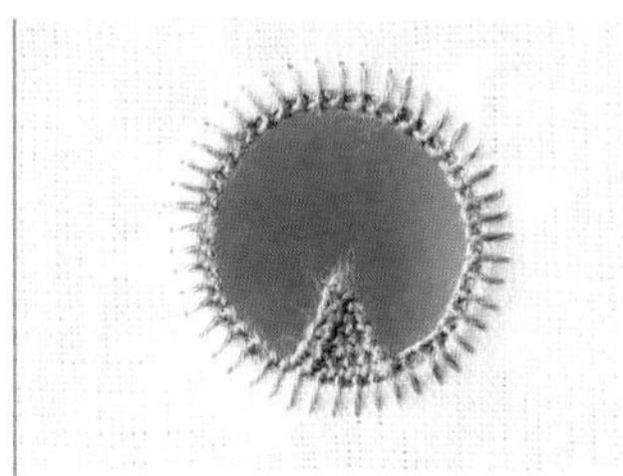

One pyramid is complete.

8

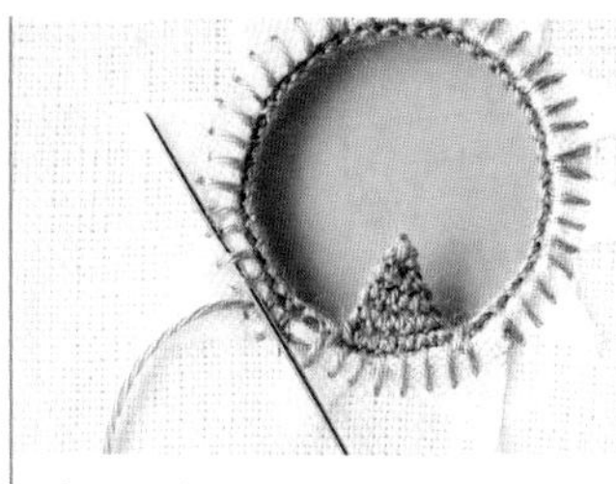

If you wish to complete your work at this point, secure floss at back (refer to page 63). To continue making more pyramids, bring needle back and slide it under the stitching until it is at desired start position for next pyramid.

Star

Wrap floss around Hedebo ring stick to make a ring-shaped foundation. Make pyramids to fill out the perimeter of the ring.

1 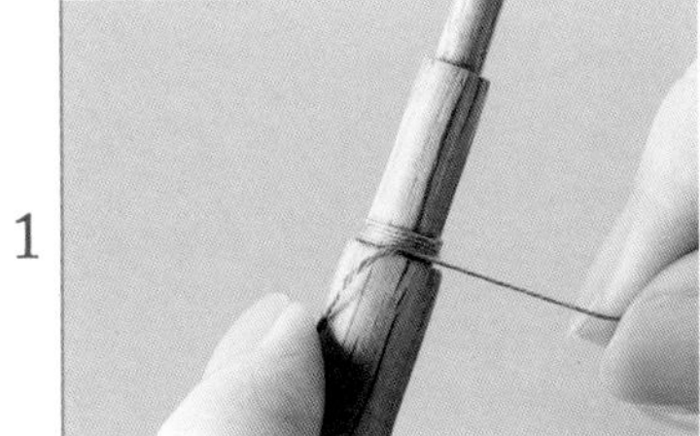

Wrap floss around Hedebo ring stick five times. If a Hedebo ring stick isn't available, use a tubular-shaped object such as a pen.

2 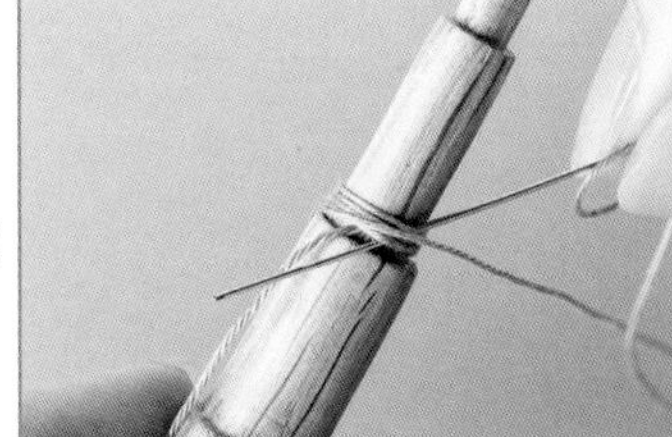

Inset needle between the stick and ring.

3 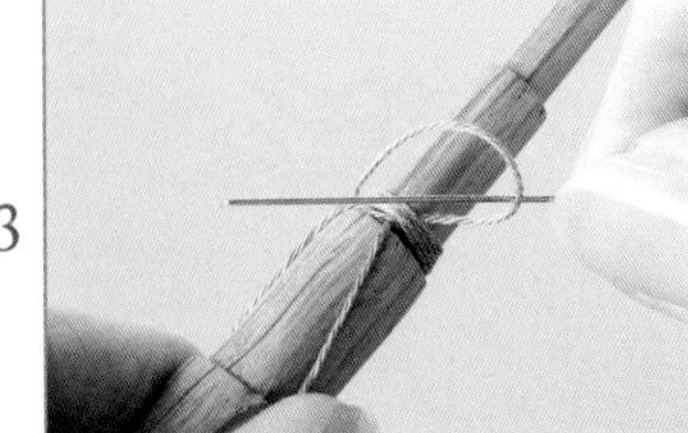

Pull floss through. Leave a small loop and insert needle through that loop from back to front.

4 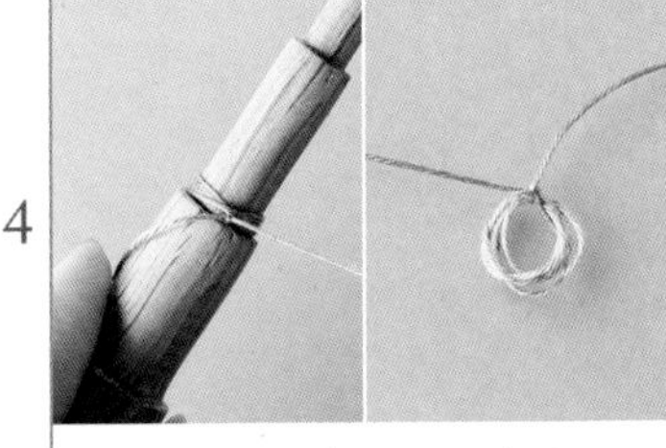

Pull floss taut and remove stick. One Hedebo buttonhole stitch is done.

5 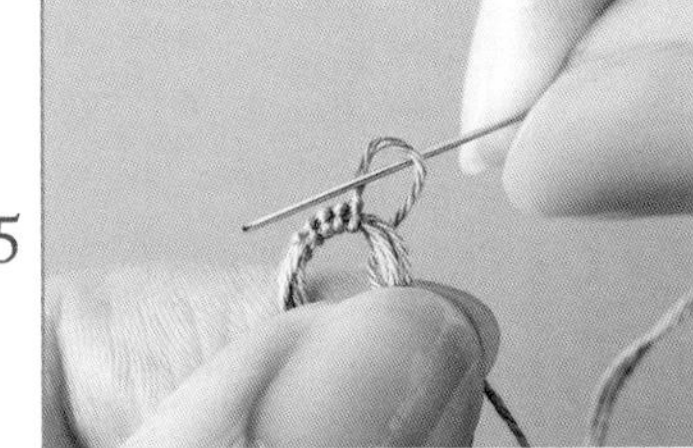

Make five Hedebo buttonhole stitches, moving clockwise. This is the first row of the pyramid.

6 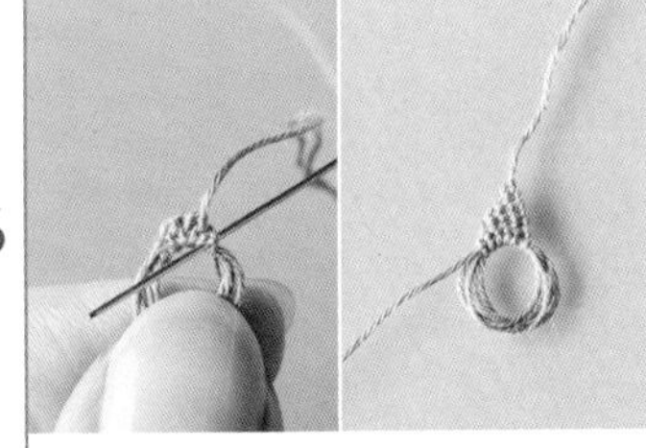

Make a pyramid, using steps similar to those on page 49.

7 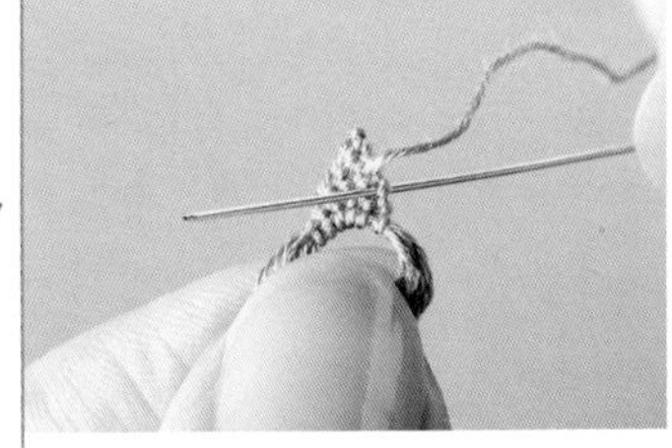

Once you reach the fifth row, pass needle through rightmost stitch from back to front. Insert needle into rightmost stitch one row below to descend.

8 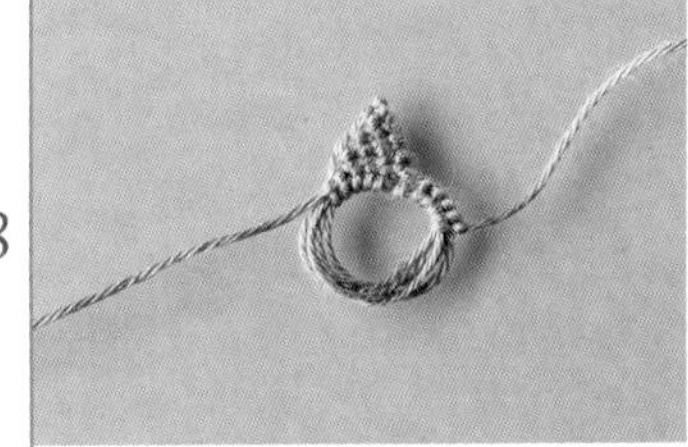

Once you have made it back down to the foundation, make five Hedebo buttonhole stitches and continue on to next pyramid.

9 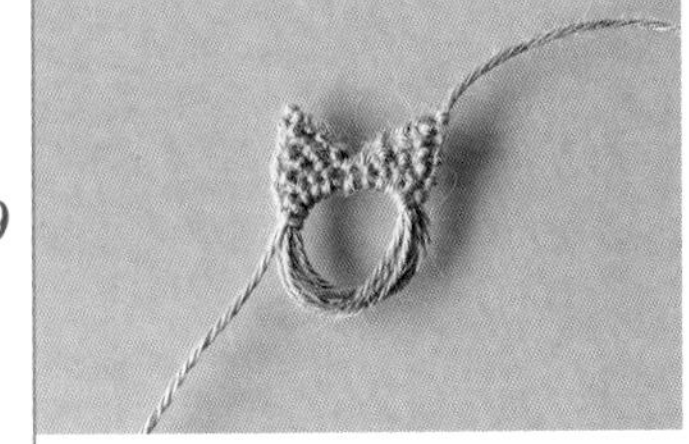

The second pyramid is complete. Make three more pyramids to make a full star.

Drawn Threadwork

The word "drawn" is used in the sense meaning "pulled out." Some of the threads in the fabric are pulled out and cut off, and the stitches on the remaining threads are used to make band-like shapes. This technique is often used for border decorations on handkerchiefs and for hems on garments. In some cases, threads are drawn over a large area, but this section uses a technique where the wefts are pulled out in thin strips and the warps are stitched to produce simple patterns.

a
b
c
d

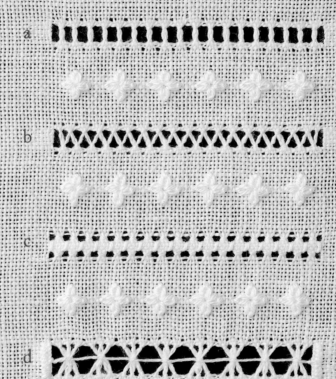

Stitches 1

a Ladder Hemstitch (bind four warp threads at both top and bottom edge)
b Zigzag Hemstitch (the ends gather two warp threads, but everywhere else uses four warps)
c Four-Sided Stitch (bind four threads in both the weft and warp direction)
d Ladder Hemstitch + Coral Knot (bind three warps along both top and bottom edge + chain middle of band)

page 104

The photo above is enlarged to 130%

e
f
g
h

Stitches 2

e Hemstitch (bind four warp threads along bottom edge)
f Coral Knot (bind along middle of band)
g Four-Sided Stitch + Coral Knot (bind three warps at top and bottom edge + Coral Knot)
h Ladder Hemstitch + Four-Sided Stitch (bind four warps on top and bottom edge + four-sided stitch along middle of band)

page 104

The photo above is enlarged to 130%

Dalecarlian Horse Hoop

21. / How To page 105

Framing your embroidery with a hoop makes for a wonderful interior accent.
The central strips of drawn threadwork look great against the simple Dalecarlian horses.

Ribbon & Ribbon Brooch

22. / How To page 106

Drawn threadwork on linen tape makes for an exquisite ribbon. When long enough, this lovely ribbon can be used for exquisite gift wrapping. On the other hand, when made shorter, the ribbon can be used to make a brooch or barrette.

Withdraw weft thread across desired width of pattern and stitch to outline the band.
Just outlining the band creates a pattern, but stitching inside that band will create a really intricate pattern. Use blunt-pointed needles.

1. Withdraw Weft

1
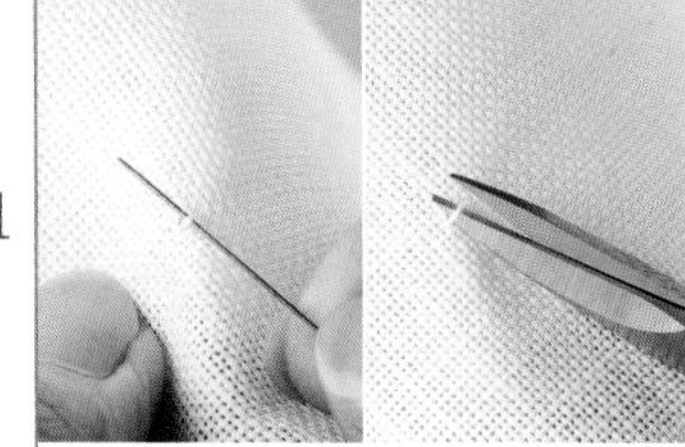

Flip fabric backside up. Pull up midpoint of weft thread you intend to withdraw with needle. Cut pulled-out section, while being careful not to cut other threads.

2
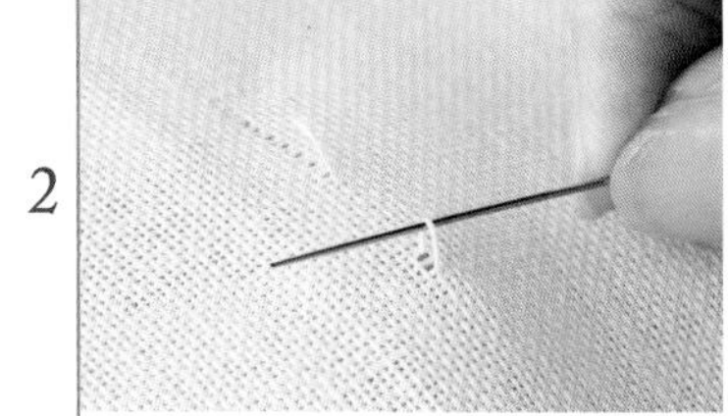

Little by little, unweave the snipped weft thread to the left.

3

Once edge is reached, thread needle with withdrawn weft. Dispose of thread at band edge.

4
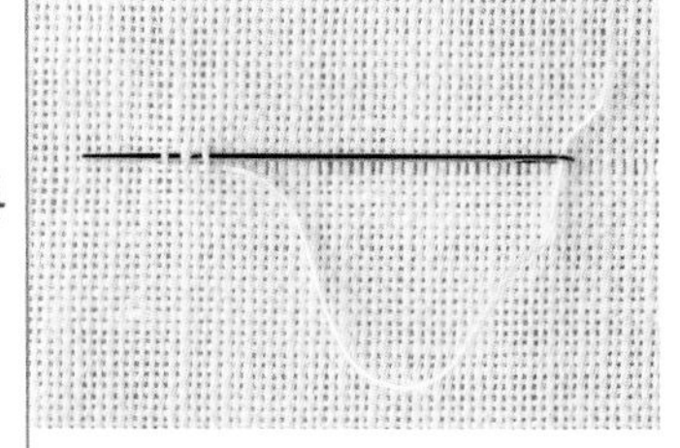

Push needle under every other warp thread, for three threads, just above withdrawn weft. This will secure the withdrawn weft.

5

Next, do the same for the right side. Unweave and dispose of withdrawn weft.

6

Withdraw as many wefts as necessary to make hemstitches and dispose of each withdrawn weft. The hemstitch band is now ready.

2. Filling the Band

Hemstitch

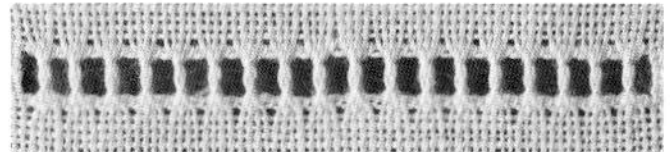

Bind warp threads, at top and bottom, inside the band created by withdrawing weft threads. Changing the top and bottom binding positions will alter look of your hemstitch.

1
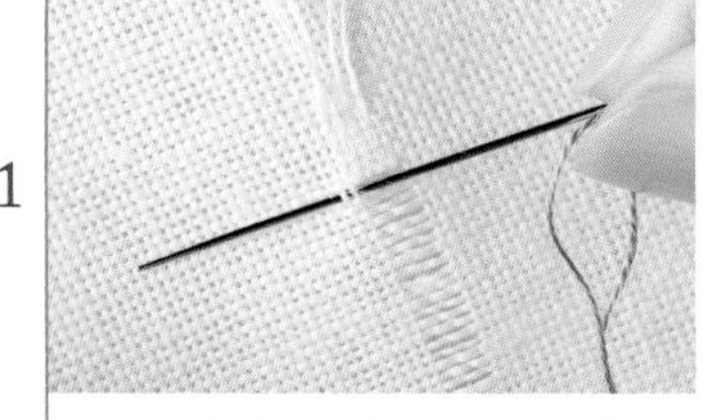

Turn backside up and position intended band vertically. Insert needle at an angle and scoop under two weft threads.

2
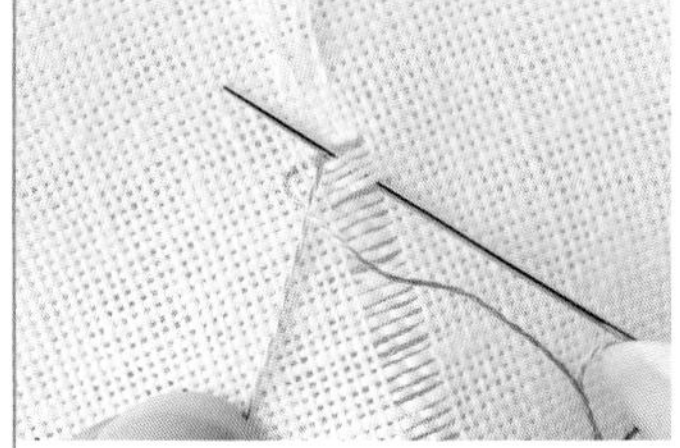

Pass needle under four warp threads and then push the tip out.

3
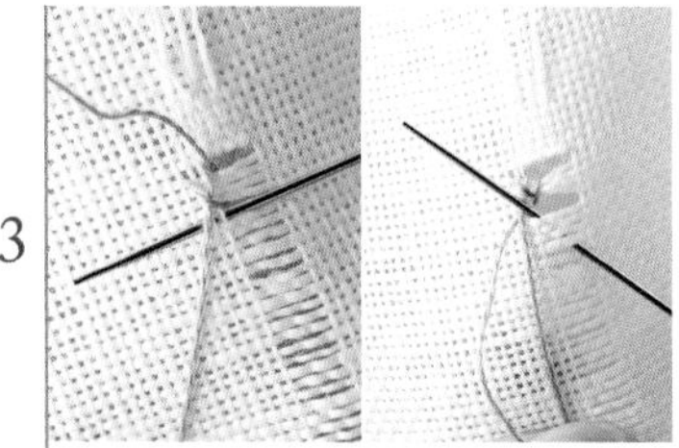

Bring needle back to previous stitch and scoop two weft threads down from edge. Pull floss taut. Subsequently, push needle under next four warp threads.

4
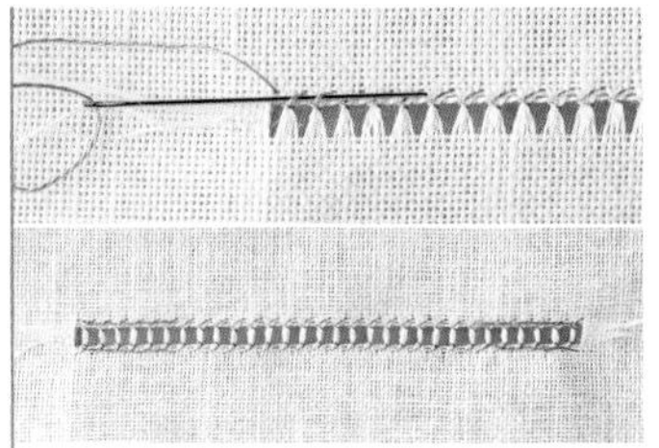

Repeat steps to stitch to other side, then secure floss. Slide needle under the stitching on backside. Do the same for the other edge and secure floss.

5
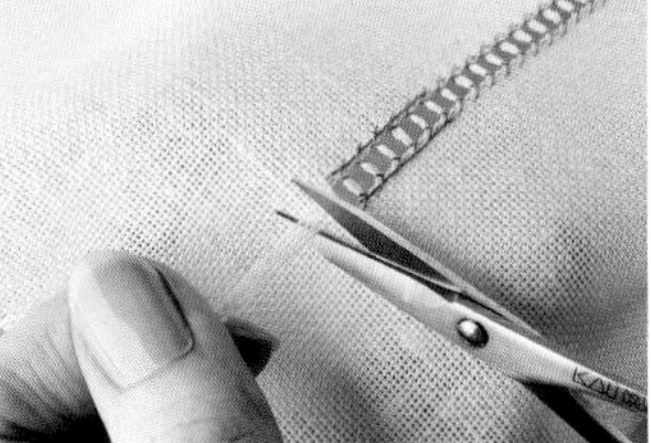

Cut off withdrawn weft strands that remain on each side. The reason we leave the withdrawn threads is so that they can be redone if we mistakenly withdraw the wrong number of threads.

Buttonhole Stitch

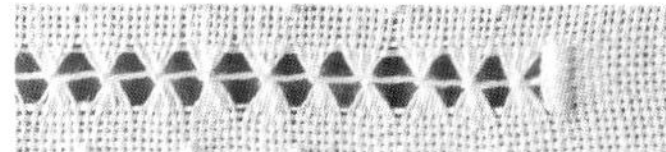

Both ends of the band are stitched. This is used when coral knot runs the length of the band.

1

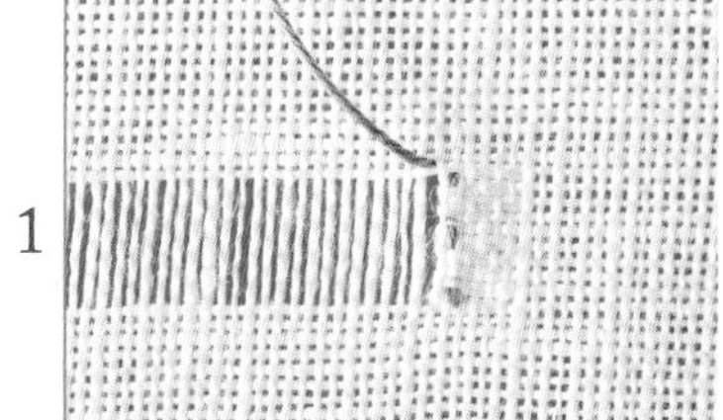

With the fabric front side up, make a few running stitches to bind corner. Pull floss through but leave a little tail at bottom edge of band.

2

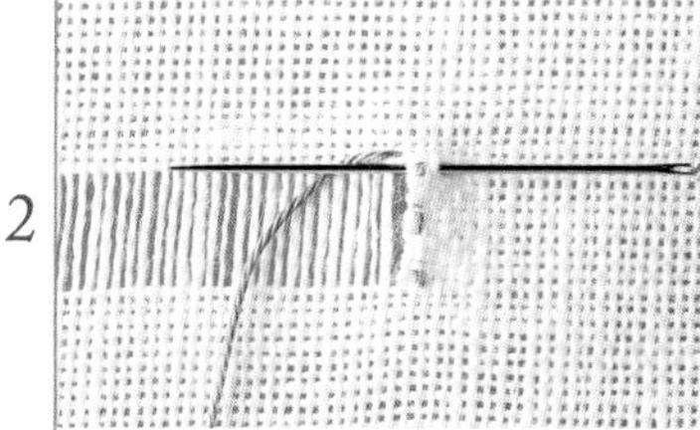

Push needle under three warp threads, from right to left, and reemerge. Lay floss under needle. Pull both needle and floss all the way through.

3

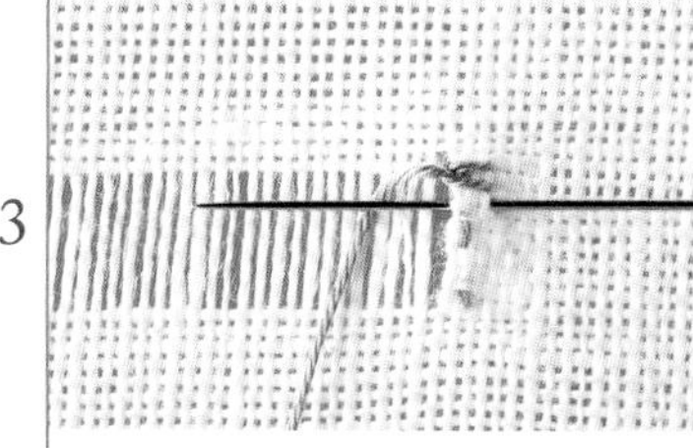

Repeat steps for entire height of band.

4

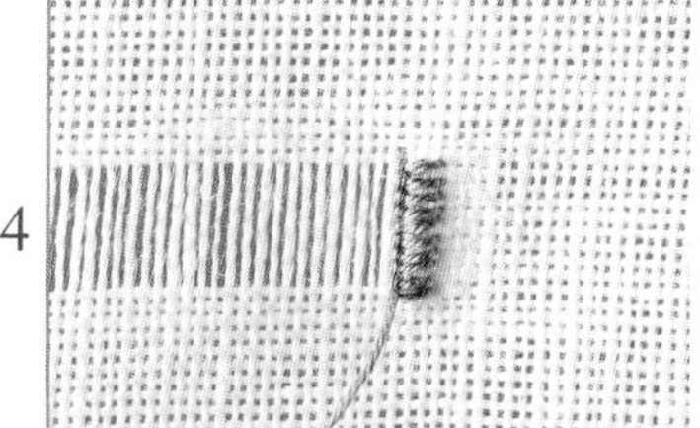

The binding is complete (see photo above). Bring needle back and slide it under stitching at backside to secure floss. Do the same for the other end.

3. Work Filling Stitches

Coral Knot

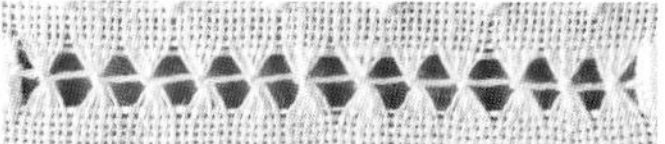

Buttonhole-stitch both band ends, then start to bind a few warp threads at a time inside the band.

1

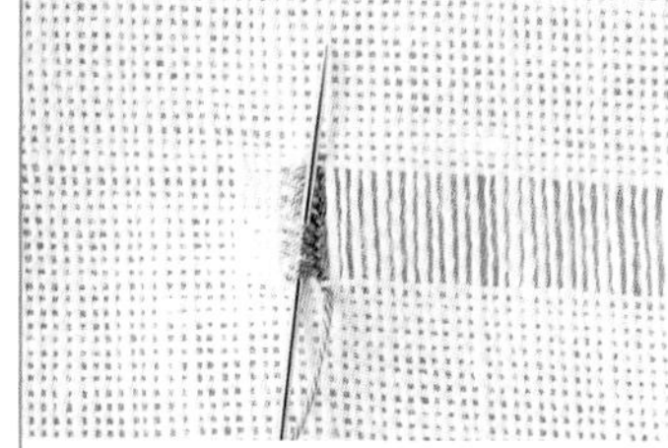

After making buttonhole stitches on both band ends, bring needle back and slide it under the stitching. Push needle up at middle.

2

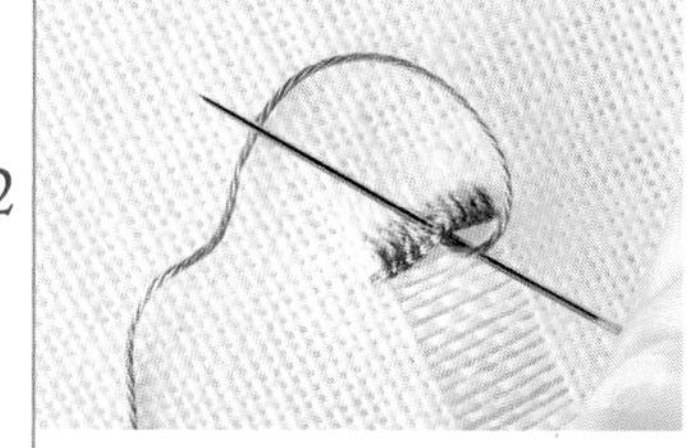

Turn fabric front side up. Force needle through buttonhole stiches and pull floss taut.

3

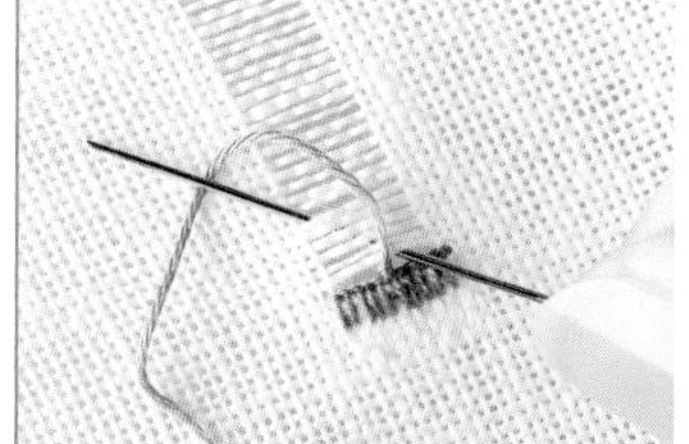

Push needle under six warp threads inside band and then lay floss under needle.

4

Pull floss taut and bind warp threads at middle. Repeat until you reach the other side.

5

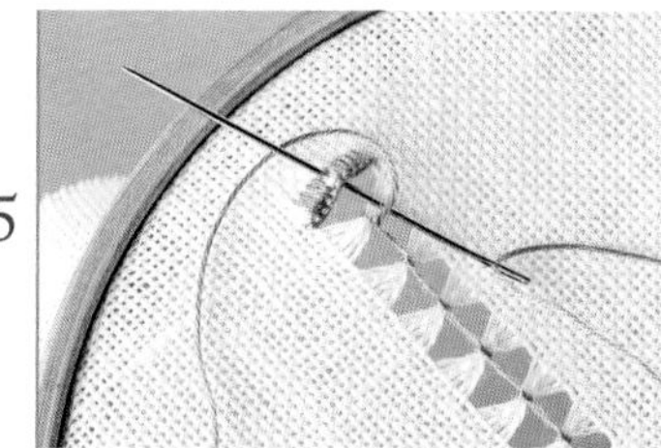

Finally, anchor floss to buttonhole stitch and secure floss at backside to complete.

Four-Sided Stitch

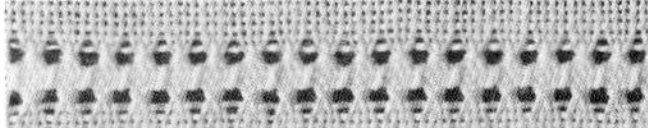

This stitch forms a square. It is often used not only in the middle of the band, but also along the top and bottom edges.

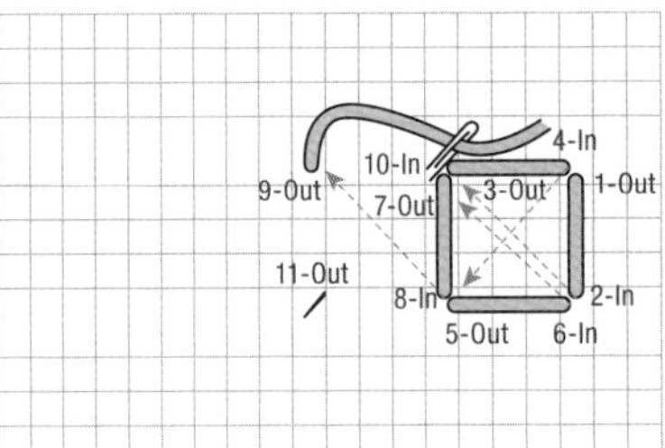
4-In
10-In
9-Out
7-Out
3-Out
1-Out
11-Out
8-In
2-In
5-Out
6-In

1

Withdraw one weft thread at the top and one at the bottom of the band. Inside the band, there should still be four weft threads.

2

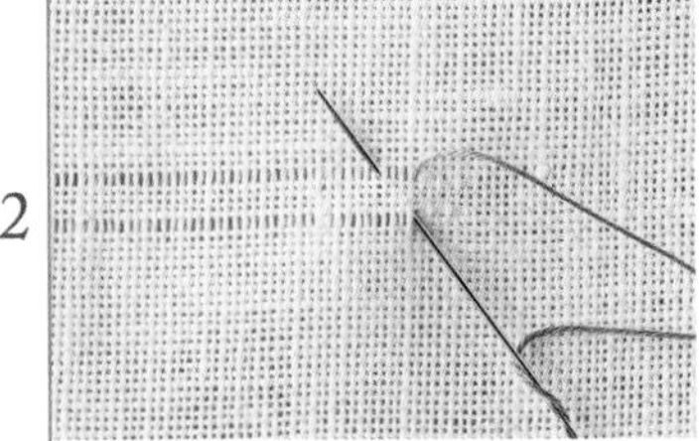

Bring needle up at top corner where weft was withdrawn. Bring needle back through bottom corner where other weft was withdrawn. Reemerge from four weft threads up and four warp threads to left.

3

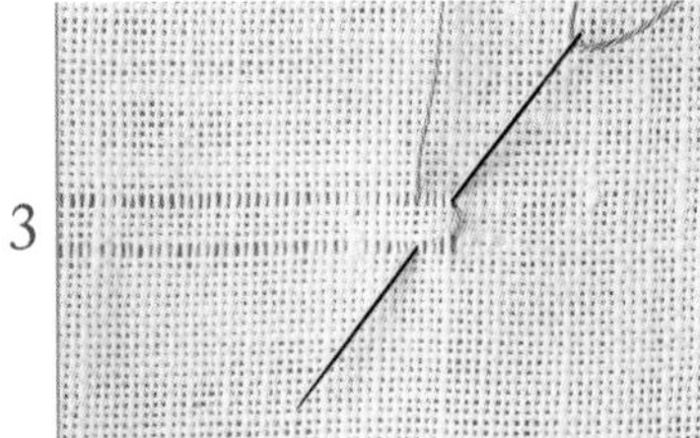

Insert needle at corner at initial exit point in step 1. Reemerge from four weft threads down and four warp threads to left.

4

Insert needle at bottom corner and reemerge at same point as in step 2 (four weft threads up and four warp threads to left).

5

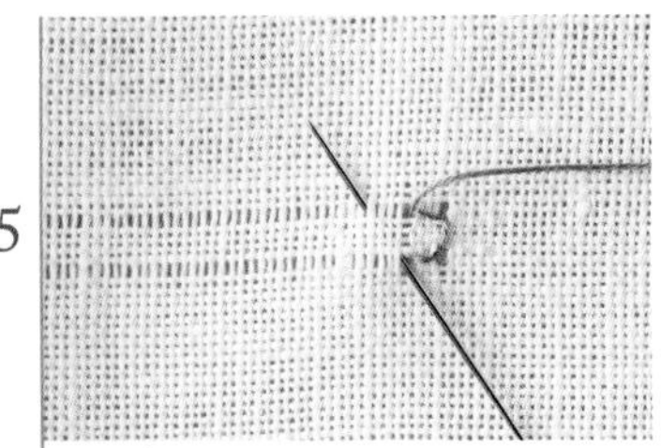

Insert needle at four weft threads down. Reemerge at four weft threads up and four warp threads to left.

6

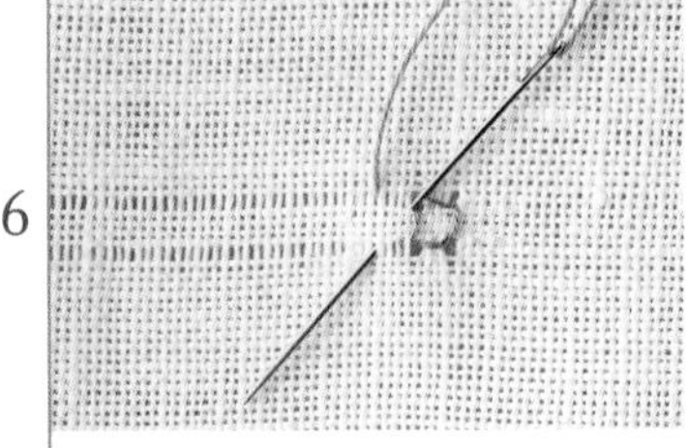

Repeat stitching sequences all the way to the other side.

7

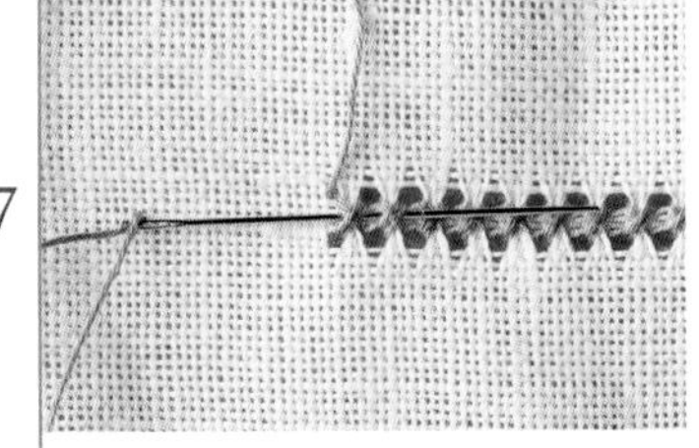

You should see consecutive X shapes on the backside of the piece. Once stitch is complete, bring needle back and slide it under the intersection of a few Xs to secure.

Embroidery on Felt

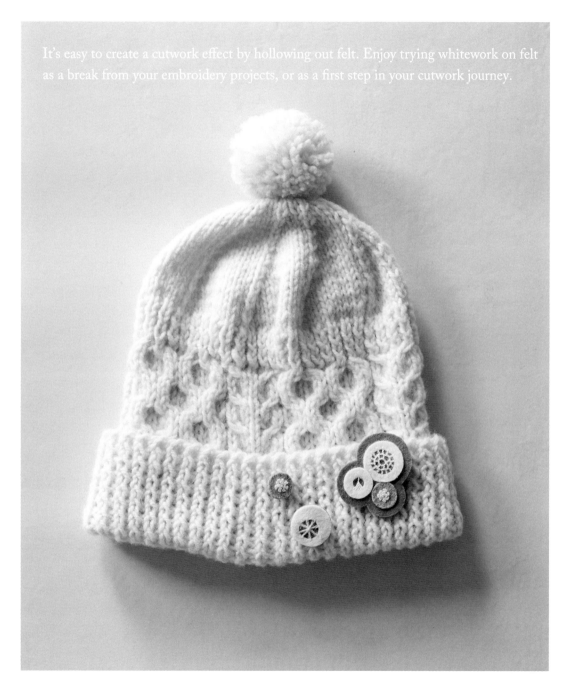

It's easy to create a cutwork effect by hollowing out felt. Enjoy trying whitework on felt as a break from your embroidery projects, or as a first step in your cutwork journey.

Simple felt brooches are so eye-catching when grouped together. Hollow out the felt and then make Hedebo stitches to fill the empty space out a bit.

23.
How To
page 108

Brooch

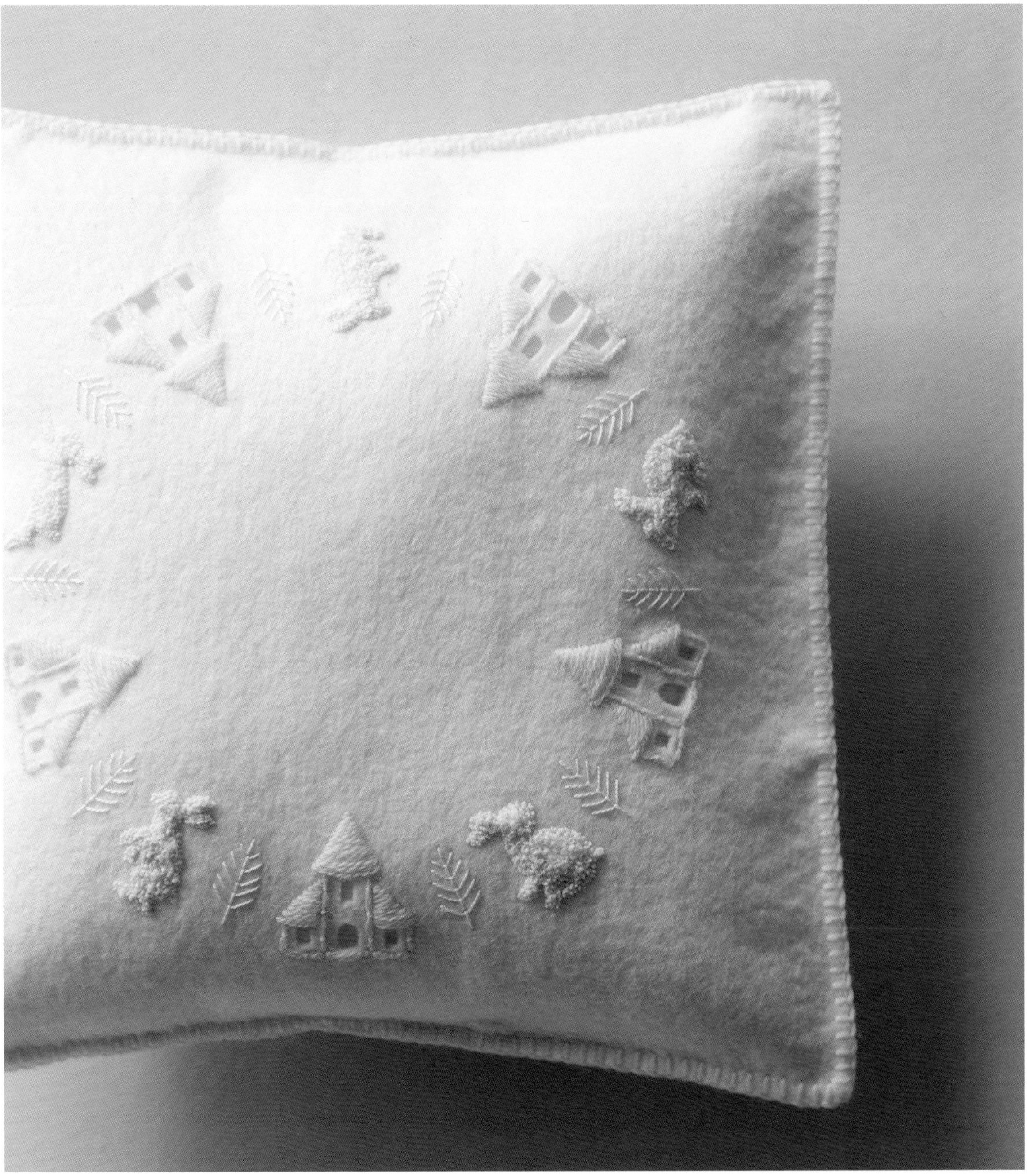

Wool embroidery floss and yarn can produce the needed volume for this felt cushion cover. Use buttonhole stitches to sew the cover together at the edges.

24.
How To
page 110

Cushion Cover

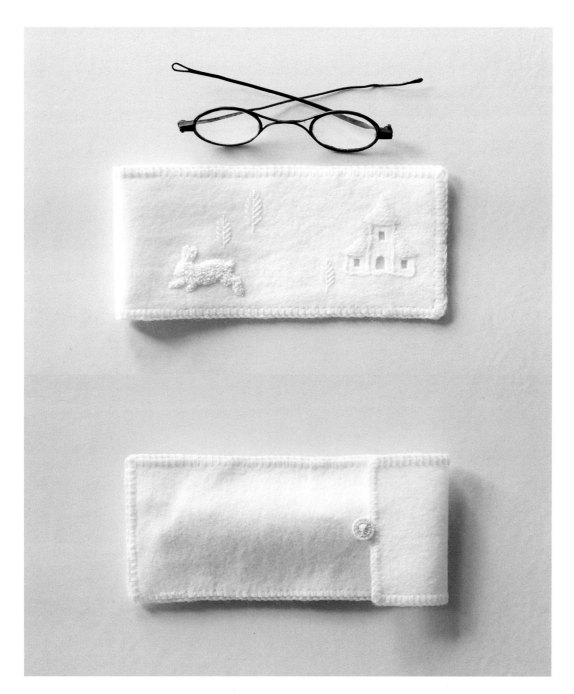

This felt eyeglass case features similar designs to the cushion on page 60. The button that fastens the flap is also made of thread to maintain the gentle appearance.

How To page 107

Glasses Case

Tools and Materials

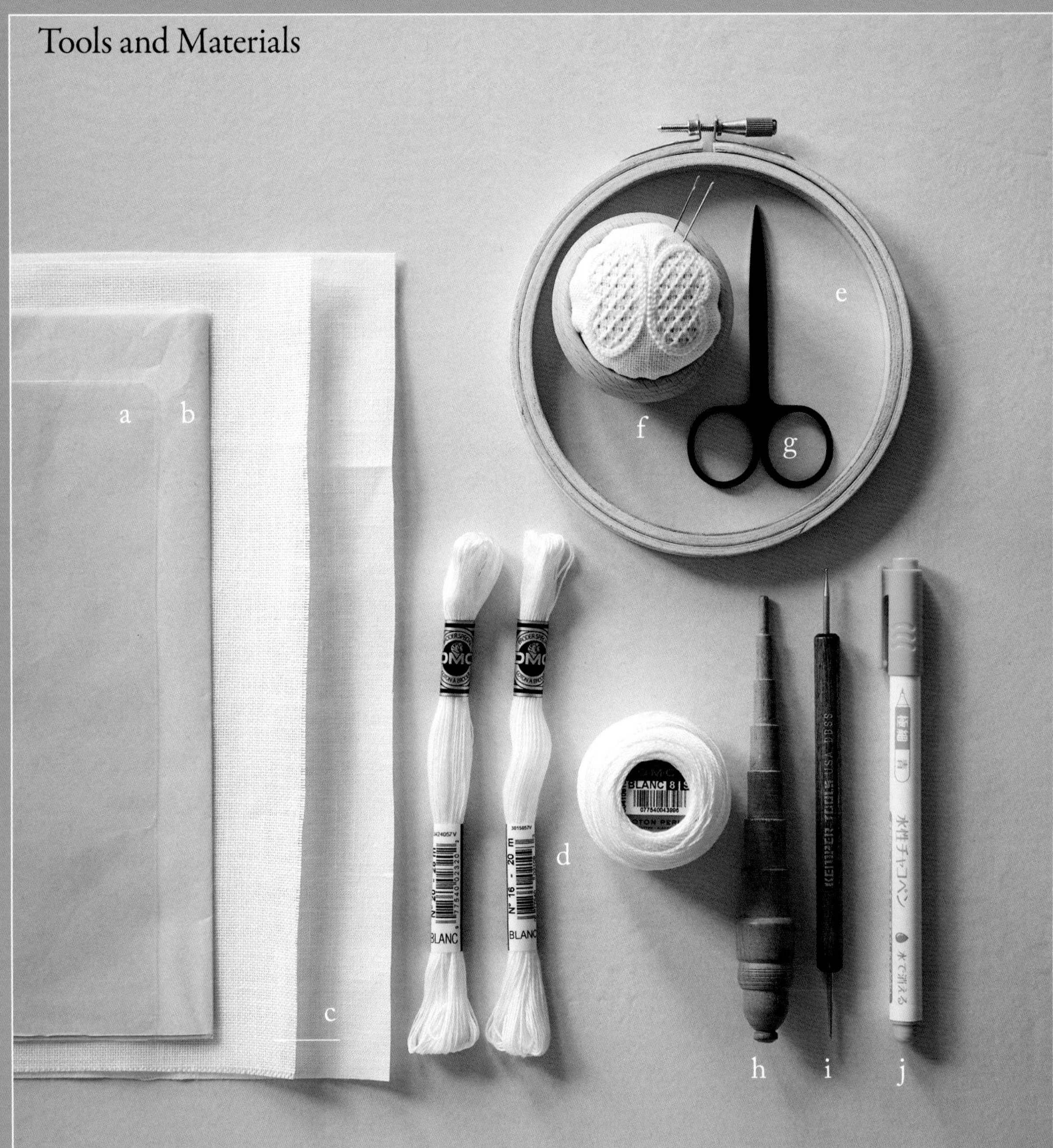
a
b
c
d
e
f
g
h
i
j

a, b. Cellophane, transfer paper: Used to transfer patterns onto fabric

c. Linen/Plain Weave Fabric

Use linen that has 12 to 14 threads per 1 cm / ⅜" for Schwalm and drawn threadwork. Ajour embroidery is pulled threadwork, so you can choose coarse fabric that has 10 to 11 threads per 1 cm / ⅜". As far as Hedebo embroidery is concerned, chose tightly woven fabric, since you aren't required to count the number of threads in the fabric. Be sure to choose fabric with an even weave, regardless of the type of embroidery you do.

d. Embroidery floss: Use No. 25 embroidery floss for Ajour. embroidery. Along with No. 25, this book uses Nos. 16, 20, 25, and 30 for *Coton a Broder*. For free stitching, I use No. 25 embroidery floss, Pearl Cotton No. 8, or my favorite wool embroidery floss and yarn.

e. Embroidery Hoop: Various sizes are available. 10 cm (4") hoops are the norm. Choose your preferred size.

f. Needles and Pincushions: Use two types of needle: one with a sharp point and one with a blunt tip. See page 63.

g. Scissors: You need both embroidery scissors and fabric shears. Use sharp embroidery scissors with a pointed tip.

h. Hedebo Ring Stick: Used to make Hedebo rings and stars.

i. Stylus: Used to trace the pattern on cellophane, which is then transferred onto fabric.

j. Sewing marker: Used to transfer, or draw, patterns on fabric.

About Needles

On the left is a blunt-tipped needle. On the right, a sharp-pointed needle. Use the blunt-tipped needle to stitch inside of outlined areas. Use the sharp-pointed needle to outline the pattern and for basic embroidery stitches.

Transferring Patterns

On the fabric, layer transfer paper, the pattern, and cellophane in that order. Trace the pattern with a stylus. If the pattern can be seen under the fabric, you can copy it with a sewing marker.

Finishing Your Stitching

Do not tie a knot in the floss tail, since the knot might make a bump in the stitch. Slide the needle under the stitching a few times at backside to secure.

1

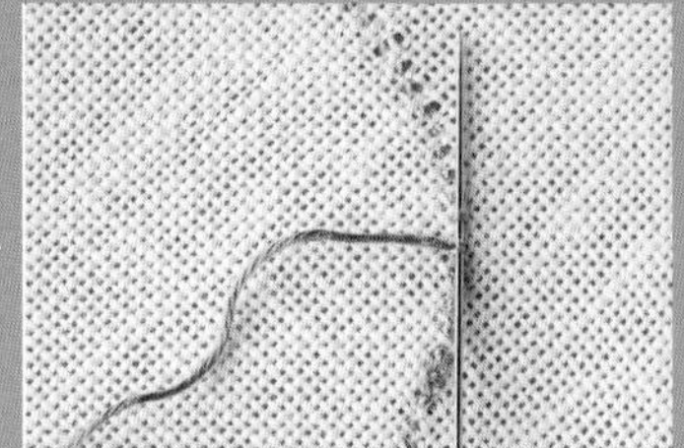

Push needle through to back and slide it under one stitch, like a backstitch.

2

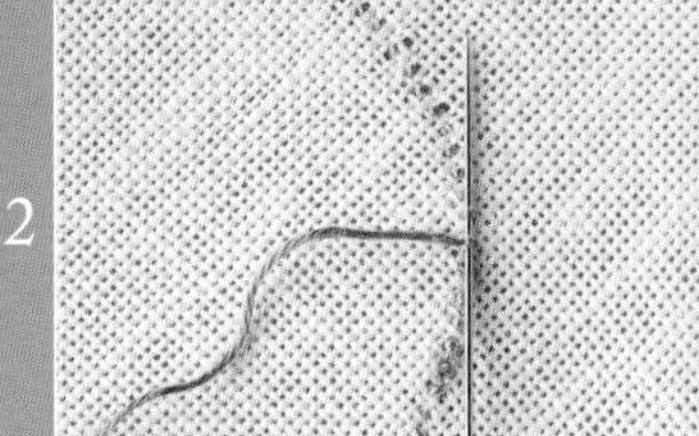

Similarly, you can slide the needle under the next stitch and back, similar to a backstitch.

3

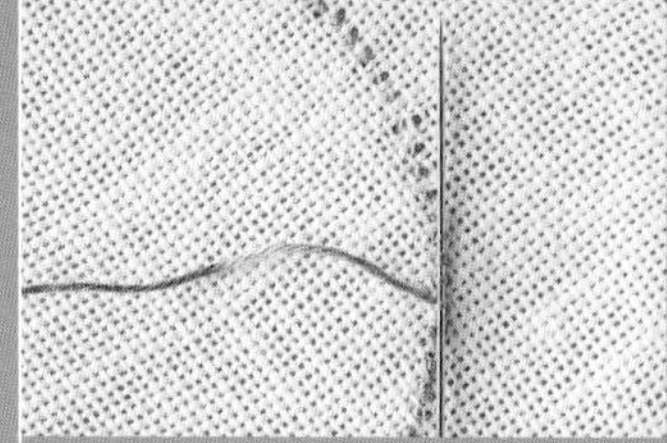

Slide needle under stitching a few stitches away.

4

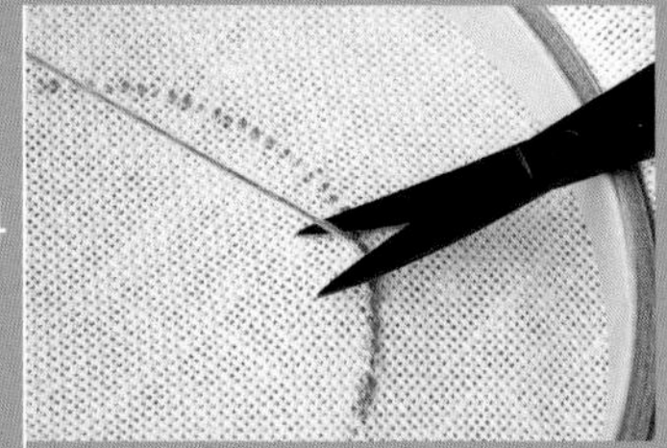

Cut off floss tail. This will secure the floss without making a knot.

Moving to Next Row

When stitching a single row and then moving on to the next, such as with Schwalm and Ajour embroidery, the needle should be pushed to the back, slid under the outline stitches, and then moved on to the next position. If the next position is too far away, secure and cut the thread on the back and start stitching again near the next position.

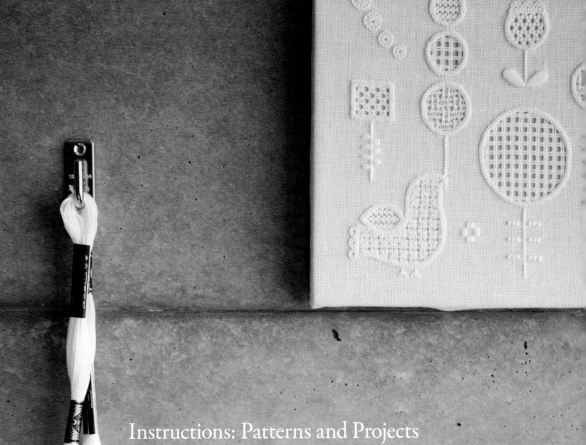

Instructions: Patterns and Projects

- This section introduces stitching diagrams for Schwalm and Ajour embroidery, in addition to a few basic stitches that haven't been explained in the step-by-step photographs in previous pages.
- The majority of patterns provided are full size. However, please enlarge patterns as specified whenever a pattern indicates a reduction ratio.
- The letter "S" in a diagram stands for stitch. The number after the number sign (#) is the color number for the embroidery floss. The abbreviation RS stands for right side of fabric, and WS stands for wrong side of fabric.
- This book uses DMC embroidery floss and Appleton wool floss. You can use other brands of floss, of course; just make sure they are the same type of floss as DMC or Appleton.
- Units of measurement are primarily cm. Even though this book provides measurements in inches, remember that they are approximate conversions only.
- Figure dimensions and patterns do not include seam allowances unless otherwise indicated. Add 1 cm / ⅜" seam allowance. Cut fabric without adding a seam allowance where labeled "No Seam Allowance."
- Fabric sizes given on patterns have some room for adjustment. Prepare fabric that is thick enough to be stable when placed in an embroidery hoop.
- Completed work dimensions may differ from measurements given on diagrams.

Basic Embroidery Stitches

Outline Stitch
Outline Filling Stitch

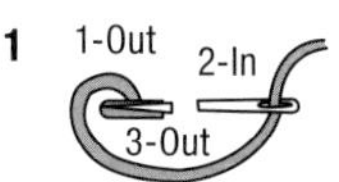
1
1-Out
2-In
3-Out
2

Outline filling stitch: Work outline stitches in layers to fill area.

Couching Stitch

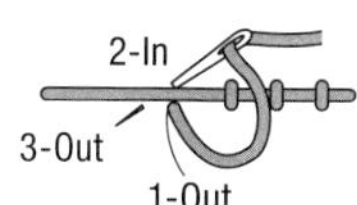
2-In
3-Out
1-Out

Coral Stitch

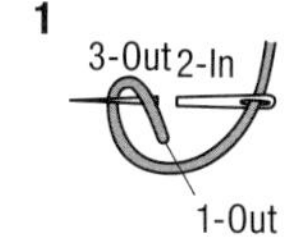
1
3-Out
2-In
1-Out

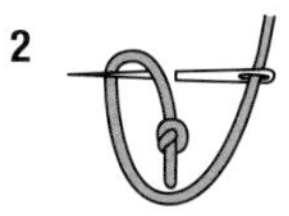
2

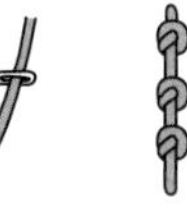

Satin Stitch

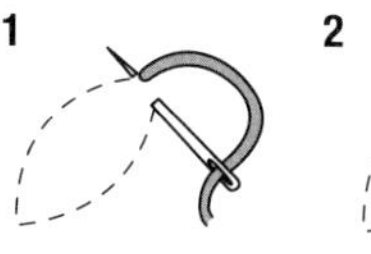
1

2

Straight Stitch

1
2

Chain Stitch

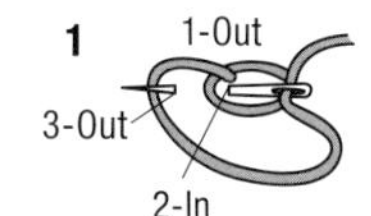
1
1-Out
3-Out
2-In

2

Whipped Chain Stitch

Pass the needle under each chain stitch.

Fly Stitch

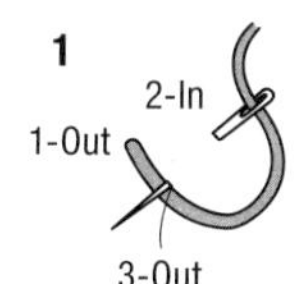
1
2-In
1-Out
3-Out

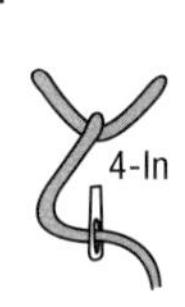
2
4-In

French Knot Stitch

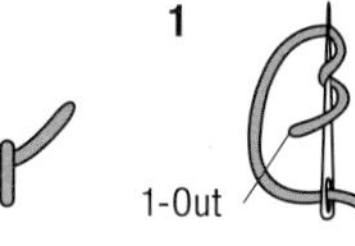
3
1
1-Out

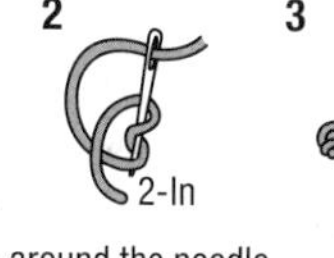
2
2-In
3

Wind the floss around the needle.

Buttonhole Stitch

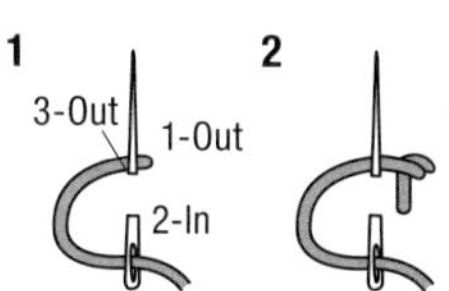
1
3-Out
1-Out
2-In
2

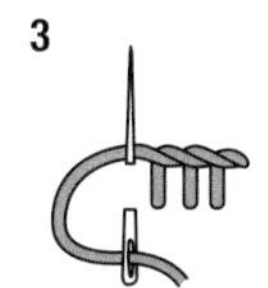
3

In a Circular Shape

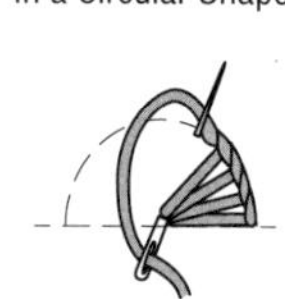

Running Stitch

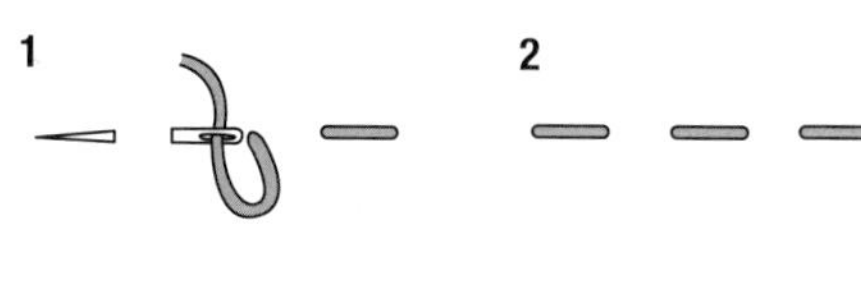
1
2

Lazy Daisy Stitch

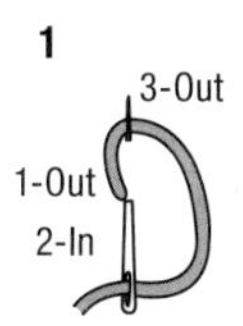
1
3-Out
1-Out
2-In

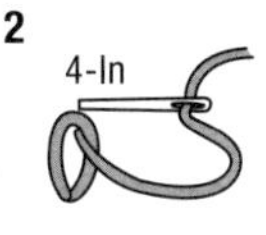
2
4-In

3

Lazy Daisy Stitch + Straight Stitch

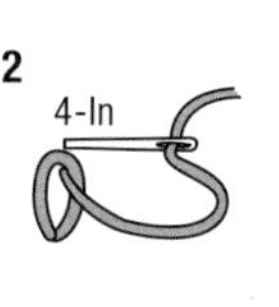
1
3-Out
1-Out
2-In
2
4-In
3
6-In
5-Out

Long & Short Stitch

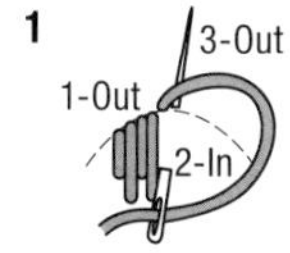
1
3-Out
1-Out
2-In

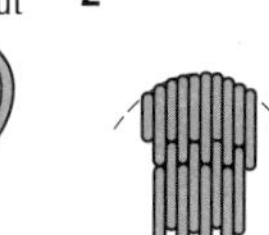
2

Schwalm Embroidery

Wrapping Stitch:

To form grid, withdraw 1 in every 5 warp threads (look closely at underlying grid).

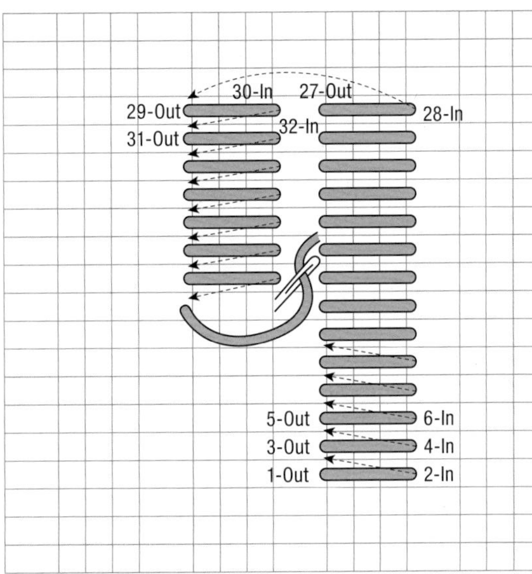
30-In
27-Out
29-Out
28-In
32-In
31-Out
5-Out
6-In
3-Out
4-In
1-Out
2-In

Basic Stitch (to bind threads):

To form grid, withdraw 2 in every 4 threads in both warp and weft.

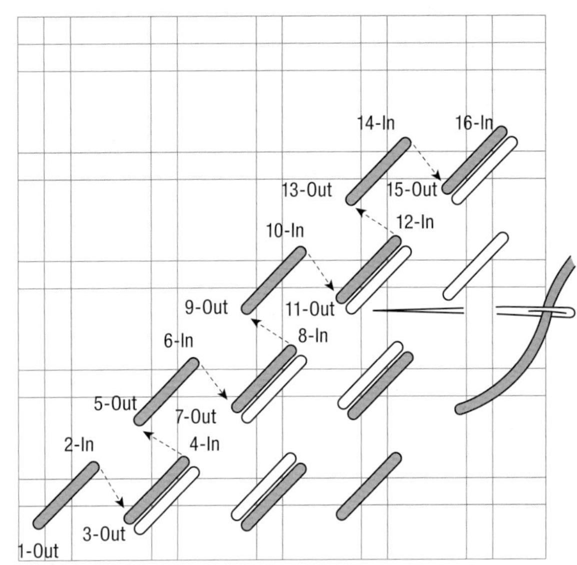
14-In
16-In
13-Out
15-Out
12-In
10-In
9-Out
11-Out
8-In
6-In
5-Out
7-Out
2-In
4-In
3-Out
1-Out

Double Wrapping Stitch:

To form grid, withdraw 1 in every 4 threads in both warp and weft direction.

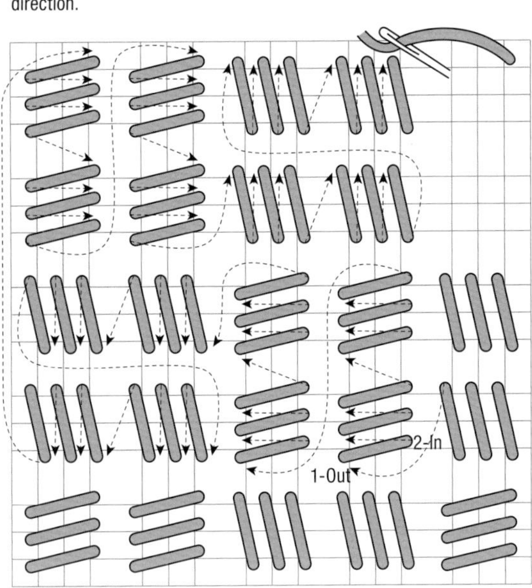
2-In
1-Out

Rose Stitch:

To form grid, withdraw 1 in every 4 threads in both warp and weft.

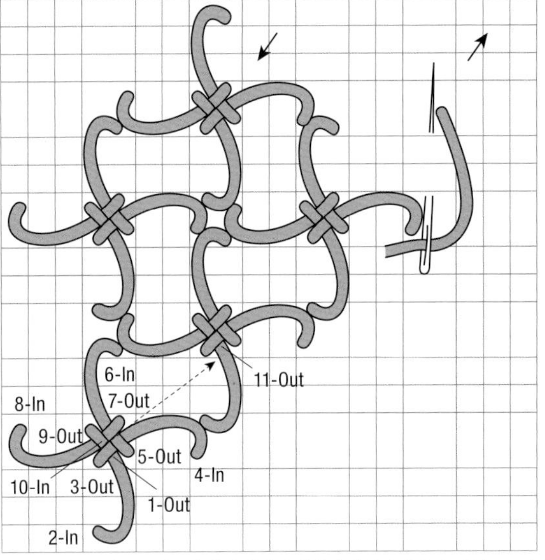
6-In
11-Out
8-In
7-Out
9-Out
5-Out
4-In
10-In
3-Out
1-Out
2-In

The positions denoted as 1-Out, 3-Out, 5-Out, 7-Out, 9-Out, 10-In apply to each subsequent stitch.

Star Rose Stitch:

To form grid, withdraw 1 in every 5 threads in both warp and weft direction.

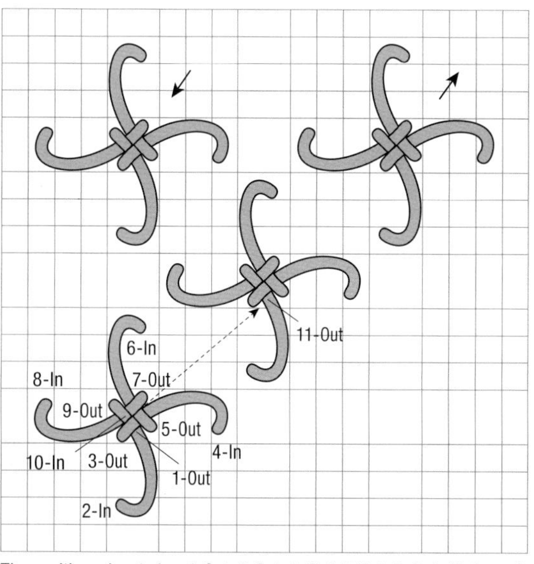
11-Out
6-In
8-In
7-Out
9-Out
5-Out
4-In
10-In
3-Out
1-Out
2-In

The positions denoted as 1-Out, 3-Out, 5-Out, 7-Out, 9-Out, 10-In apply to each subsequent stitch. Same as Rose Stitch.

Mosquito Stitch:

To form grid, withdraw 1 in every 4 weft threads.

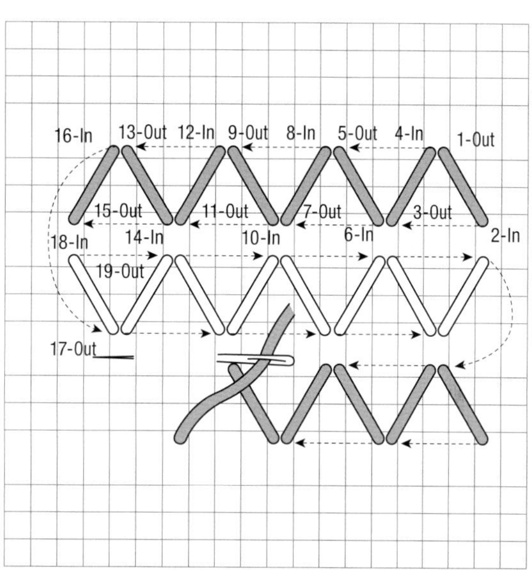
16-In
13-Out
12-In
9-Out
8-In
5-Out
4-In
1-Out
15-Out
11-Out
7-Out
3-Out
18-In
14-In
10-In
6-In
2-In
19-Out
17-Out

Waffle Stitch:

To form grid, withdraw 1 weft thread every 4 weft threads.

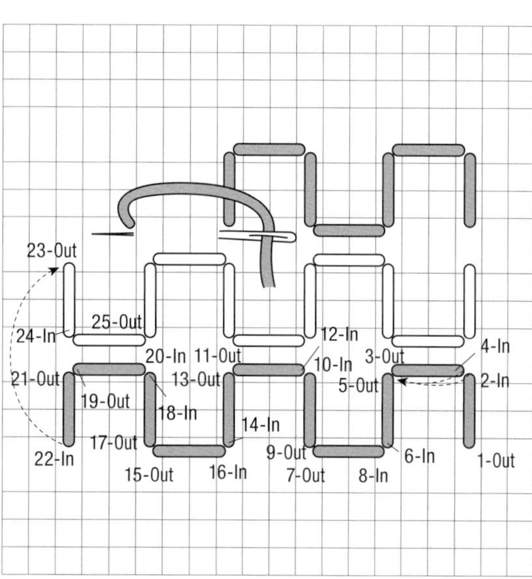
23-Out
25-Out
24-In
12-In
4-In
20-In
11-Out
10-In
3-Out
21-Out
13-Out
5-Out
2-In
19-Out
18-In
14-In
17-Out
9-Out
6-In
22-In
1-Out
15-Out
16-In
7-Out
8-In

Checker Filling Stitch

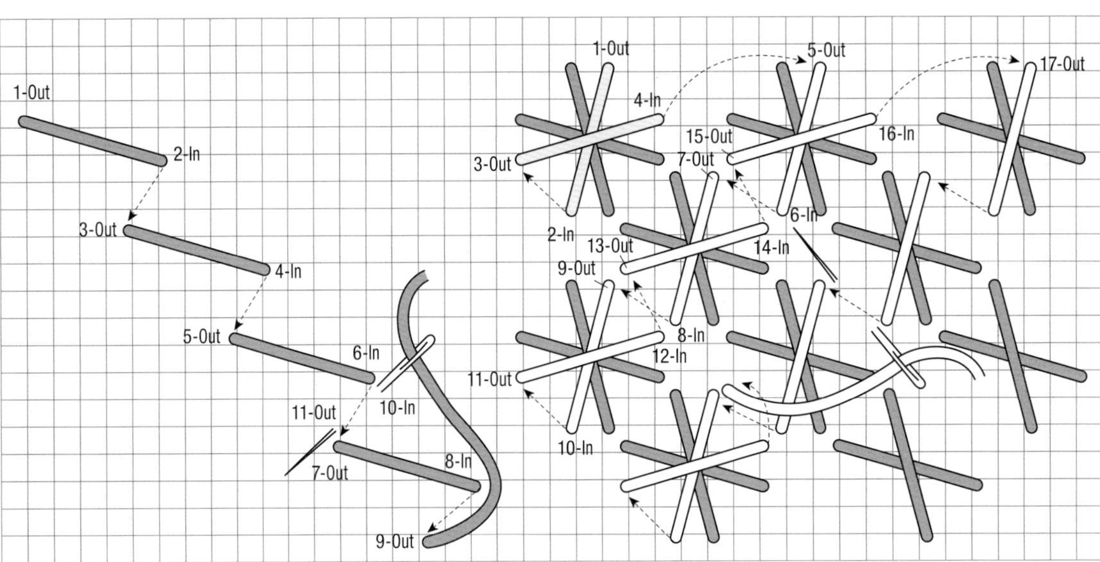
1-Out
2-In
3-Out
4-In
5-Out
6-In
10-In
11-Out
7-Out
8-In
9-Out
1-Out
4-In
3-Out
2-In
5-Out
15-Out
7-Out
16-In
17-Out
6-In
13-Out
14-In
9-Out
8-In
12-In
11-Out
10-In

Mosaic Filling Stitch

10-In
4-In
2-In
1-Out
12-In
11-Out
3-Out
40-In
20-In
21-Out
31-Out
32-In
22-In
30-In
47-Out
44-In
42-In
48-In
41-Out
46-In
43-Out
45-Out
50-In
52-In
51-Out
49-Out
54-In
53-Out

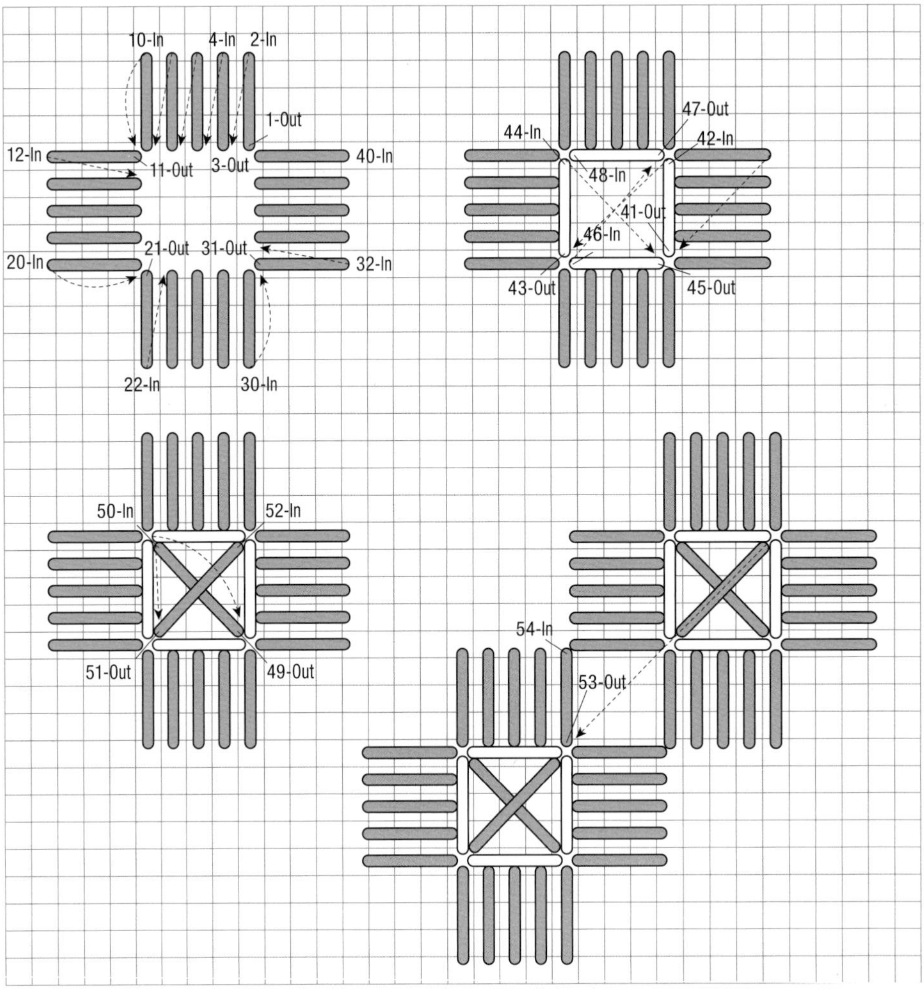

Reverse Wave Stitch

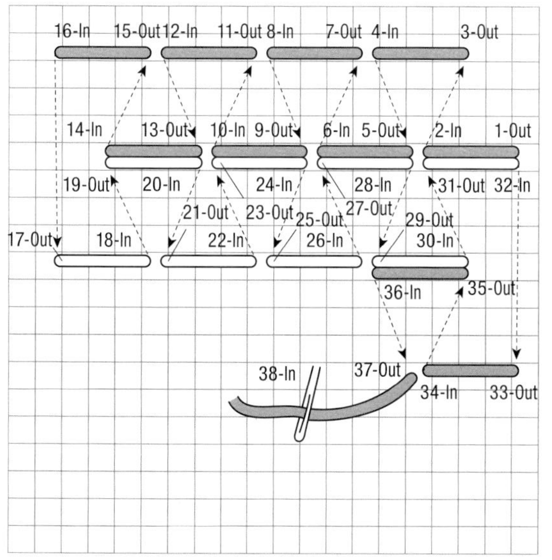
16-In
15-Out
12-In
11-Out
8-In
7-Out
4-In
3-Out
14-In
13-Out
10-In
9-Out
6-In
5-Out
2-In
1-Out
19-Out
20-In
24-In
28-In
31-Out
32-In
21-Out
23-Out
25-Out
27-Out
29-Out
17-Out
18-In
22-In
26-In
30-In
36-In
35-Out
38-In
37-Out
34-In
33-Out

Pebble Filling Stitch

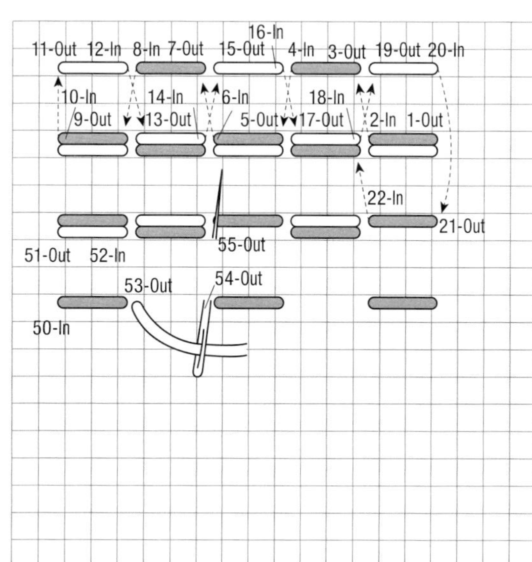
16-In
11-Out
12-In
8-In
7-Out
15-Out
4-In
3-Out
19-Out
20-In
10-In
14-In
6-In
18-In
9-Out
13-Out
5-Out
17-Out
2-In
1-Out
22-In
21-Out
55-Out
51-Out
52-In
53-Out
54-Out
50-In

Drawn Buttonhole Stitch

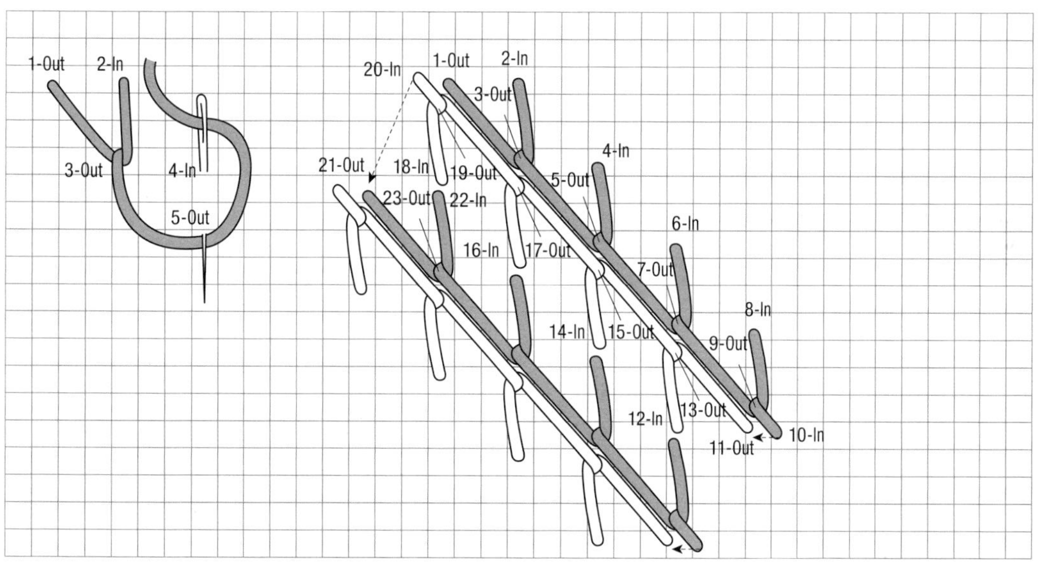
1-Out
2-In
3-Out
4-In
5-Out
20-In
1-Out
2-In
3-Out
4-In
21-Out
18-In
19-Out
5-Out
23-Out
22-In
6-In
16-In
17-Out
7-Out
8-In
14-In
15-Out
9-Out
12-In
13-Out
11-Out
10-In

Stitches 1 / page 6 Schwalm Embroidery

Materials Fabric (white plain-weave linen, 12 threads per cm for both warp and weft / 30 threads per inch (TPI) for both warp and weft)
DMC *Coton a Broder* B5200 #16, 20, 25

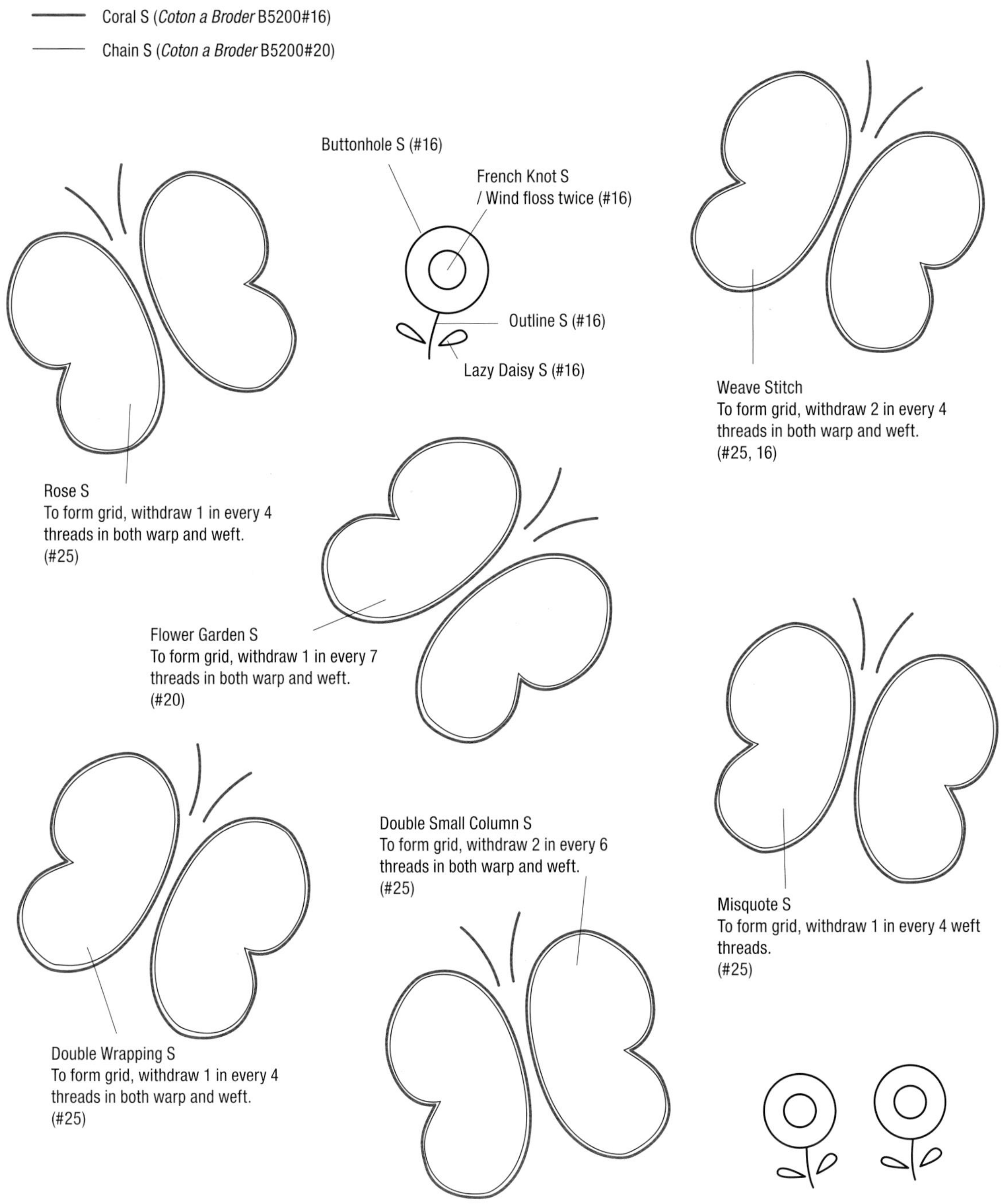

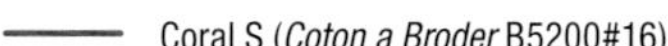

Coral S (*Coton a Broder* B5200#16)
Chain S (*Coton a Broder* B5200#20)

Buttonhole S (#16)

French Knot S / Wind floss twice (#16)

Outline S (#16)

Lazy Daisy S (#16)

Weave Stitch
To form grid, withdraw 2 in every 4 threads in both warp and weft.
(#25, 16)

Rose S
To form grid, withdraw 1 in every 4 threads in both warp and weft.
(#25)

Flower Garden S
To form grid, withdraw 1 in every 7 threads in both warp and weft.
(#20)

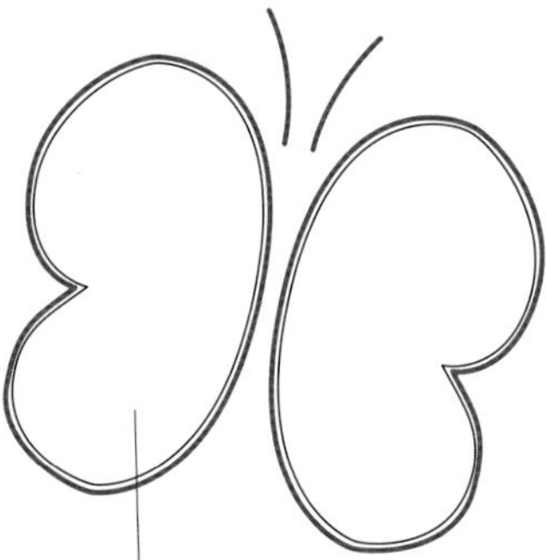

Misquote S
To form grid, withdraw 1 in every 4 weft threads.
(#25)

Double Small Column S
To form grid, withdraw 2 in every 6 threads in both warp and weft.
(#25)

Double Wrapping S
To form grid, withdraw 1 in every 4 threads in both warp and weft.
(#25)

Stitches 2/ page 7 Schwalm Embroidery

Materials Fabric (white plain-weave linen, 12 threads per cm for both warp and weft / 30 TPI for both warp and weft)
DMC *Coton a Broder* B5200 #16, 20, 25

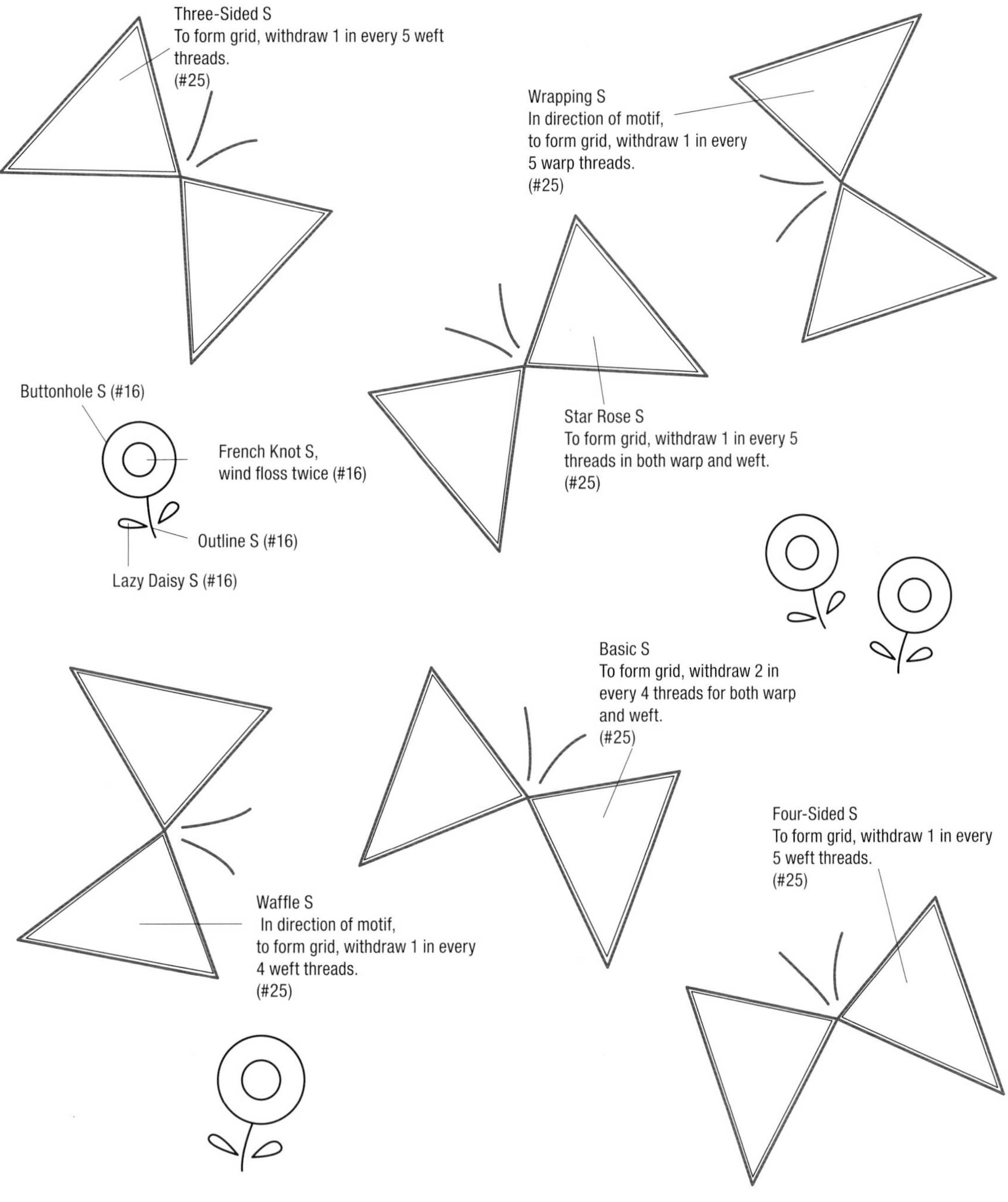

Coral S (Coton a Broder B5200 #16)
Chain S (Coton a Broder B5200 #20)
Three-Sided S
To form grid, withdraw 1 in every 5 weft threads.
(#25)
Wrapping S
In direction of motif,
to form grid, withdraw 1 in every 5 warp threads.
(#25)
Buttonhole S (#16)
French Knot S,
wind floss twice (#16)
Outline S (#16)
Lazy Daisy S (#16)
Star Rose S
To form grid, withdraw 1 in every 5 threads in both warp and weft.
(#25)
Basic S
To form grid, withdraw 2 in every 4 threads for both warp and weft.
(#25)
Four-Sided S
To form grid, withdraw 1 in every 5 weft threads.
(#25)
Waffle S
In direction of motif,
to form grid, withdraw 1 in every 4 weft threads.
(#25)

1. / page 8 Schwalm Embroidery: Poodle and Cat

Materials Fabric (white plain-weave linen, 14 threads per cm for both warp and weft / 35 TPI for both warp and weft)
DMC *Coton a Broder* B5200 #16, 20, 25, 30
DMC No. 25 Embroidery Floss BLANC

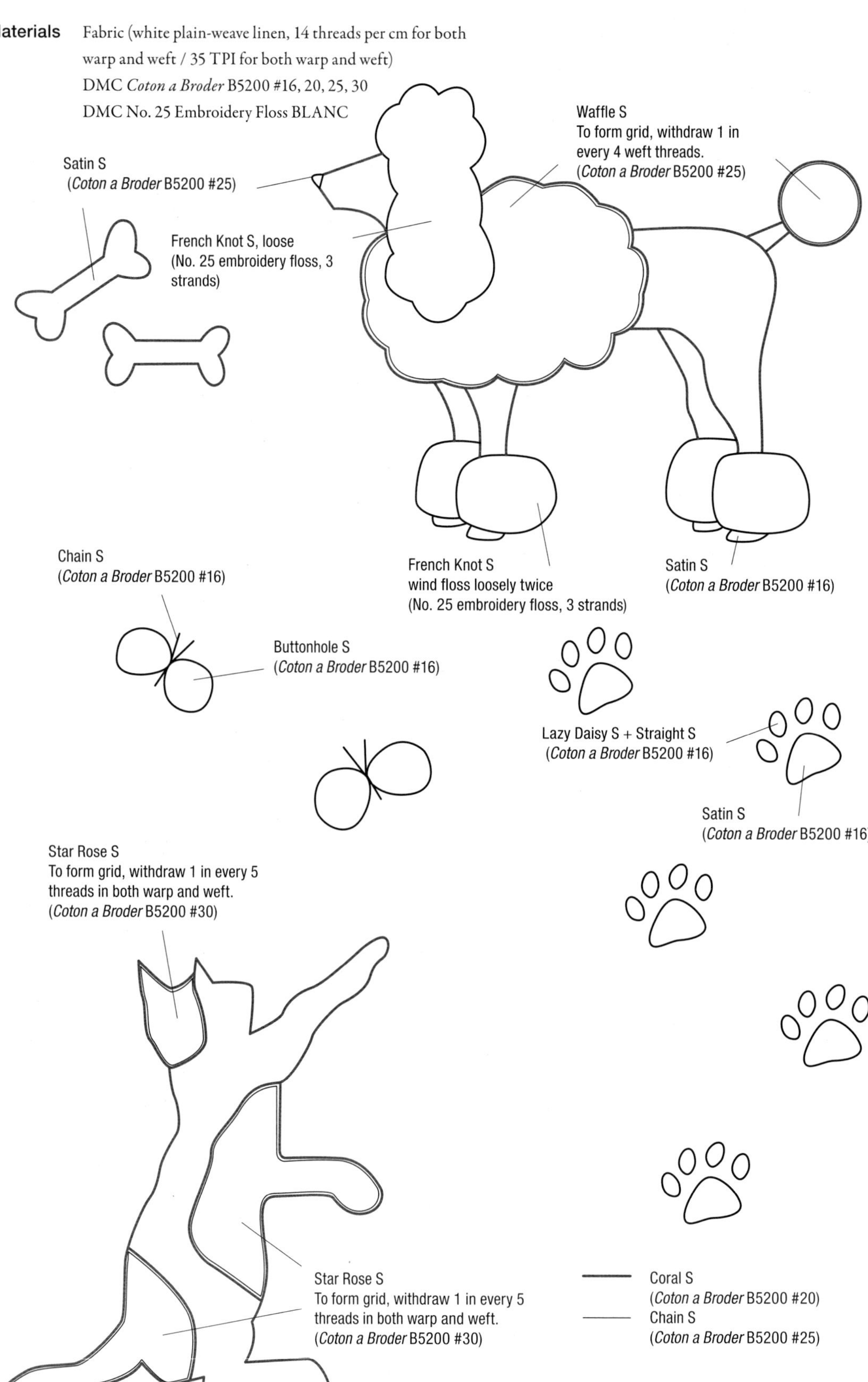

Satin S
(*Coton a Broder* B5200 #25)
French Knot S, loose
(No. 25 embroidery floss, 3 strands)
Waffle S
To form grid, withdraw 1 in every 4 weft threads.
(*Coton a Broder* B5200 #25)
Chain S
(*Coton a Broder* B5200 #16)
French Knot S
wind floss loosely twice
(No. 25 embroidery floss, 3 strands)
Satin S
(*Coton a Broder* B5200 #16)
Buttonhole S
(*Coton a Broder* B5200 #16)
Lazy Daisy S + Straight S
(*Coton a Broder* B5200 #16)
Satin S
(*Coton a Broder* B5200 #16)
Star Rose S
To form grid, withdraw 1 in every 5 threads in both warp and weft.
(*Coton a Broder* B5200 #30)
Star Rose S
To form grid, withdraw 1 in every 5 threads in both warp and weft.
(*Coton a Broder* B5200 #30)
Coral S
(*Coton a Broder* B5200 #20)
Chain S
(*Coton a Broder* B5200 #25)

3. / page 10 Schwalm Embroidery: Donkey, Duck, Sheep

Materials

Fabric (white plain-weave linen, 14 threads per cm for both warp and weft / 35 TPI for both warp and weft)
DMC 4 *Coton a Broder* BLANC #20, 25
DMC No. 25 Embroidery Floss BLANC
DMC Pearl Cotton BLANC #8, 12
DMC Light Effects E677
DMC Diamant D3821

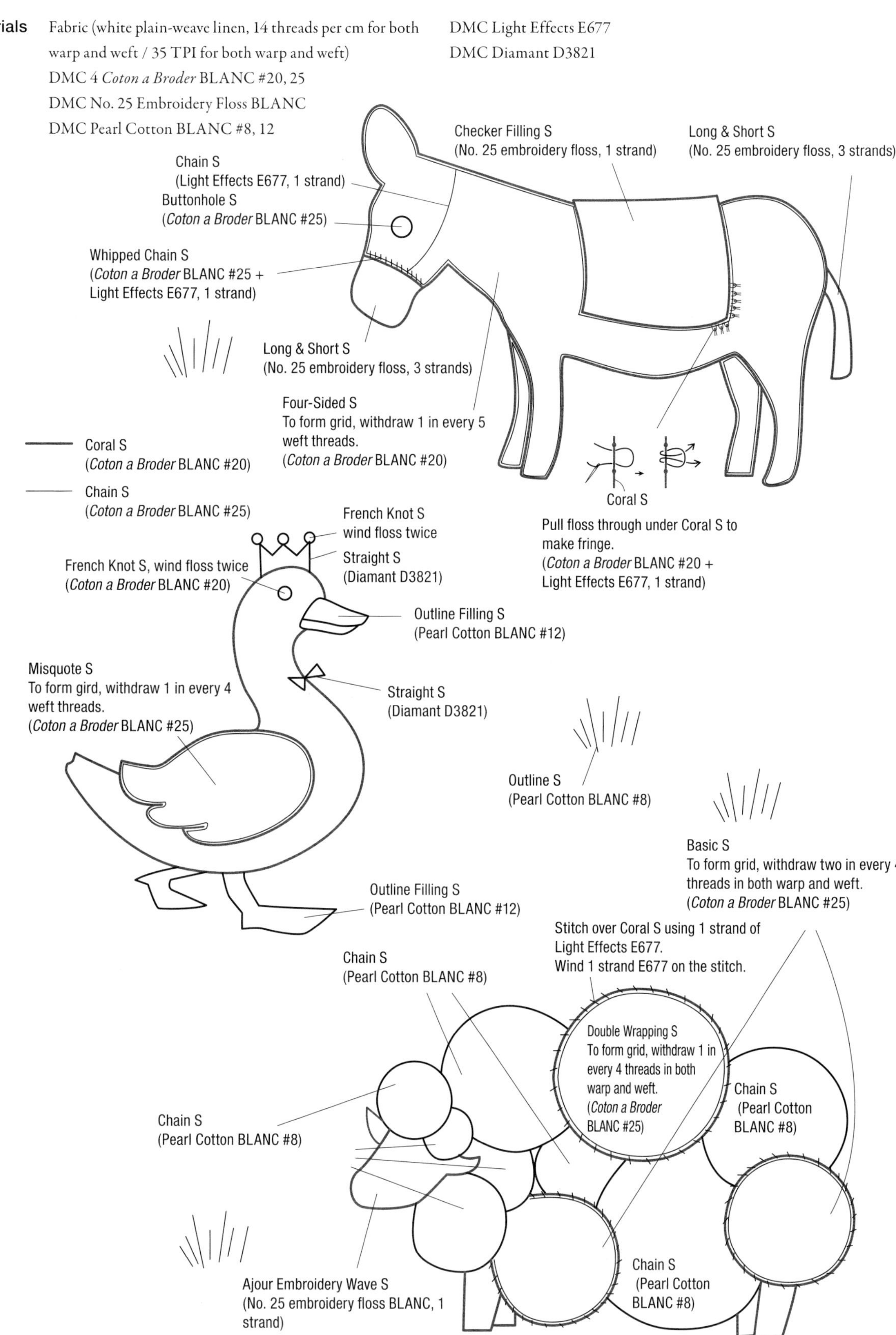

Checker Filling S
(No. 25 embroidery floss, 1 strand)
Long & Short S
(No. 25 embroidery floss, 3 strands)
Chain S
(Light Effects E677, 1 strand)
Buttonhole S
(Coton a Broder BLANC #25)
Whipped Chain S
(Coton a Broder BLANC #25 + Light Effects E677, 1 strand)
Long & Short S
(No. 25 embroidery floss, 3 strands)
Four-Sided S
To form grid, withdraw 1 in every 5 weft threads.
(Coton a Broder BLANC #20)
Coral S
(Coton a Broder BLANC #20)
Chain S
(Coton a Broder BLANC #25)
Coral S
Pull floss through under Coral S to make fringe.
(Coton a Broder BLANC #20 + Light Effects E677, 1 strand)
French Knot S
wind floss twice
Straight S
(Diamant D3821)
French Knot S, wind floss twice
(Coton a Broder BLANC #20)
Outline Filling S
(Pearl Cotton BLANC #12)
Misquote S
To form gird, withdraw 1 in every 4 weft threads.
(Coton a Broder BLANC #25)
Straight S
(Diamant D3821)
Outline S
(Pearl Cotton BLANC #8)
Basic S
To form grid, withdraw two in every 4 threads in both warp and weft.
(Coton a Broder BLANC #25)
Outline Filling S
(Pearl Cotton BLANC #12)
Stitch over Coral S using 1 strand of Light Effects E677.
Wind 1 strand E677 on the stitch.
Chain S
(Pearl Cotton BLANC #8)
Double Wrapping S
To form grid, withdraw 1 in every 4 threads in both warp and weft.
(Coton a Broder BLANC #25)
Chain S
(Pearl Cotton BLANC #8)
Chain S
(Pearl Cotton BLANC #8)
Chain S
(Pearl Cotton BLANC #8)
Ajour Embroidery Wave S
(No. 25 embroidery floss BLANC, 1 strand)

2. / page 9 Schwalm Embroidery: Circus

Materials Fabric (white plain-weave linen, 14 threads per cm for both warp and weft / 35 TPI for both warp and weft)
DMC *Coton a Broder* B5200 #16, 20, 25, BLANC #25
DMC Light Effects E677, E168
DMC Diamant D301
Appleton Crewel Wool 991B

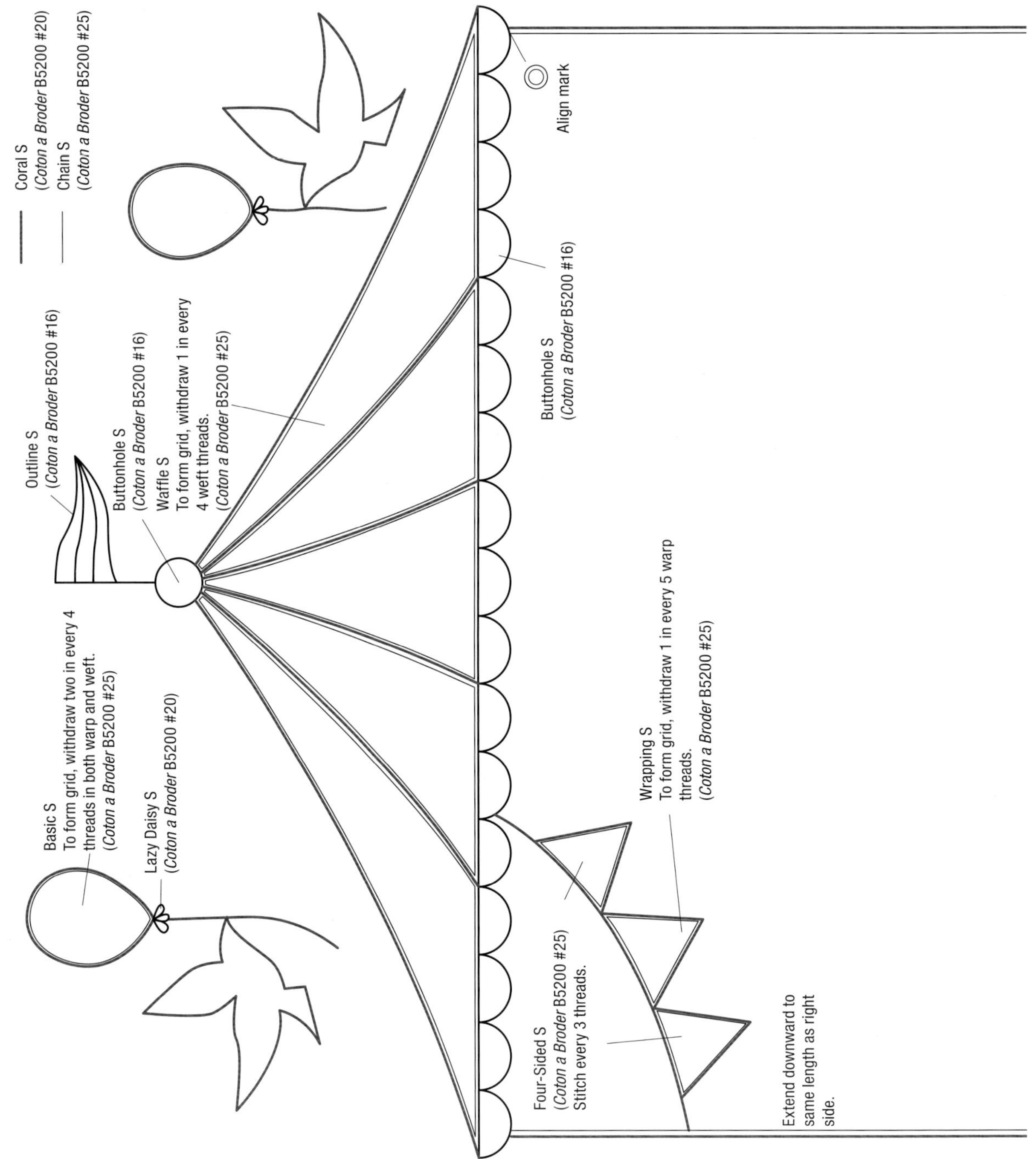

Coral S
(Coton a Broder B5200 #20)
Chain S
(Coton a Broder B5200 #25)
Align mark
Outline S
(Coton a Broder B5200 #16)
Buttonhole S
(Coton a Broder B5200 #16)
Waffle S
To form grid, withdraw 1 in every 4 weft threads.
(Coton a Broder B5200 #25)
Buttonhole S
(Coton a Broder B5200 #16)
Basic S
To form grid, withdraw two in every 4 threads in both warp and weft.
(Coton a Broder B5200 #25)
Lazy Daisy S
(Coton a Broder B5200 #20)
Wrapping S
To form grid, withdraw 1 in every 5 warp threads.
(Coton a Broder B5200 #25)
Four-Sided S
(Coton a Broder B5200 #25)
Stitch every 3 threads.
Extend downward to same length as right side.

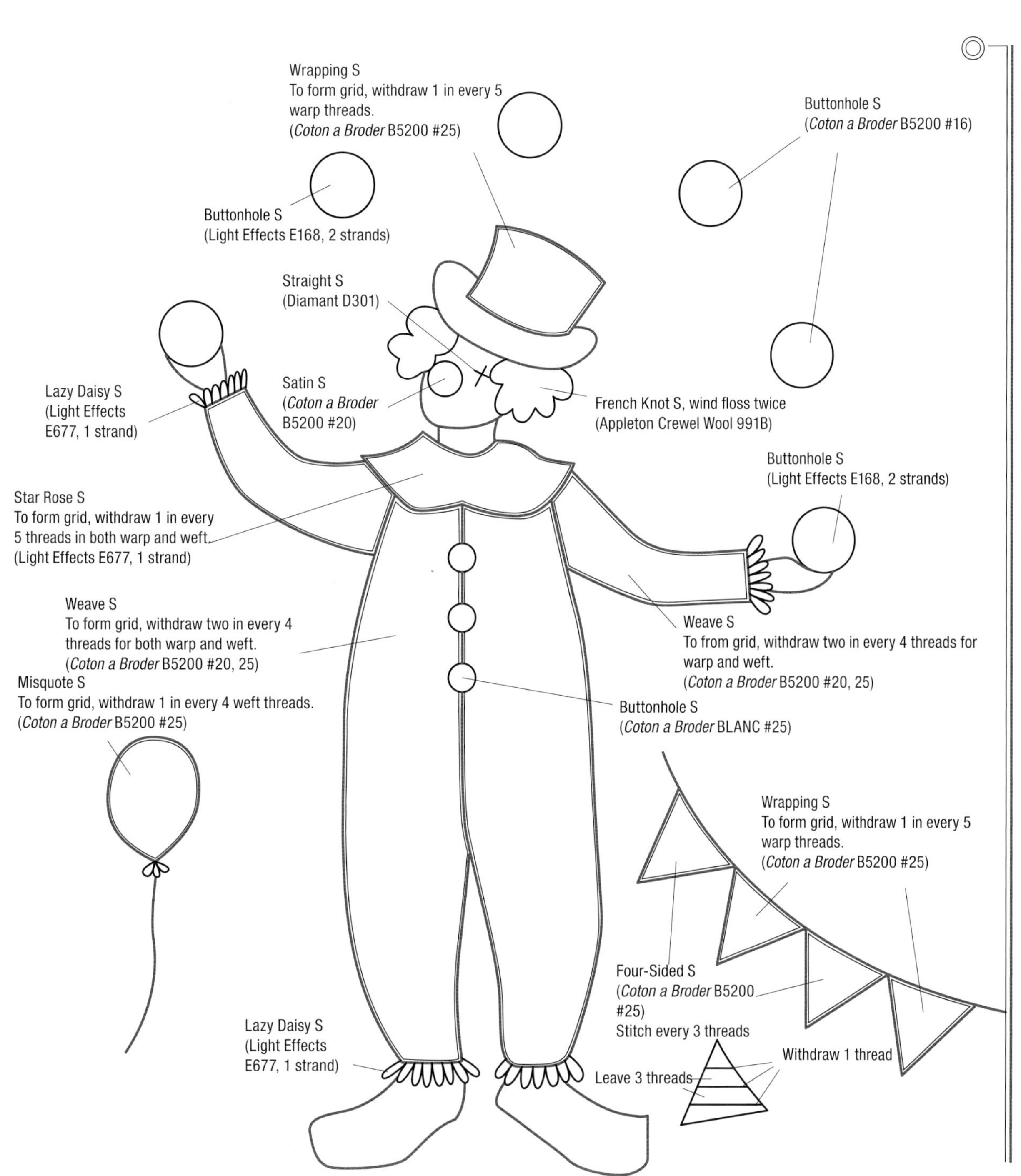
Coral S
(*Coton a Broder* B5200 #20)
Chain S
(*Coton a Broder* B5200 #25)
Wrapping S
To form grid, withdraw 1 in every 5 warp threads.
(*Coton a Broder* B5200 #25)
Buttonhole S
(*Coton a Broder* B5200 #16)
Buttonhole S
(Light Effects E168, 2 strands)
Straight S
(Diamant D301)
Lazy Daisy S
(Light Effects E677, 1 strand)
Satin S
(*Coton a Broder* B5200 #20)
French Knot S, wind floss twice
(Appleton Crewel Wool 991B)
Buttonhole S
(Light Effects E168, 2 strands)
Star Rose S
To form grid, withdraw 1 in every 5 threads in both warp and weft.
(Light Effects E677, 1 strand)
Weave S
To form grid, withdraw two in every 4 threads for both warp and weft.
(*Coton a Broder* B5200 #20, 25)
Weave S
To from grid, withdraw two in every 4 threads for warp and weft.
(*Coton a Broder* B5200 #20, 25)
Misquote S
To form grid, withdraw 1 in every 4 weft threads.
(*Coton a Broder* B5200 #25)
Buttonhole S
(*Coton a Broder* BLANC #25)
Wrapping S
To form grid, withdraw 1 in every 5 warp threads.
(*Coton a Broder* B5200 #25)
Four-Sided S
(*Coton a Broder* B5200 #25)
Stitch every 3 threads
Lazy Daisy S
(Light Effects E677, 1 strand)
Withdraw 1 thread
Leave 3 threads

4. / page 11 Duck Zippered Pouch

Materials Outer Fabric (Blue plain weave linen, 12 threads per cm for both warp and weft / 30 TPI for both warp and weft) 25 × 30 cm / 9⅞" ×11⅞"
Lining Fabric 25 × 30cm / 9⅞" × 11⅞"
One 20 cm / 7⅞" long zipper
DMC *Coton a Broder* ECRU #20, 25
DMC Pearl Cotton ECRU #8

Finished Size 13 × 20 cm / 5⅛" × 7⅞"

Steps

1. Embroider on outer fabric.
2. Install zipper on top edge of outer and lining fabric.
3. Sew both sides.
4. Turn right side out. Close opening.

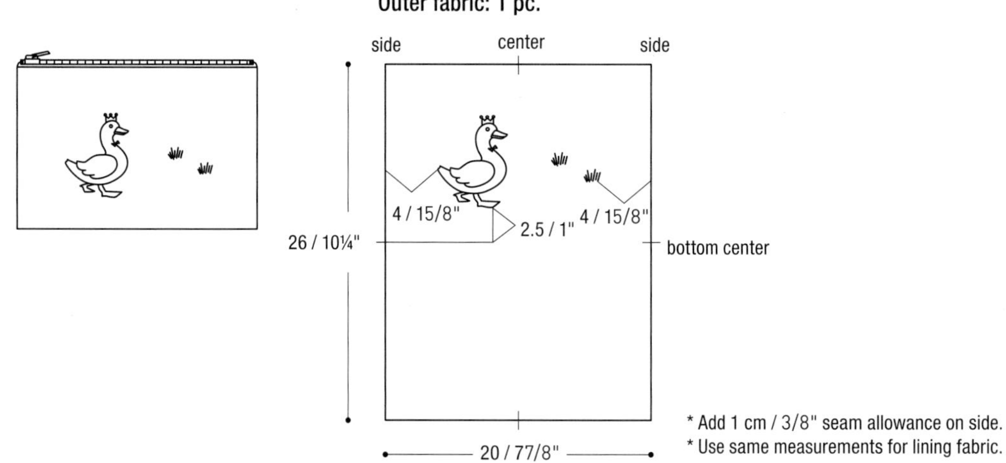
Outer fabric: 1 pc.
side
center
side
4 / 15/8"
2.5 / 1"
4 / 15/8"
26 / 10¼"
bottom center
20 / 77/8"
* Add 1 cm / 3/8" seam allowance on side.
* Use same measurements for lining fabric.

Sewing Steps

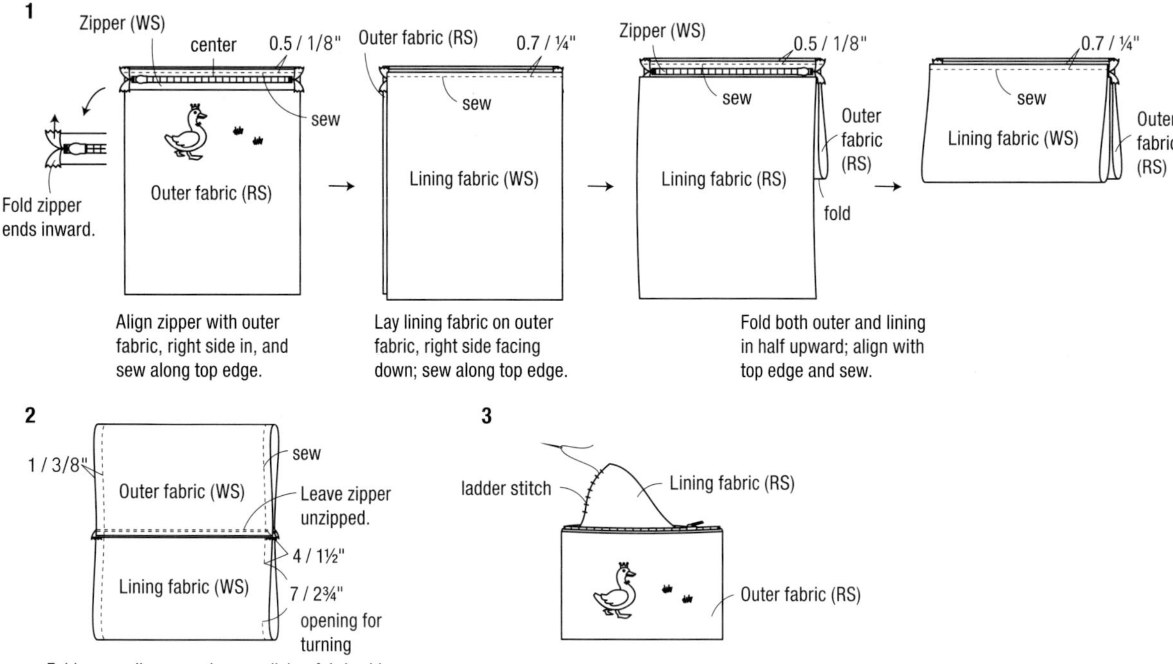
1
Zipper (WS)
center
0.5 / 1/8"
sew
Fold zipper ends inward.
Outer fabric (RS)
Align zipper with outer fabric, right side in, and sew along top edge.
Outer fabric (RS)
0.7 / ¼"
sew
Lining fabric (WS)
Lay lining fabric on outer fabric, right side facing down; sew along top edge.
Zipper (WS)
0.5 / 1/8"
sew
Lining fabric (RS)
Outer fabric (RS)
fold
Fold both outer and lining in half upward; align with top edge and sew.
0.7 / ¼"
sew
Lining fabric (WS)
Outer fabric (RS)
2
1 / 3/8"
sew
Outer fabric (WS)
Leave zipper unzipped.
4 / 1½"
Lining fabric (WS)
7 / 2¾"
opening for turning
Fold seam allowance down on lining-fabric side. Sew sides as shown in figure above, leaving an opening for turning.
3
ladder stitch
Lining fabric (RS)
Outer fabric (RS)
Turn right side out. Close opening.

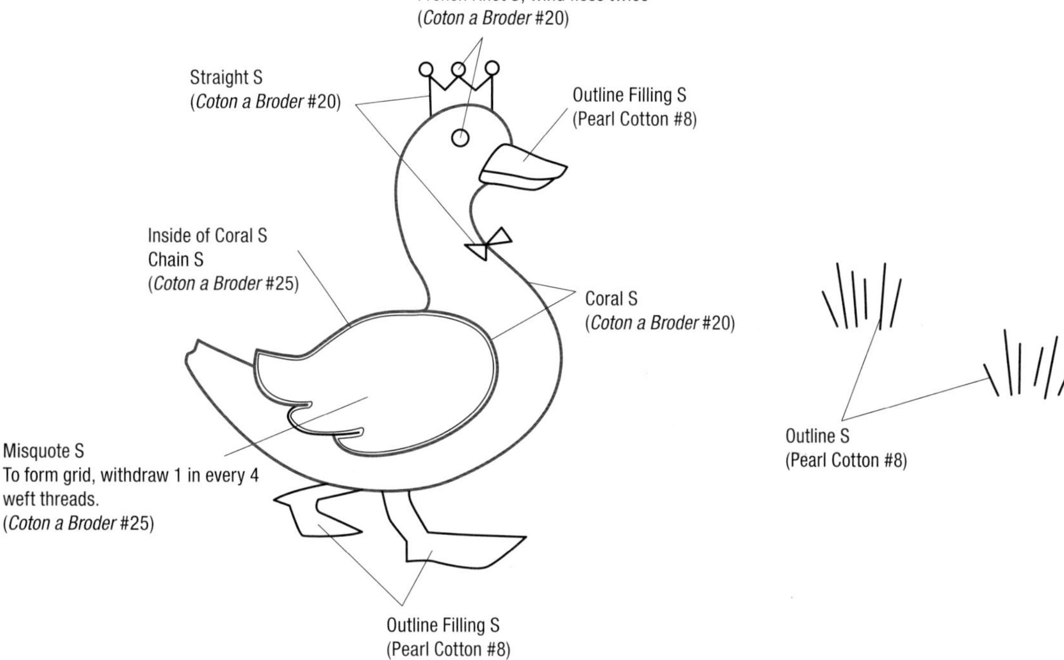
French Knot S, wind floss twice
(*Coton a Broder* #20)
Straight S
(*Coton a Broder* #20)
Outline Filling S
(Pearl Cotton #8)
Inside of Coral S
Chain S
(*Coton a Broder* #25)
Coral S
(*Coton a Broder* #20)
Outline S
(Pearl Cotton #8)
Misquote S
To form grid, withdraw 1 in every 4
weft threads.
(*Coton a Broder* #25)
Outline Filling S
(Pearl Cotton #8)

5. / page 12 Schwalm Embroidery: Plants and Bird

Materials Fabric (white plain-weave linen, 12 threads per cm for both warp and weft / 30 TPI for both warp and weft)
DMC *Coton a Broder* B5200 #16, 20, 25

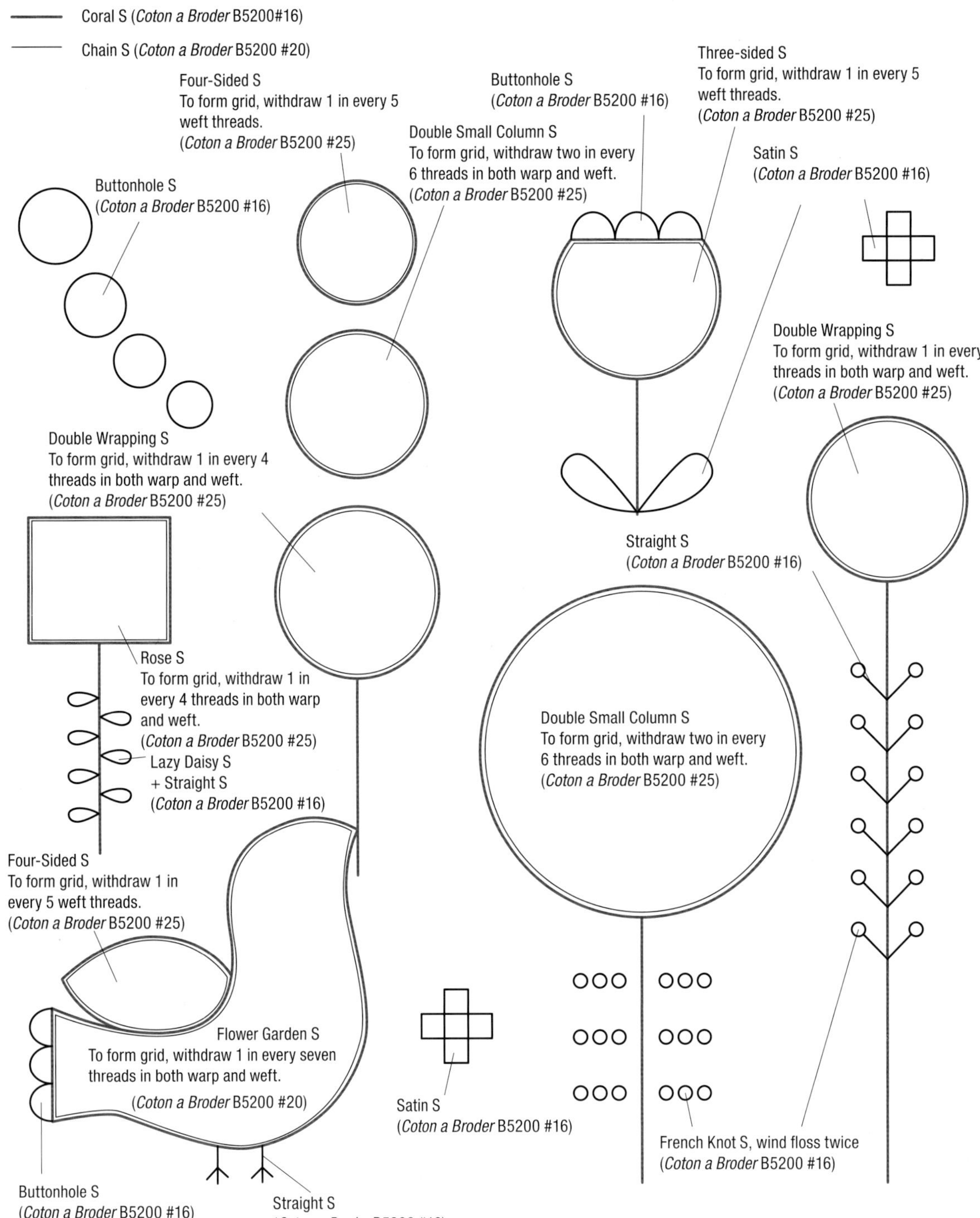

Coral S (Coton a Broder B5200#16)
Chain S (Coton a Broder B5200 #20)
Four-Sided S
To form grid, withdraw 1 in every 5 weft threads.
(Coton a Broder B5200 #25)
Buttonhole S
(Coton a Broder B5200 #16)
Three-sided S
To form grid, withdraw 1 in every 5 weft threads.
(Coton a Broder B5200 #25)
Double Small Column S
To form grid, withdraw two in every 6 threads in both warp and weft.
(Coton a Broder B5200 #25)
Satin S
(Coton a Broder B5200 #16)
Buttonhole S
(Coton a Broder B5200 #16)
Double Wrapping S
To form grid, withdraw 1 in every 4 threads in both warp and weft.
(Coton a Broder B5200 #25)
Double Wrapping S
To form grid, withdraw 1 in every 4 threads in both warp and weft.
(Coton a Broder B5200 #25)
Straight S
(Coton a Broder B5200 #16)
Rose S
To form grid, withdraw 1 in every 4 threads in both warp and weft.
(Coton a Broder B5200 #25)
Lazy Daisy S
+ Straight S
(Coton a Broder B5200 #16)
Double Small Column S
To form grid, withdraw two in every 6 threads in both warp and weft.
(Coton a Broder B5200 #25)
Four-Sided S
To form grid, withdraw 1 in every 5 weft threads.
(Coton a Broder B5200 #25)
Flower Garden S
To form grid, withdraw 1 in every seven threads in both warp and weft.
(Coton a Broder B5200 #20)
Satin S
(Coton a Broder B5200 #16)
French Knot S, wind floss twice
(Coton a Broder B5200 #16)
Buttonhole S
(Coton a Broder B5200 #16)
Straight S
(Coton a Broder B5200 #16)

6. / page 13 Plants and Bird Panel

Materials Outer Fabric (white plain-weave linen, 12 threads per cm for both warp and weft / 30 TPI for both warp and weft) 30 × 30 cm / 11¾" × 11¾"
Backing Fabric (Light blue heavy plain weave linen) 20 × 20cm / 7⅞" × 7⅞"
One 18 × 18cm / 7⅛" × 7⅛" panel
DMC *Coton a Broder* B5200 #16, 20, 25

Finished Size 18 × 18cm / 7⅛" × 7⅛"

Steps

1. Embroider same design as page 78.
2. Lay down backing fabric, warp panel, and secure fabric with staples at back.

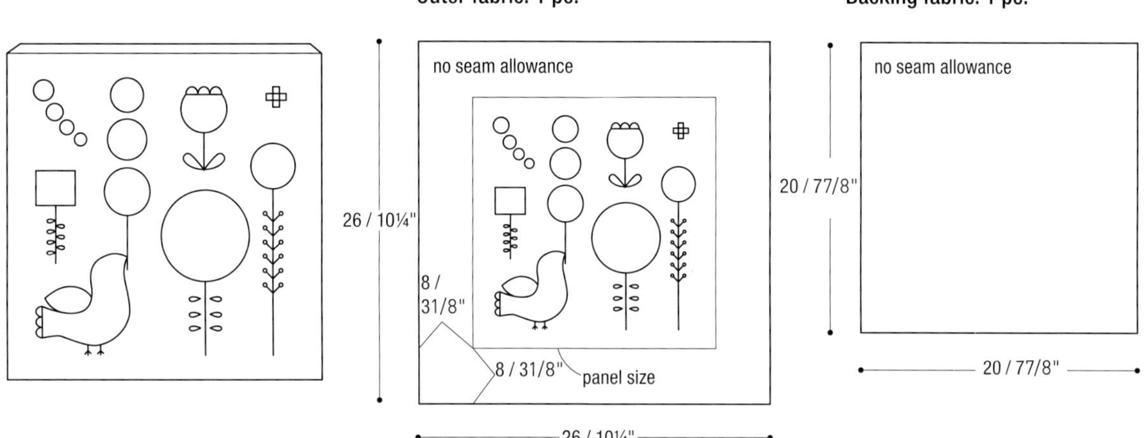
Outer fabric: 1 pc.
no seam allowance
26 / 10¼"
8 / 31/8"
8 / 31/8"
panel size
26 / 10¼"
Backing fabric: 1 pc.
no seam allowance
20 / 77/8"
20 / 77/8"

Mounting Steps

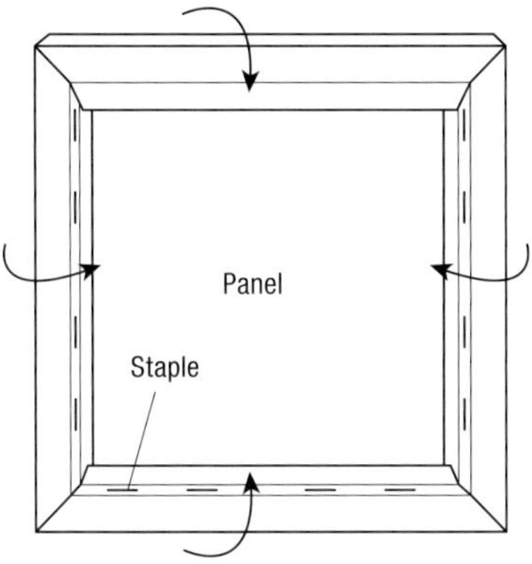
Panel
Staple

Lay down outer fabric on backing fabric, warp panel, and secure fabric with staples at back.

Stitches 1 / page 22 Ajour Embroidery

Materials Fabric (white plain-weave linen, 11 threads per cm for both warp and weft / 28 TPI for both warp and weft)
DMC No. 25 Embroidery Floss B5200

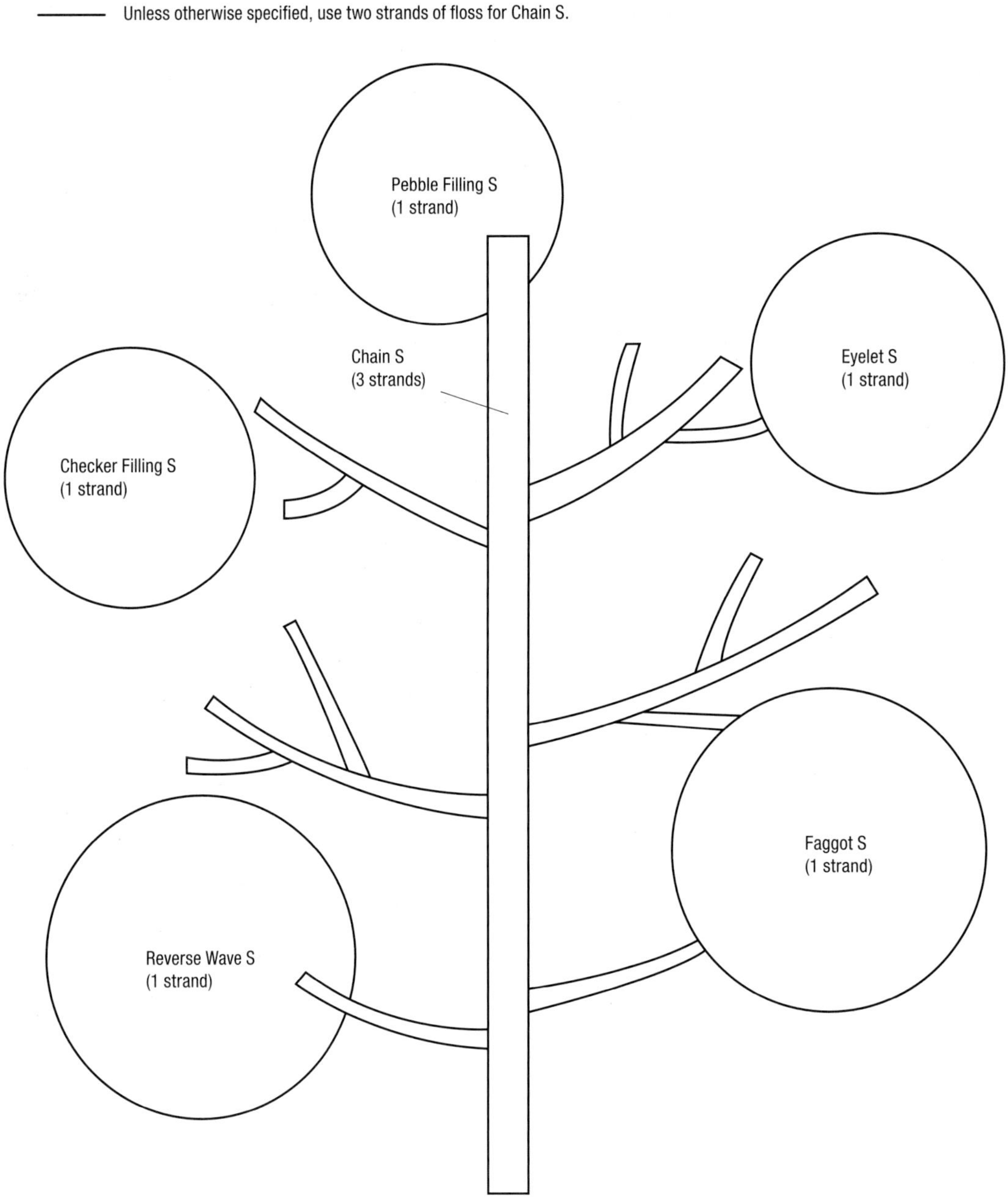

Unless otherwise specified, use two strands of floss for Chain S.
Pebble Filling S (1 strand)
Chain S (3 strands)
Eyelet S (1 strand)
Checker Filling S (1 strand)
Faggot S (1 strand)
Reverse Wave S (1 strand)

Stitches 2 / page 23 Ajour Embroidery

Materials Fabric (white plain-weave linen, 11 threads per cm for both warp and weft / 28 TPI for both warp and weft)
DMC No. 25 Embroidery Floss B5200

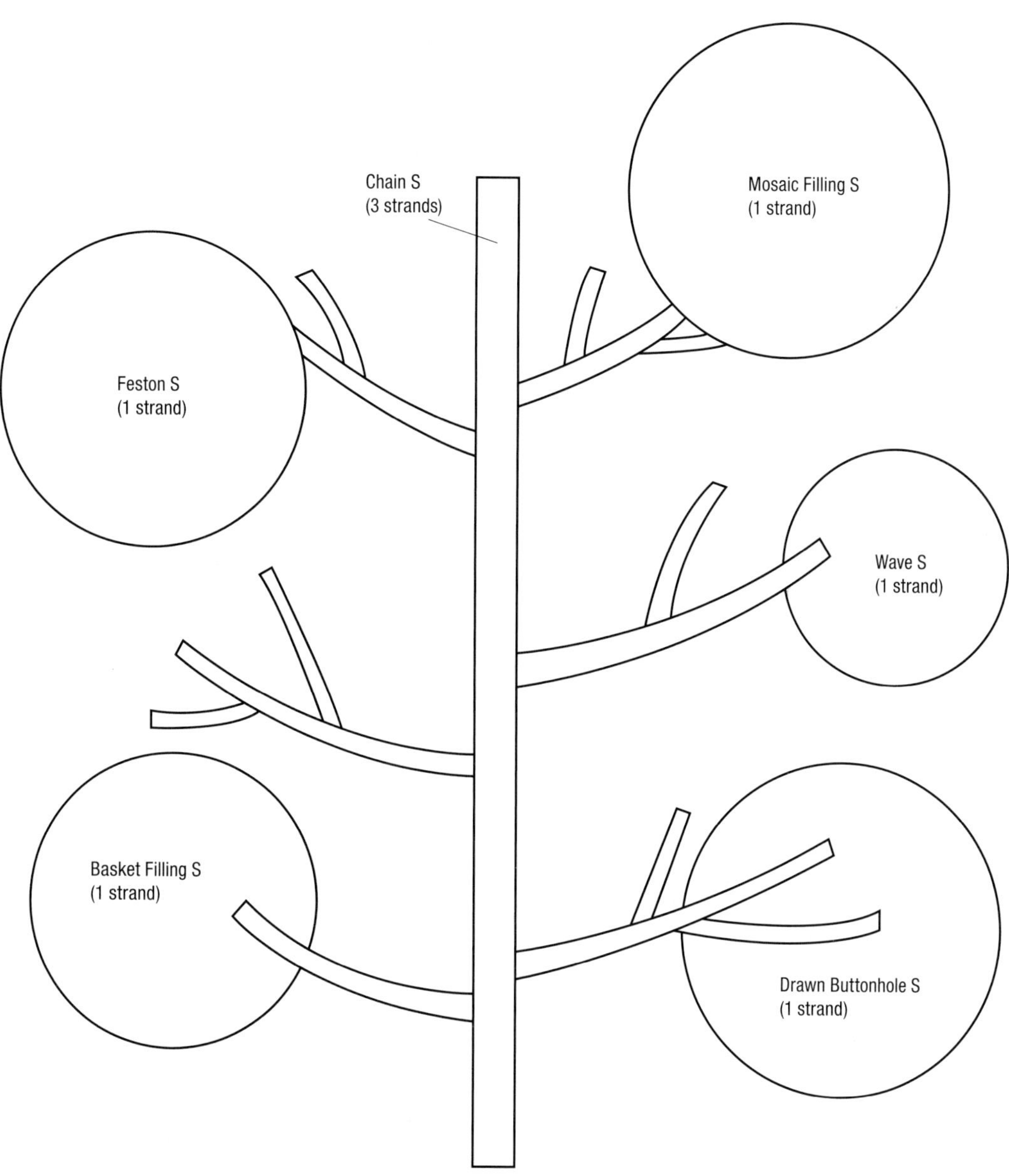
Unless otherwise specified, use two strands of floss for Chain S.
Chain S
(3 strands)
Mosaic Filling S
(1 strand)
Feston S
(1 strand)
Wave S
(1 strand)
Basket Filling S
(1 strand)
Drawn Buttonhole S
(1 strand)

7. / page 24 Ajour Embroidery: Townscape

Materials Fabric (white plain-weave linen, 12 threads per cm for both warp and weft / 30 TPI for both warp and weft)
DMC No. 25 Embroidery Floss BLANC

95% Scale Pattern.
Enlarge the 95% scale pattern to 105% to produce a full-sized pattern.
——— Unless otherwise specified, use two strands of floss for Chain S.

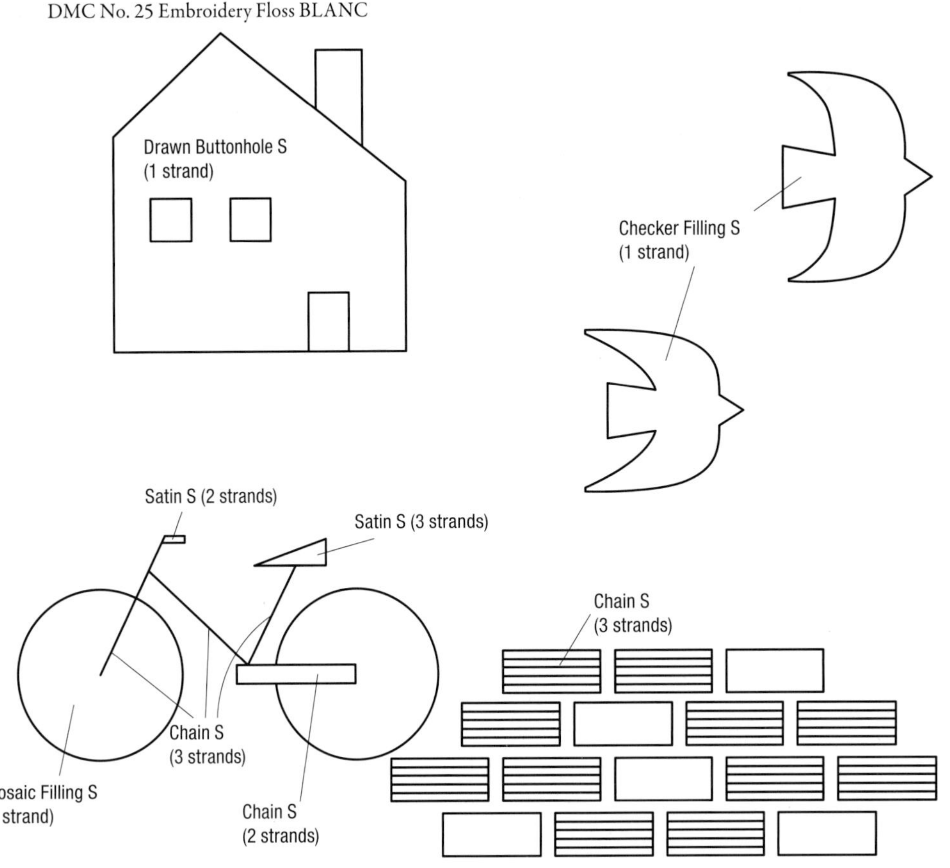
Drawn Buttonhole S
(1 strand)
Checker Filling S
(1 strand)
Satin S (2 strands)
Satin S (3 strands)
Chain S
(3 strands)
Chain S
(3 strands)
Mosaic Filling S
(1 strand)
Chain S
(2 strands)

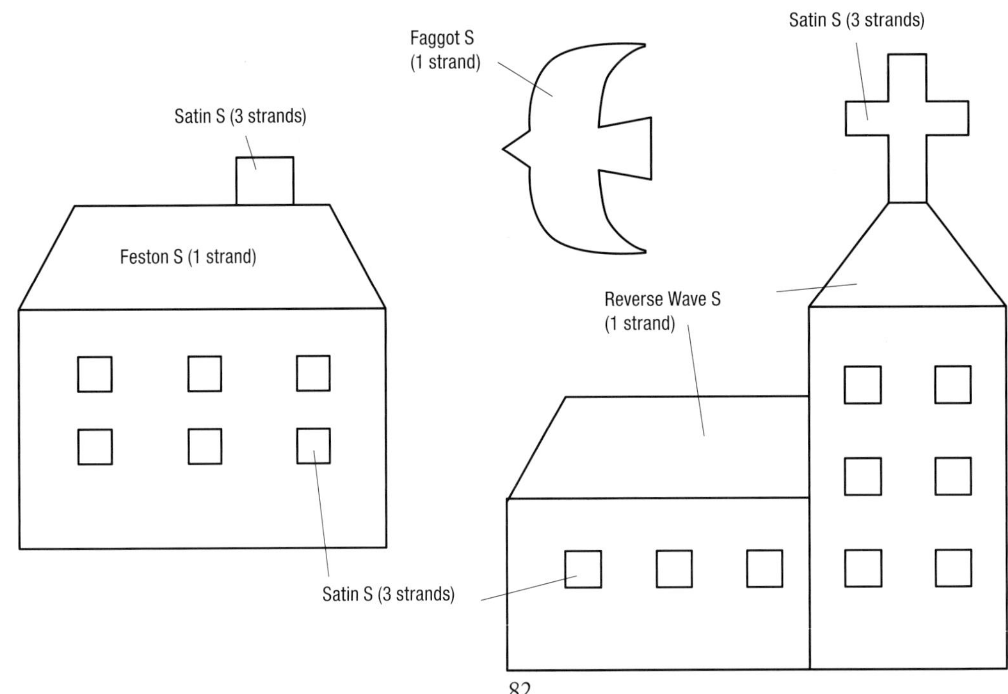
Faggot S
(1 strand)
Satin S (3 strands)
Satin S (3 strands)
Feston S (1 strand)
Reverse Wave S
(1 strand)
Satin S (3 strands)

8. / page 25 Ajour Embroidery Getting Ready for Winter

Materials Fabric (white plain-weave linen, 12 threads per cm for both warp and weft / 30 TPI for both warp and weft)
DMC No. 25 Embroidery Floss BLANC, Apple Crewel Wool 991B

95% Scale Pattern.
Enlarge the 95% scale pattern to 105% to produce a full-sized pattern.
——— Unless otherwise specified, use two strands of floss for Chain S.
Unless otherwise specified, use DMC No. 25 embroidery floss BLANC.

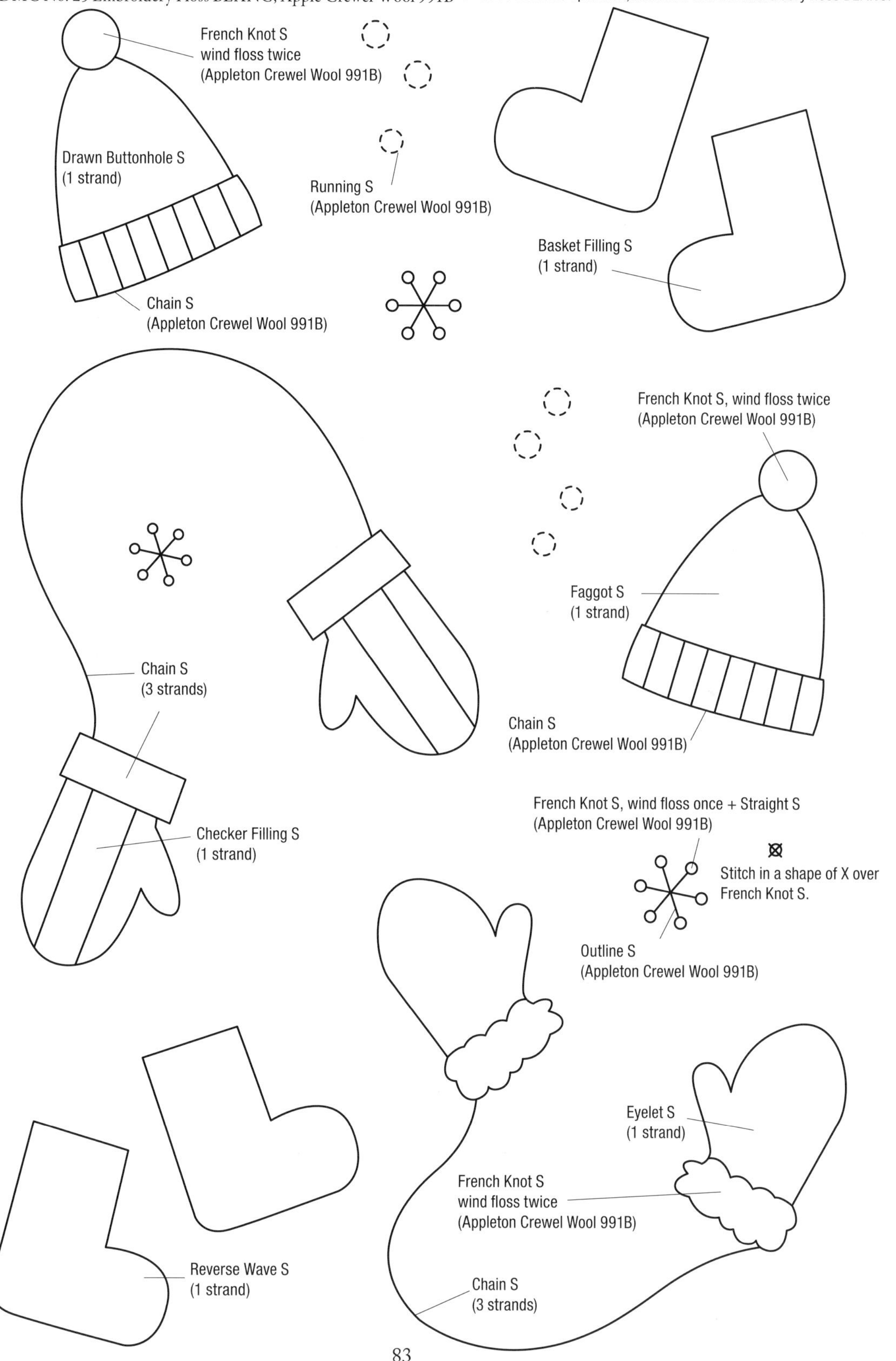
French Knot S
wind floss twice
(Appleton Crewel Wool 991B)
Drawn Buttonhole S
(1 strand)
Running S
(Appleton Crewel Wool 991B)
Basket Filling S
(1 strand)
Chain S
(Appleton Crewel Wool 991B)
French Knot S, wind floss twice
(Appleton Crewel Wool 991B)
Faggot S
(1 strand)
Chain S
(3 strands)
Chain S
(Appleton Crewel Wool 991B)
French Knot S, wind floss once + Straight S
(Appleton Crewel Wool 991B)
Checker Filling S
(1 strand)
Stitch in a shape of X over
French Knot S.
Outline S
(Appleton Crewel Wool 991B)
Eyelet S
(1 strand)
French Knot S
wind floss twice
(Appleton Crewel Wool 991B)
Reverse Wave S
(1 strand)
Chain S
(3 strands)

9. / page 26 Ajour Embroidery: Cute Couple

Materials Fabric (white plain-weave linen, 12 threads per cm for both warp and weft / 30 TPI for both warp and weft)
DMC No. 25 Embroidery Floss BLANC

Align mark

Lazy Daisy S + Straight S
(3 strands)

Chain S (2 strands)

Faggot S (1 strand)

Satin S
(2 strands)

Eyelet S (3 threads)
(1 strand)

Eyelet S (4 threads) (1 strand)

Feston S (1 strand)

Fly S (3 strands)

——— Unless otherwise specified, use two strands of floss and Chain S for human figures. Unless otherwise specified, use three strands of floss and Outline S for flower motifs that surround the human figures.

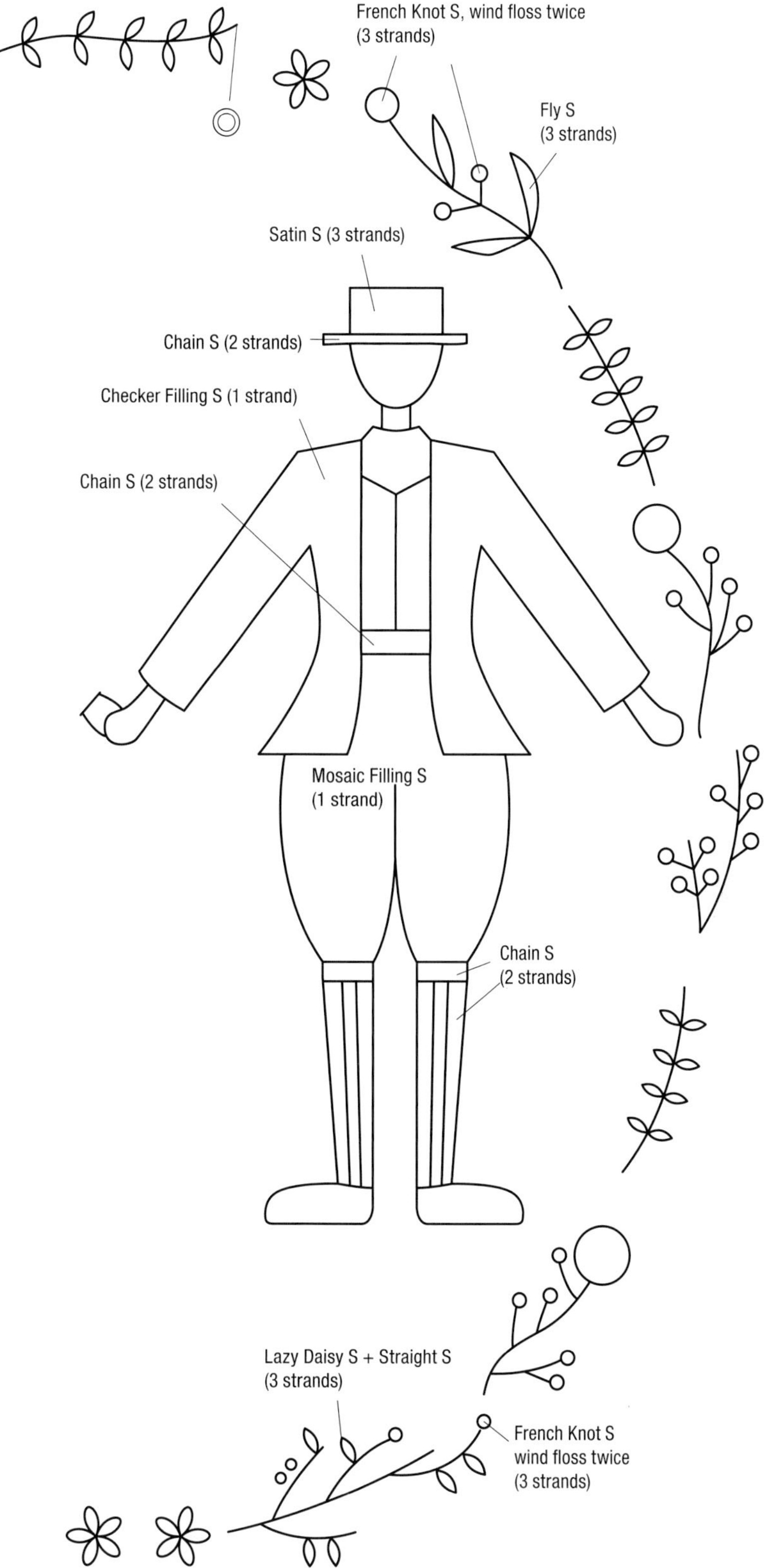
French Knot S, wind floss twice
(3 strands)
Fly S
(3 strands)
Satin S (3 strands)
Chain S (2 strands)
Checker Filling S (1 strand)
Chain S (2 strands)
Mosaic Filling S
(1 strand)
Chain S
(2 strands)
Lazy Daisy S + Straight S
(3 strands)
French Knot S
wind floss twice
(3 strands)

10. / page 27 Boy in Lederhosen Bag

Materials Outer Fabric (gray plain-weave linen, 12 threads per cm for both warp and weft / 30 TPI for both warp and weft, includes handles) 35 × 55 cm / 13¾" × 21⅝"
Lining fabric 25 × 55 cm / 9⅞" × 21⅝"
DMC No. 25 Embroidery Floss BLANC

Finished Size 25 × 18cm / 9⅞" × 7⅛"

Steps

1. Embroider on outer fabric.
2. Sew sides on both outer and lining fabric.
3. Sew handles and attach to outer fabric.
4. Insert lining into outer fabric and blind-stitch all around top edge.

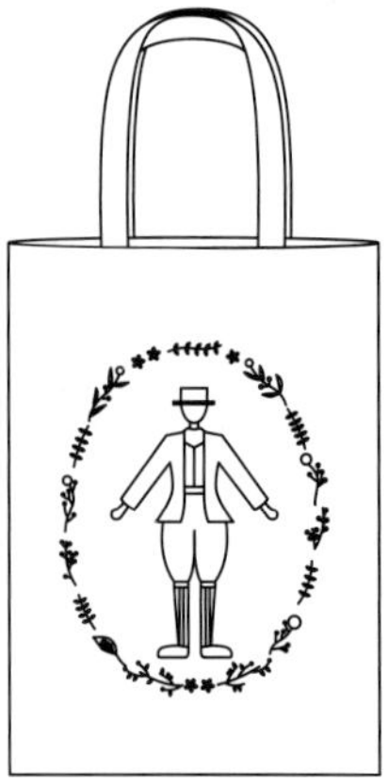

Outer fabric: 1 pc.

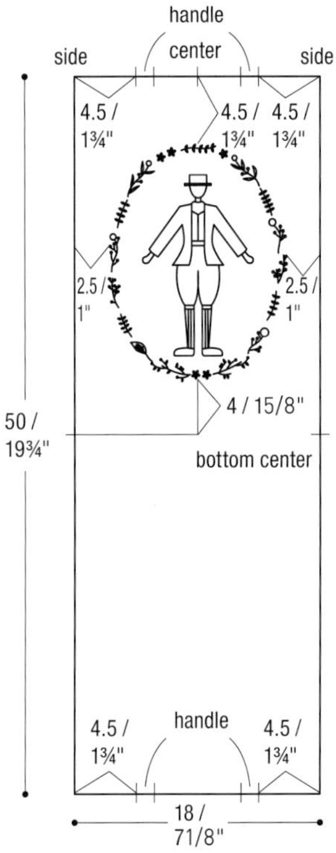

handle
side center side
4.5 / 1¾" 4.5 / 1¾" 4.5 / 1¾"
2.5 / 1" 2.5 / 1"
4 / 15/8"
50 / 19¾"
bottom center
4.5 / 1¾" handle 4.5 / 1¾"
18 / 71/8"

Lining fabric: 1pc.

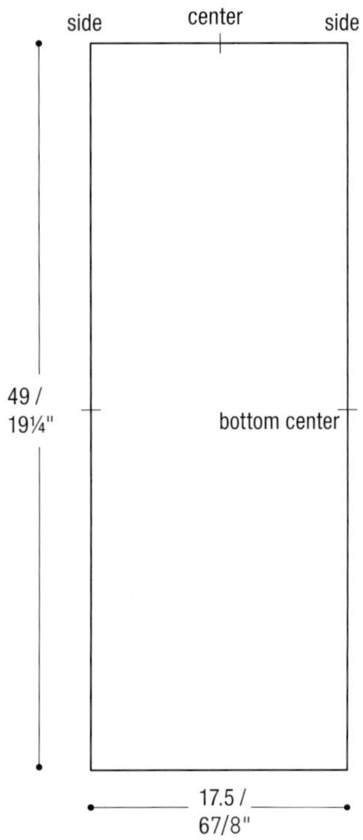

side center side
49 / 19¼"
bottom center
17.5 / 67/8"

* Add 2 cm / ¾" seam allowance on top edge, 1 cm / 3/8" on both side.

Handle: 2 pcs.

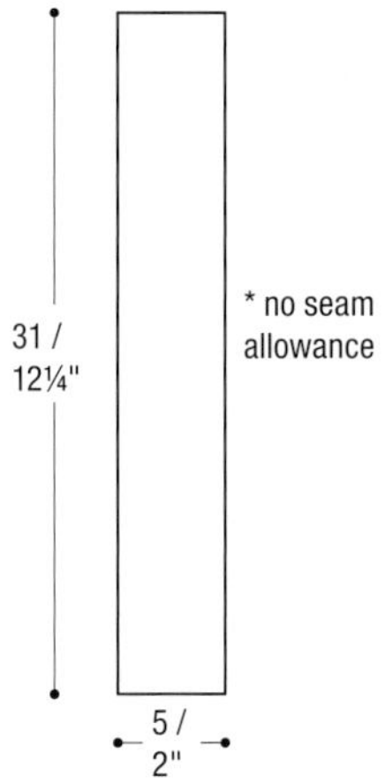

31 / 12¼"
* no seam allowance
5 / 2"

Making Handle

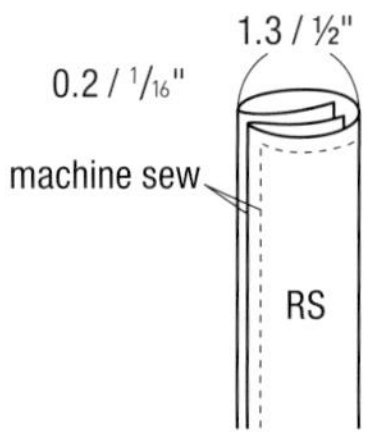

1.3 / ½"
0.2 / 1/16"
machine sew
RS

With right side facing out, fold in 4 then sew side.

Sewing Steps

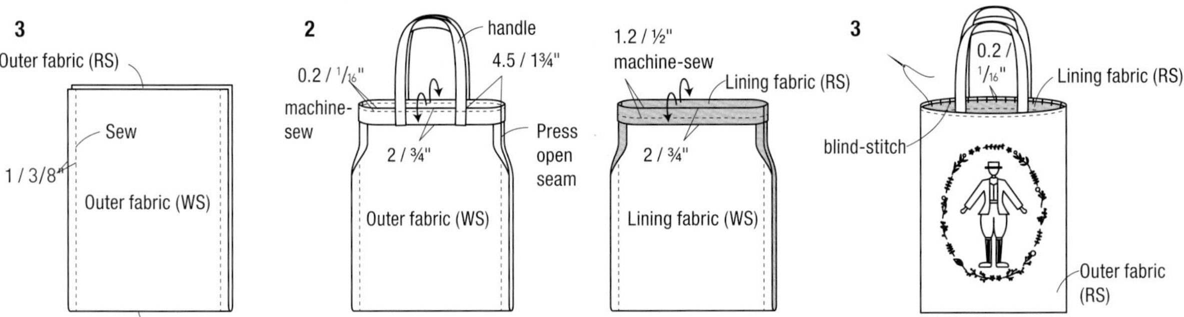

3
Outer fabric (RS)
Sew
1 / 3/8"
Outer fabric (WS)
fold
2
handle
0.2 / 1/16"
4.5 / 1¾"
machine-sew
Press open seam
2 / ¾"
Outer fabric (WS)
1.2 / ½"
machine-sew
Lining fabric (RS)
2 / ¾"
Lining fabric (WS)
3
0.2 / 1/16"
Lining fabric (RS)
blind-stitch
Outer fabric (RS)

Fold in half, right side in. Sew both sides. Do the same for the lining.

Fold down seam allowance on top edge and align handles. Sew along top edge. Do the same for the lining.

Insert lining into outer fabric; blind-stitch on top edge.

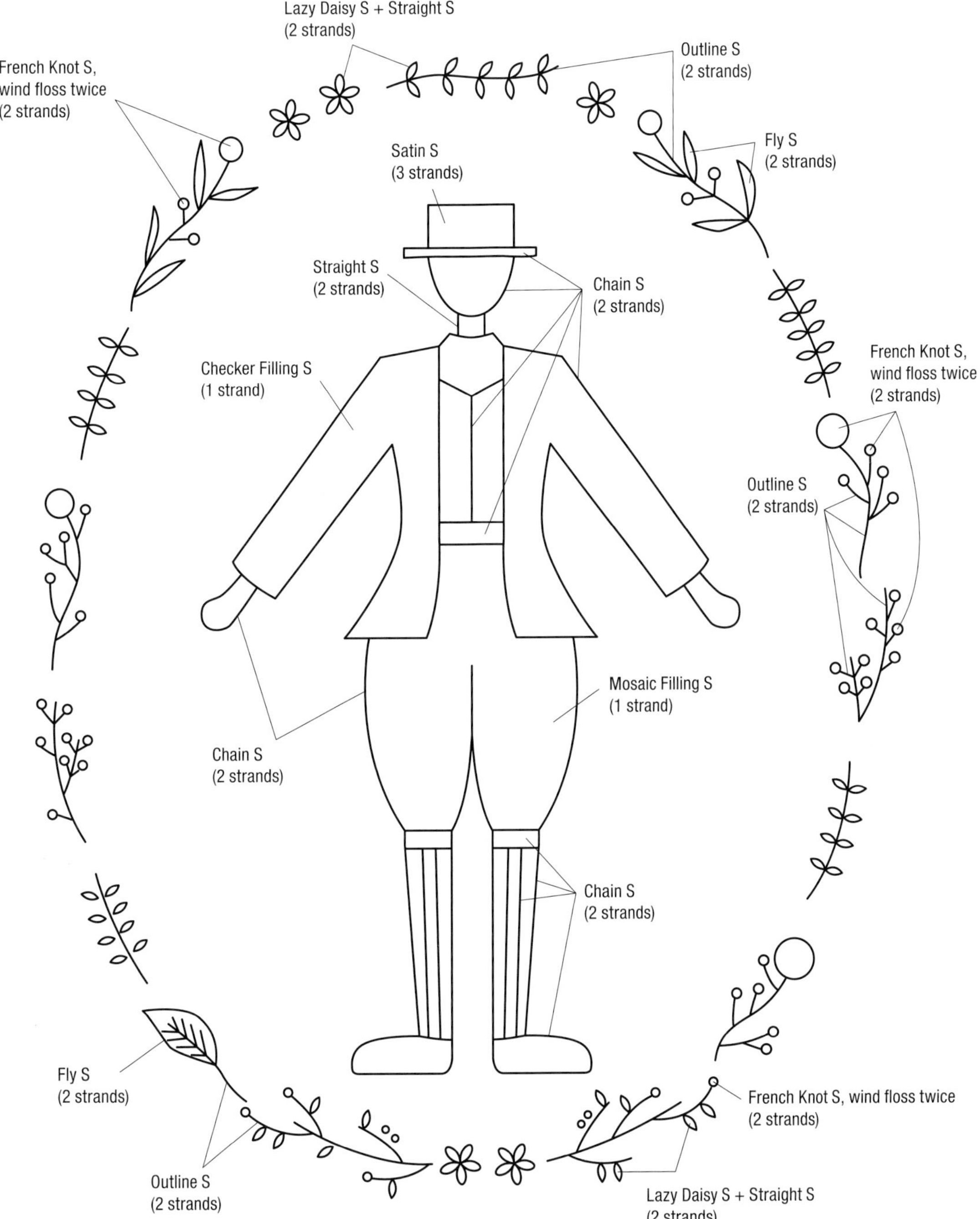
Lazy Daisy S + Straight S
(2 strands)
French Knot S,
wind floss twice
(2 strands)
Outline S
(2 strands)
Fly S
(2 strands)
Satin S
(3 strands)
Straight S
(2 strands)
Chain S
(2 strands)
Checker Filling S
(1 strand)
French Knot S,
wind floss twice
(2 strands)
Outline S
(2 strands)
Mosaic Filling S
(1 strand)
Chain S
(2 strands)
Chain S
(2 strands)
Fly S
(2 strands)
French Knot S, wind floss twice
(2 strands)
Outline S
(2 strands)
Lazy Daisy S + Straight S
(2 strands)

11. / page 28 Ajour Embroidery: Toy Soldiers

Materials Fabric (white plain-weave linen, 12 threads per cm for both warp and weft / 30 TPI for both warp and weft)
DMC No. 25 Embroidery Floss BLANC, 3865

——— Unless otherwise specified, use two strands of floss and Chain S for soldiers. Unless otherwise stated, use three strands of floss and Outline S for music notes.

Use DMC No. 25 embroidery floss BLANC unless otherwise specified.

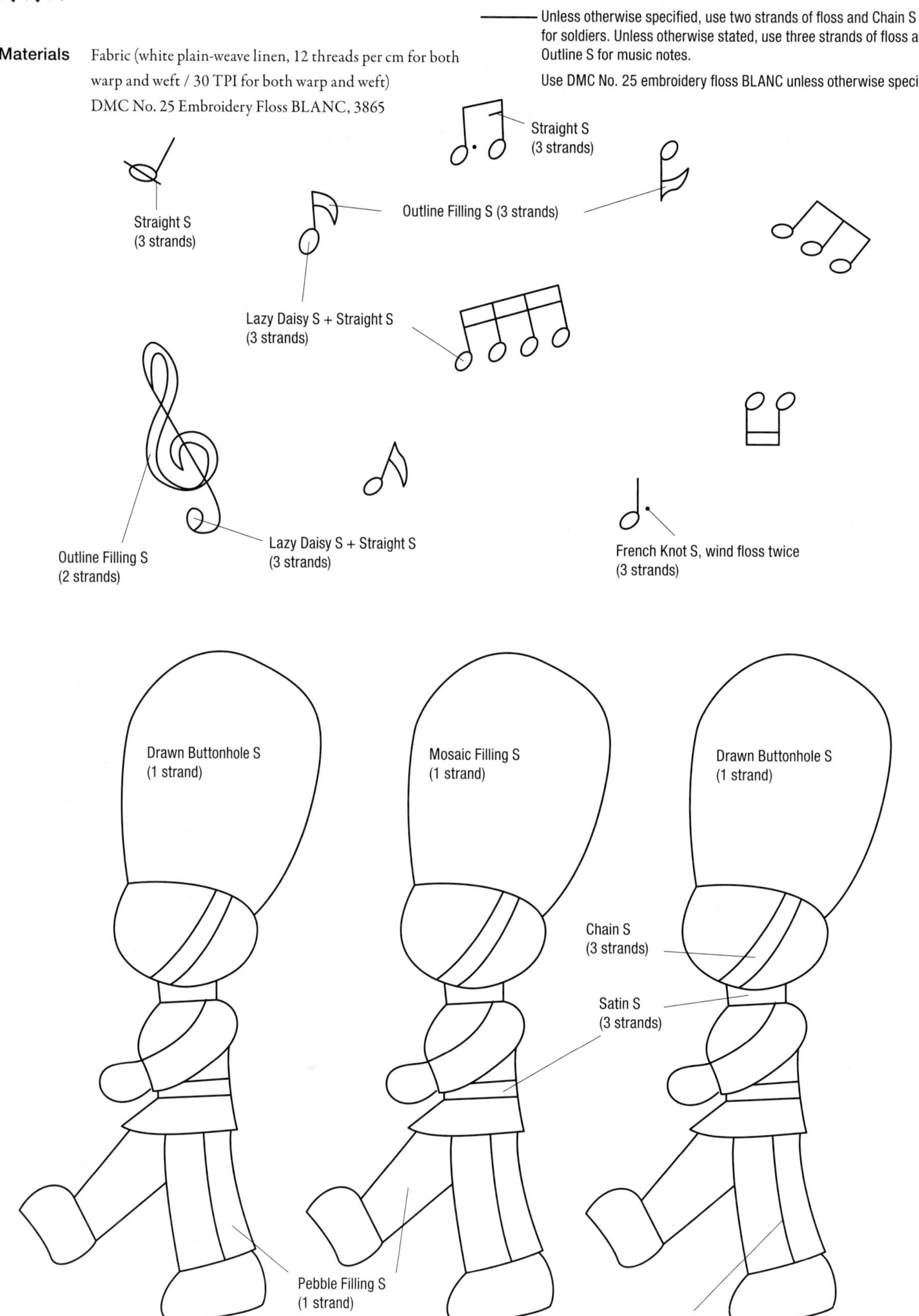
Straight S
(3 strands)
Straight S
(3 strands)
Outline Filling S (3 strands)
Lazy Daisy S + Straight S
(3 strands)
Outline Filling S
(2 strands)
Lazy Daisy S + Straight S
(3 strands)
French Knot S, wind floss twice
(3 strands)
Drawn Buttonhole S
(1 strand)
Mosaic Filling S
(1 strand)
Drawn Buttonhole S
(1 strand)
Chain S
(3 strands)
Satin S
(3 strands)
Pebble Filling S
(1 strand)
Over Pebble Filling S,
work Chain S (No. 25 floss 3865, 3 strands)

12. / page 29 Toy Soldier Bookmark

Materials For white bookmark: Fabric (white plain-weave linen, 12 threads per cm for both warp and weft / 30 TPI for both warp and weft) 20 × 20 cm / 7⅞" × 7⅞"
DMC No. 25 Embroidery Floss BLANC
For brown bookmark: Fabric (brown plain-weave linen, 12 threads per cm for both warp and weft / 30 TPI for both warp and weft) 20 × 20cm / 7⅞" × 7⅞"
DMC No. 25 Embroidery Floss 3865

Finished Size 15 × 5.5 cm / 5⅞" × 2⅛"

Steps

1. Embroider on fabric.
2. Fold right side in; sew long edge.
3. Turn right side out; stitch top edge. Fray the bottom edge.

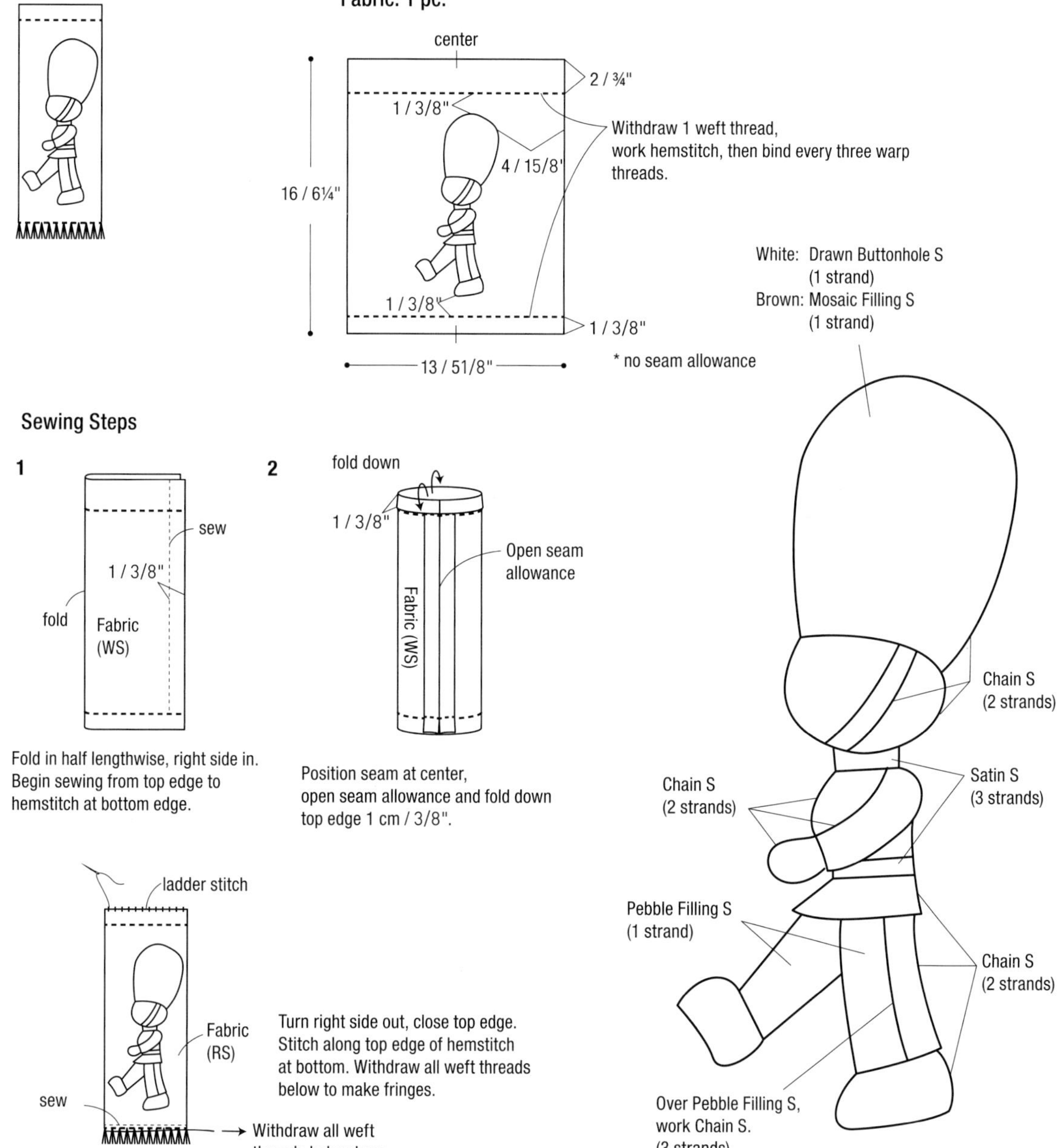
Fabric: 1 pc.
center
2 / ¾"
1 / 3/8"
Withdraw 1 weft thread, work hemstitch, then bind every three warp threads.
4 / 15/8"
16 / 6¼"
1 / 3/8"
1 / 3/8"
13 / 51/8"
* no seam allowance
White: Drawn Buttonhole S (1 strand)
Brown: Mosaic Filling S (1 strand)
Sewing Steps
1
sew
1 / 3/8"
fold
Fabric (WS)
Fold in half lengthwise, right side in. Begin sewing from top edge to hemstitch at bottom edge.
2
fold down
1 / 3/8"
Open seam allowance
Fabric (WS)
Position seam at center, open seam allowance and fold down top edge 1 cm / 3/8".
ladder stitch
Fabric (RS)
sew
Turn right side out, close top edge. Stitch along top edge of hemstitch at bottom. Withdraw all weft threads below to make fringes.
Withdraw all weft threads below here.
Chain S (2 strands)
Satin S (3 strands)
Chain S (2 strands)
Pebble Filling S (1 strand)
Chain S (2 strands)
Over Pebble Filling S, work Chain S. (3 strands)

13. / page 30 Pocket-Sized Tissue Case

Materials Fabric (white plain-weave linen, 12 threads per cm for both warp and weft / 30 TPI for both warp and weft) 70 × 20cm / 27½" × 7⅞"
DMC No. 25 Embroidery Floss BLANC
Appleton Crewel Wool 991B

Finished Size 9 × 13 cm / 3½" × 5⅛"

Steps

1. Embroider on fabric.
2. Fold inward, then fold outward. Sew edges, then turn right side out.

Front

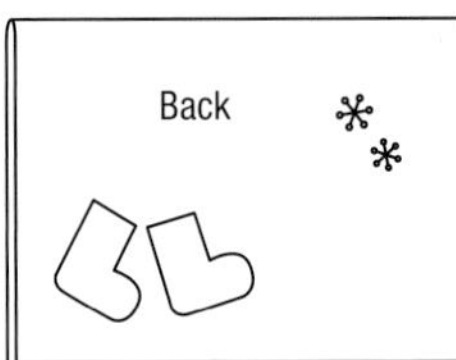
Back

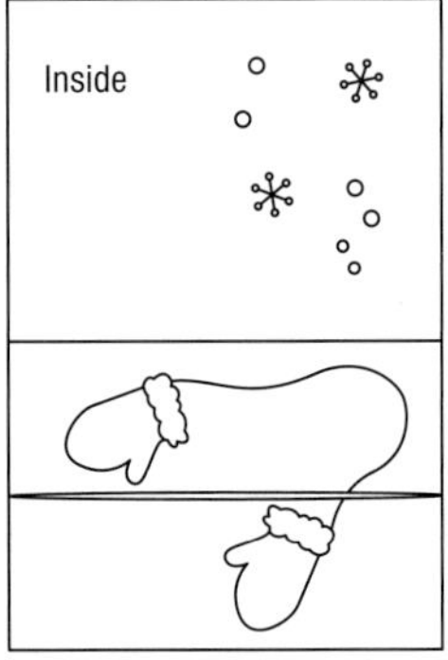
Inside

Fabric: 1 pc.

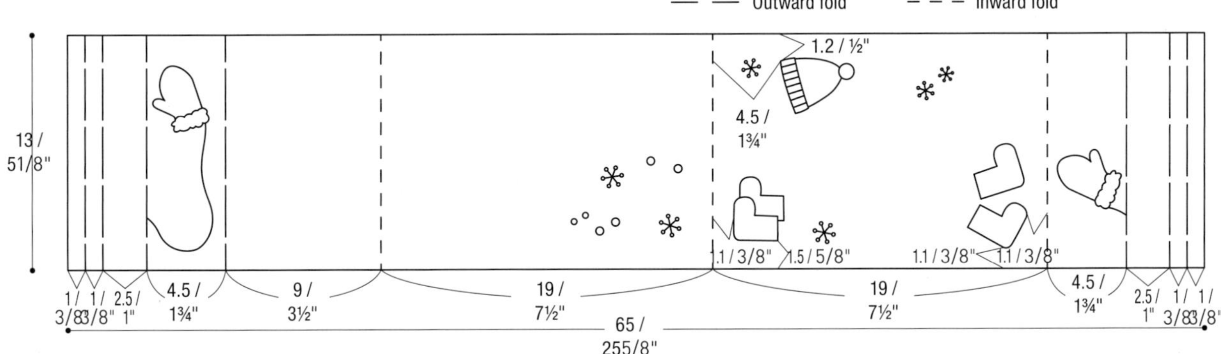
Outward fold
Inward fold
1.2 / ½"
4.5 / 1¾"
13 / 51/8"
1.1 / 3/8"
1.5 / 5/8"
1.1 / 3/8"
1.1 / 3/8"
1 / 3/8"
1 / 3/8"
2.5 / 1"
4.5 / 1¾"
9 / 3½"
19 / 7½"
19 / 7½"
4.5 / 1¾"
2.5 / 1"
1 / 3/8"
1 / 3/8"
65 / 255/8"

* Add 1 cm / 3/8" seam allowance on lengthwise edges. No seam allowance on short sides.

Sewing Steps

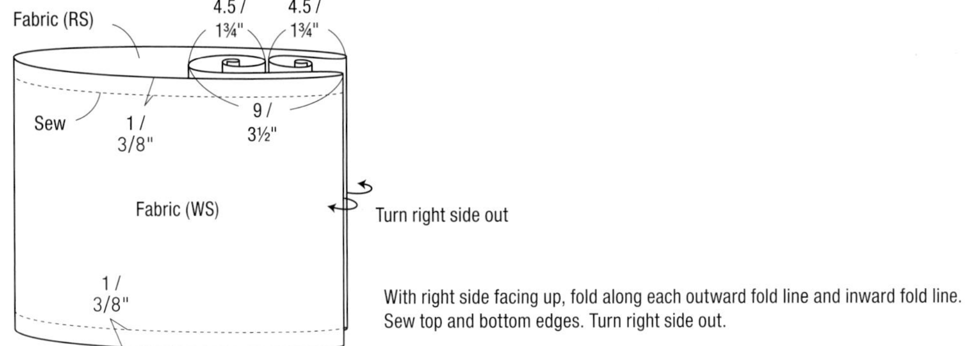
Fabric (RS)
4.5 / 1¾"
4.5 / 1¾"
Sew
1 / 3/8"
9 / 3½"
Fabric (WS)
Turn right side out
1 / 3/8"

With right side facing up, fold along each outward fold line and inward fold line. Sew top and bottom edges. Turn right side out.

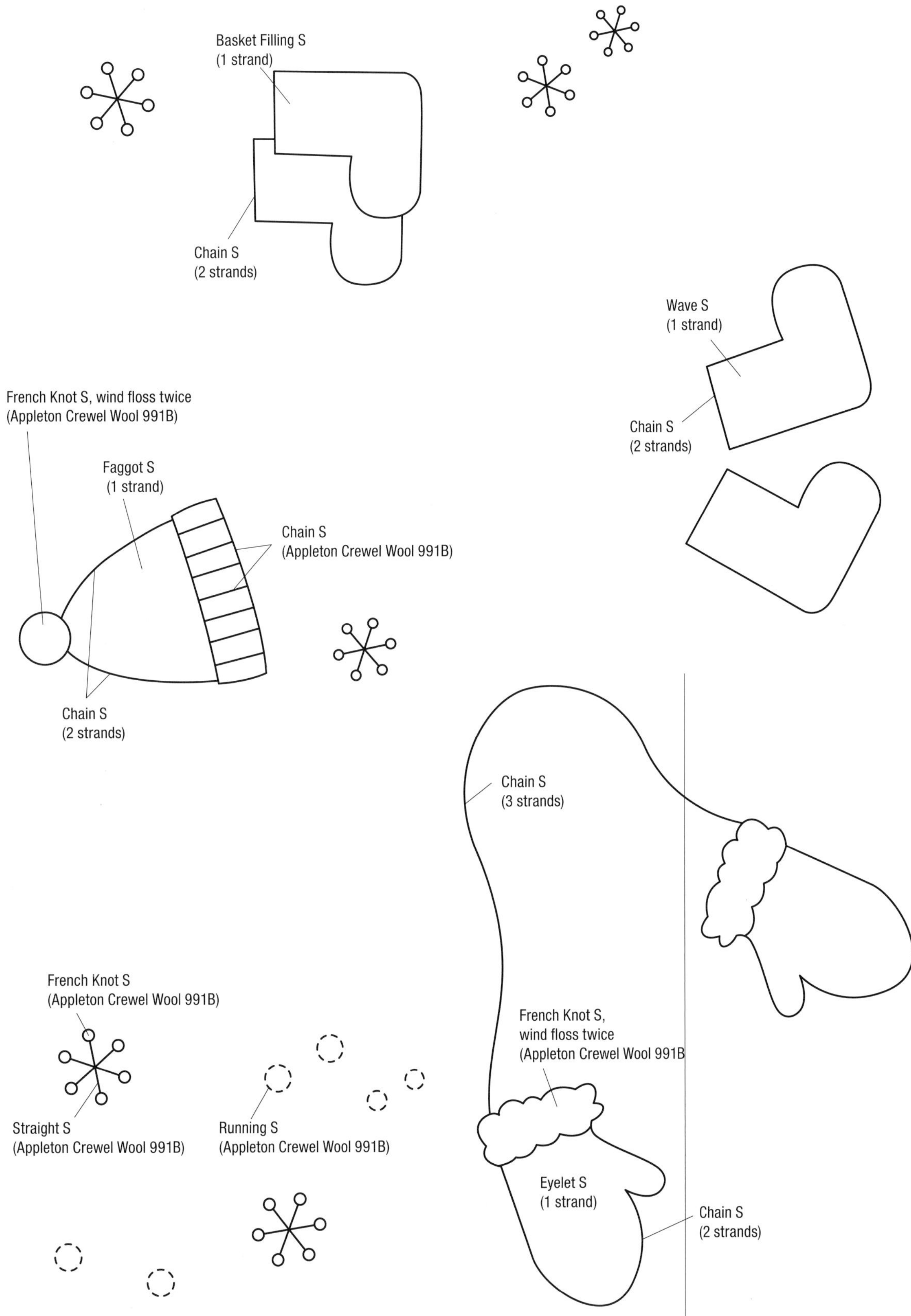
Basket Filling S
(1 strand)
Chain S
(2 strands)
Wave S
(1 strand)
Chain S
(2 strands)
French Knot S, wind floss twice
(Appleton Crewel Wool 991B)
Faggot S
(1 strand)
Chain S
(Appleton Crewel Wool 991B)
Chain S
(2 strands)
Chain S
(3 strands)
French Knot S
(Appleton Crewel Wool 991B)
French Knot S,
wind floss twice
(Appleton Crewel Wool 991B
Straight S
(Appleton Crewel Wool 991B)
Running S
(Appleton Crewel Wool 991B)
Eyelet S
(1 strand)
Chain S
(2 strands)

Stitches 1 / page 36 Hedebo Embroidery

Materials Fabric (white tightly woven linen)
DMC Coton à Broder B5200 #20

—— Hedebo Buttonhole S

Hedebo Buttonhole, Stitch 1 tier

Hedebo Buttonhole Stitch, 2 tiers

Buttonhole Scallop
Make arc with 4 stitches.

Buttonhole Scallop 2 tiers
Bottom tier: make arc with 4 stitches,
Top tier: make arc with 3 stitches.
Make bar.

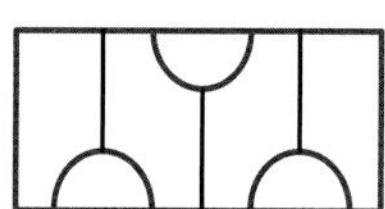

Buttonhole Scallop, make arc with 4 stitches
Make bars.

Buttonhole Scallop, make arc with 4 stitches
Make bars.

Make bars.

Buttonhole Scallop, make arc with 4 stitches
Make bars.

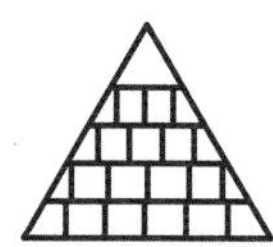

Hedebo Buttonhole Stitch, 4 tiers

Stitches 2 / page 37 Hedebo Embroidery

Materials Fabric (white tightly woven linen)
DMC *Coton a Broder* B5200 #20, 25

——— Hedebo Buttonhole S (Use #20 except where specified as *Coton a Broder* B5200)
——— Pyramids (Use #20 except where specified as *Coton a Broder* B5200)

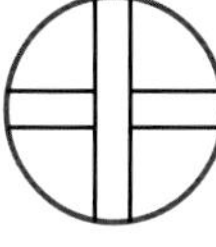

Darning Stitch

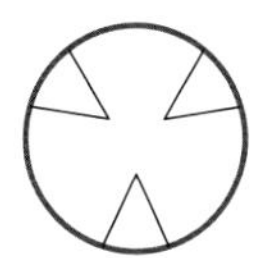

Pyramids, use 4 rows of Hedebo Buttonhole S.

Pyramids, use 6 rows of Hedebo Buttonhole S.
Make bars.

Hedebo Buttonhole Scallops, make arc with 4 stitches.
Pyramids at side—use 4 rows of Hedebo Buttonhole S. Pyramid at center—use 5 rows of Hedebo Buttonhole S (#25).
Make bars.

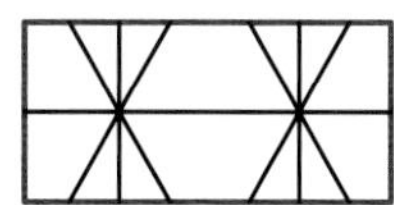

Make bars.
Coral Knot on drawn threadwork.

Star formed using 4 row pyramids on Hedebo ring (#25).
Pyramids—use 4 rows of Hedebo Buttonhole S
Make bars.

Pyramids—use 4 rows of Hedebo Buttonhole S.
Make bars.

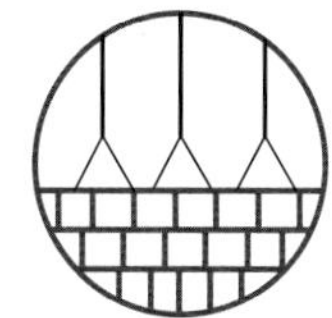

Hedeo Buttonhole Stitch, 3 tiers
Pyramids, make 4 rows of Hedebo Buttonhole S(#25).
Make bars.

14. / page 38 Hedebo Embroidery: Plants

Materials Fabric (white tightly woven linen)
DMC *Coton a Broder* B5200 #20, 25, 30

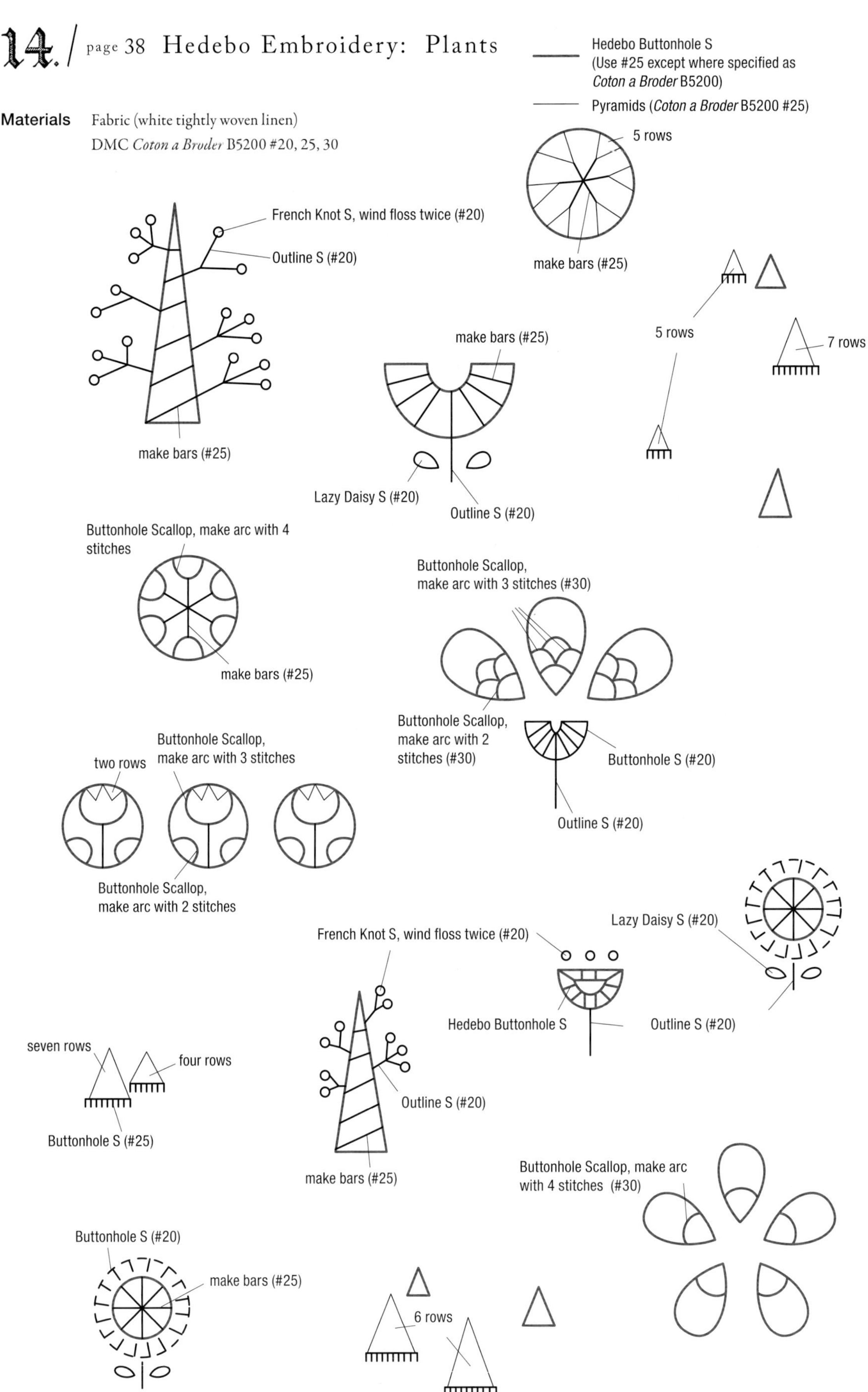

Hedebo Buttonhole S
(Use #25 except where specified as *Coton a Broder* B5200)
Pyramids (*Coton a Broder* B5200 #25)
5 rows
make bars (#25)
French Knot S, wind floss twice (#20)
Outline S (#20)
make bars (#25)
make bars (#25)
Lazy Daisy S (#20)
Outline S (#20)
5 rows
7 rows
Buttonhole Scallop, make arc with 4 stitches
make bars (#25)
Buttonhole Scallop,
make arc with 3 stitches (#30)
Buttonhole Scallop,
make arc with 2 stitches (#30)
Buttonhole S (#20)
Outline S (#20)
two rows
Buttonhole Scallop,
make arc with 3 stitches
Buttonhole Scallop,
make arc with 2 stitches
French Knot S, wind floss twice (#20)
Lazy Daisy S (#20)
Hedebo Buttonhole S
Outline S (#20)
seven rows
four rows
Buttonhole S (#25)
Outline S (#20)
make bars (#25)
Buttonhole Scallop, make arc
with 4 stitches (#30)
Buttonhole S (#20)
make bars (#25)
6 rows

15. / page 39 Hedebo Embroidery: Bird

Materials Fabric (white tightly woven linen)
DMC *Coton a Broder* B5200 #25, 30

——— Hedebo Buttonhole S (Use #25 except where specified as *Coton a Broder* B5200)
——— Pyramids (*Coton a Broder* B5200 #25)

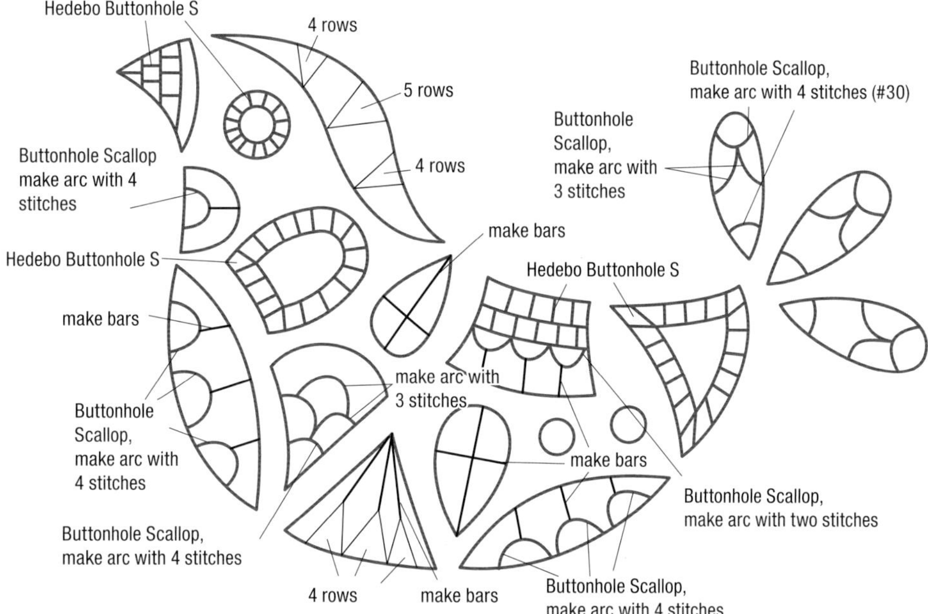
Hedebo Buttonhole S
4 rows
5 rows
4 rows
Buttonhole Scallop, make arc with 4 stitches (#30)
Buttonhole Scallop, make arc with 3 stitches
Buttonhole Scallop make arc with 4 stitches
make bars
Hedebo Buttonhole S
Hedebo Buttonhole S
make bars
make arc with 3 stitches
Buttonhole Scallop, make arc with 4 stitches
make bars
Buttonhole Scallop, make arc with two stitches
Buttonhole Scallop, make arc with 4 stitches
4 rows
make bars
Buttonhole Scallop, make arc with 4 stitches

16. / page 40 Hedebo Embroidery: Night Sky

Materials Fabric (white tightly woven linen)
DMC *Coton a Broder* B5200 #16, 20, 25, 30

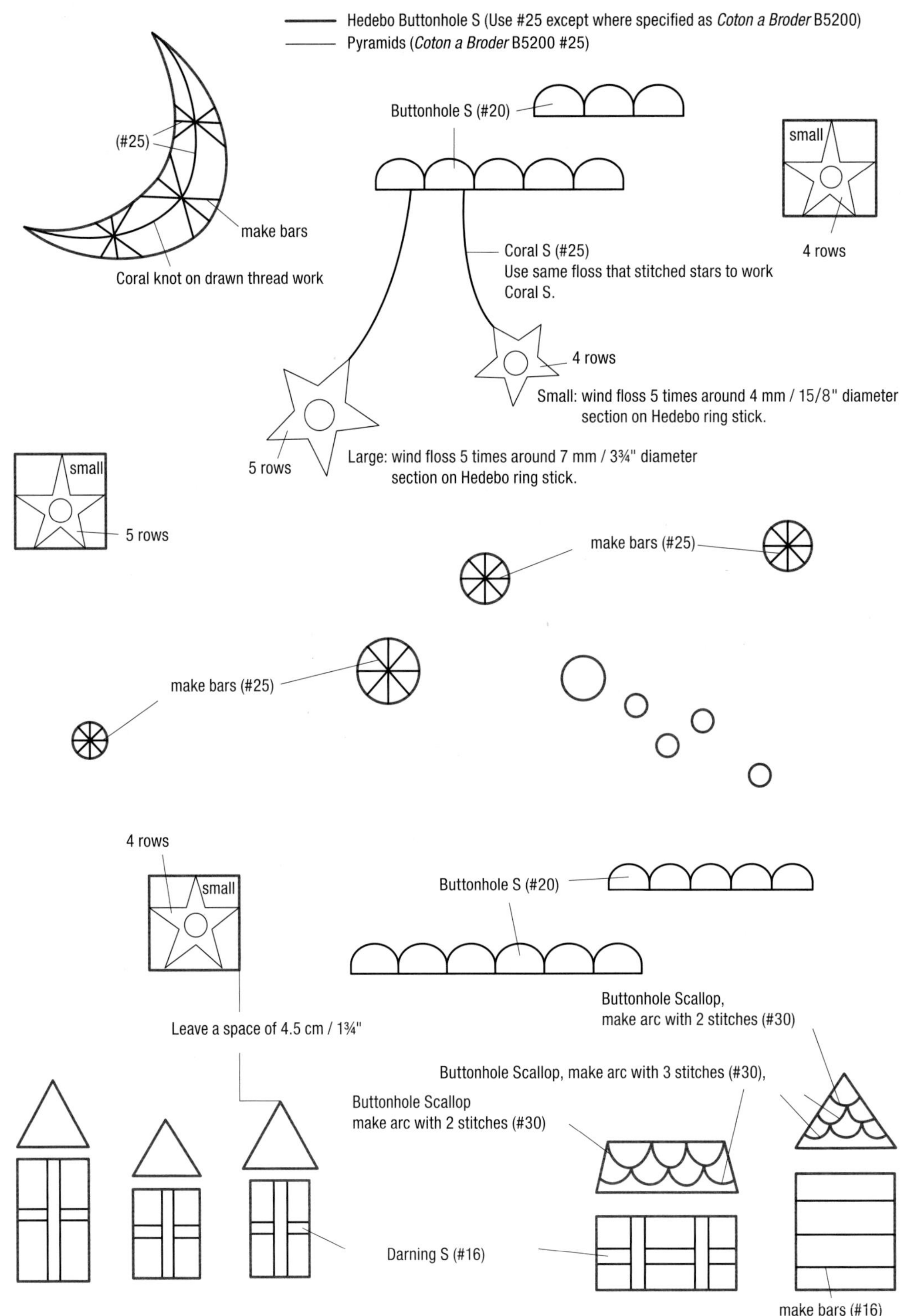

Hedebo Buttonhole S (Use #25 except where specified as Coton a Broder B5200)
Pyramids (Coton a Broder B5200 #25)
(#25)
make bars
Coral knot on drawn thread work
Buttonhole S (#20)
small
4 rows
Coral S (#25)
Use same floss that stitched stars to work
Coral S.
4 rows
Small: wind floss 5 times around 4 mm / 15/8" diameter
section on Hedebo ring stick.
5 rows
Large: wind floss 5 times around 7 mm / 3¾" diameter
section on Hedebo ring stick.
small
5 rows
make bars (#25)
make bars (#25)
4 rows
small
Buttonhole S (#20)
Leave a space of 4.5 cm / 1¾"
Buttonhole Scallop,
make arc with 2 stitches (#30)
Buttonhole Scallop, make arc with 3 stitches (#30),
Buttonhole Scallop
make arc with 2 stitches (#30)
Darning S (#16)
make bars (#16)

17. / page 41 Hedebo Embroidery: Cross

Materials Fabric (white tightly woven linen)
DMC *Coton a Broder* B5200 #20, 25

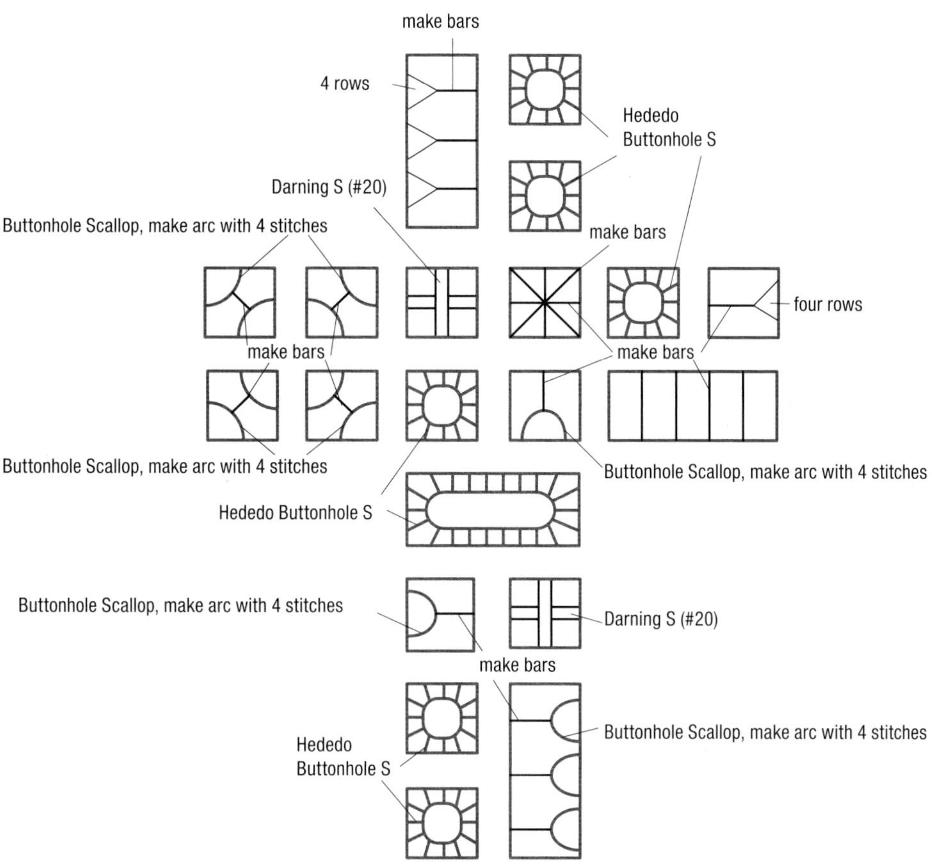

Hedebo Buttonhole S (*Coton a Broder* B5200 #25)
Pyramids (*Coton a Broder* B5200 #25)
make bars
4 rows
Hededo
Buttonhole S
Darning S (#20)
Buttonhole Scallop, make arc with 4 stitches
make bars
four rows
make bars
make bars
Buttonhole Scallop, make arc with 4 stitches
Buttonhole Scallop, make arc with 4 stitches
Hededo Buttonhole S
Buttonhole Scallop, make arc with 4 stitches
Darning S (#20)
make bars
Hededo
Buttonhole S
Buttonhole Scallop, make arc with 4 stitches

18. / page 42 Embroidery Hoop Case

Materials Outer Fabric (Brown linen) 35 × 45cm / 13¾" ×17¾"
Embroidery Fabric (white tightly woven linen) 20 × 15cm / 7⅞" × 5⅞"
DMC *Coton a Broder* B5200 #25
DMC No. 25 Embroidery Floss B5200

Finished Size 14 × 15 cm / 5½" × 5⅞"

Steps

1. Embroider and then sew embroidered fabric on outer fabric.
2. Sew bottom edge, right side in. Fold along folding line. Sew side edges.
3. Turn right side out; close opening.

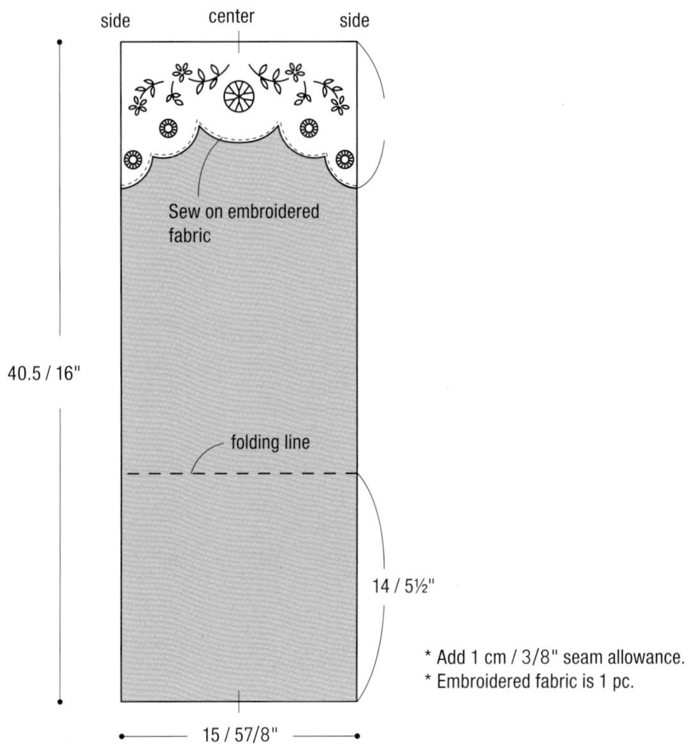

Fabric: 1 pc.
side
center
side
Sew on embroidered fabric
40.5 / 16"
folding line
14 / 5½"
15 / 57/8"
* Add 1 cm / 3/8" seam allowance.
* Embroidered fabric is 1 pc.

Sewing Steps

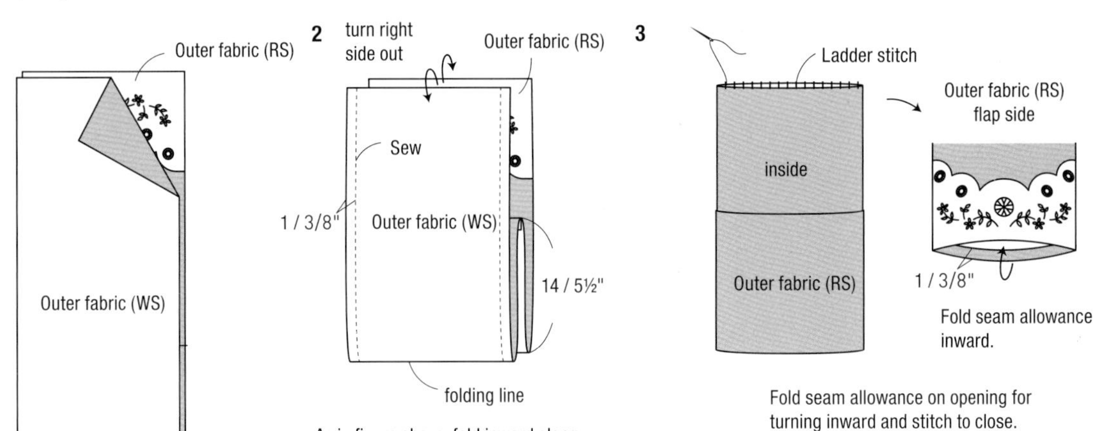

1
Outer fabric (RS)
Outer fabric (WS)
1 / 3/8"
Sew
2
turn right side out
Outer fabric (RS)
Sew
1 / 3/8"
Outer fabric (WS)
14 / 5½"
folding line
3
Ladder stitch
Outer fabric (RS) flap side
inside
Outer fabric (RS)
1 / 3/8"
Fold seam allowance inward.

Put 2 pieces of outer fabric together, right side in.
Sew bottom edge.

As in figure above, fold inward along folding line.
Sew side edges. Turn right side out.

Fold seam allowance on opening for turning inward and stitch to close.

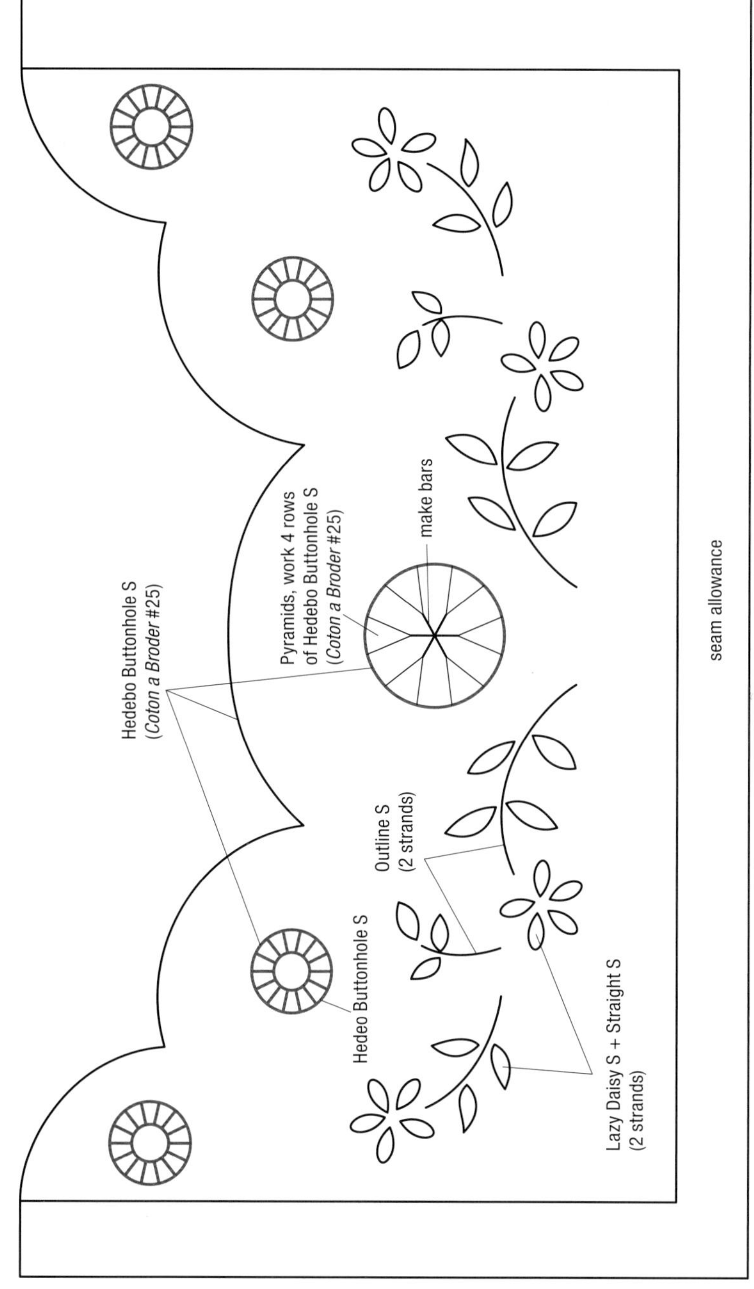
Hedebo Buttonhole S
(*Coton a Broder* #25)
Pyramids, work 4 rows
of Hedebo Buttonhole S
(*Coton a Broder* #25)
make bars
Outline S
(2 strands)
Hedebo Buttonhole S
Hedeo Buttonhole S
Lazy Daisy S + Straight S
(2 strands)
seam allowance

19. / page 43 Cross Motif Drawstring Pouch

Materials Outer Fabric (white plain-weave linen, 16 threads per cm for both warp and weft / 40 TPI for both warp and weft)
20 × 40cm / 7⅞" × 15¾"
Lining Fabric (purple tightly woven plain-weave linen)
20 × 50cm / 7⅞" × 19¾"
DMC *Coton a Broder* B5200 #16, 20, 25, 30
85 cm / 33½" long string

Finished Size 20 × 15 cm / 7⅞" × 5⅞"

Steps

1. Embroider on outer fabric.
2. Fold outer fabric in half, right side in. Sew side edges. Do the same for lining fabric.
3. Work buttonhole scallops along top edge of outer fabric.
4. Insert lining into outer fabric and blind stitch all around top edge. Thread string.

Outer fabric: 1 pc.

Lining fabric: 1 pc.

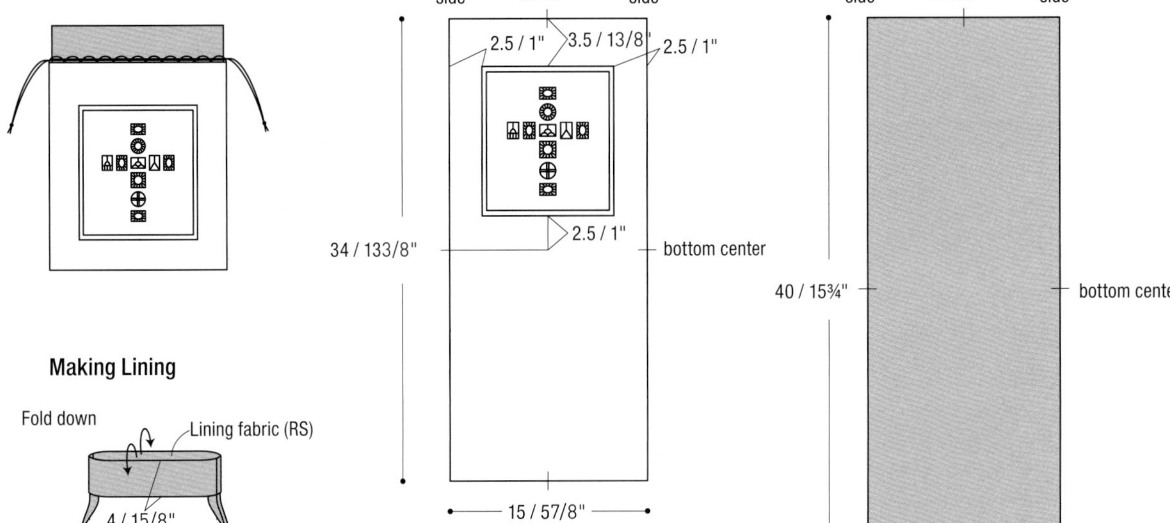
side
center
side
2.5 / 1"
3.5 / 13/8"
2.5 / 1"
34 / 133/8"
2.5 / 1"
bottom center
15 / 57/8"
* Add 1 cm / 3/8" seam allowance.
side
center
side
40 / 15¾"
bottom center
14.5 / 5¾"
* Add 4 cm / 15/8" seam allowance on top edge, 1cm / 3/8" on both sides.

Making Lining

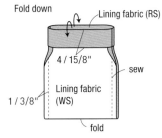

Fold down
Lining fabric (RS)
4 / 15/8"
sew
Lining fabric (WS)
1 / 3/8"
fold

Fold in half, right side in, and sew side edges. Fold down seam allowance on top edge.

Threading String

Thread string alternately in and out through each scallop.

Sewing Steps

1

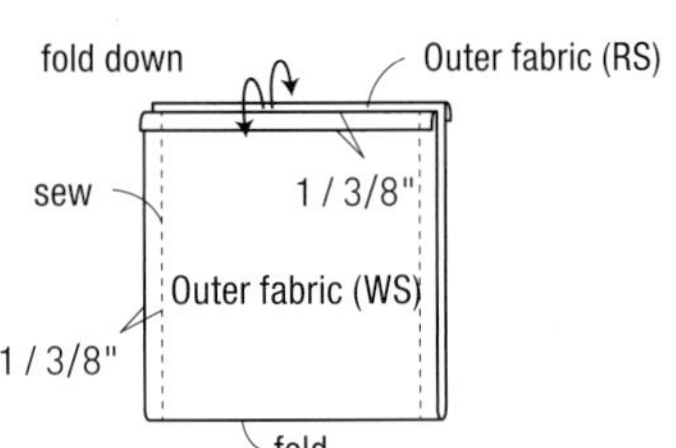
fold down
Outer fabric (RS)
sew
1 / 3/8"
Outer fabric (WS)
1 / 3/8"
fold

Fold outer fabric in half, right side in. Fold seam allowance on top edge down; sew side edges.

2

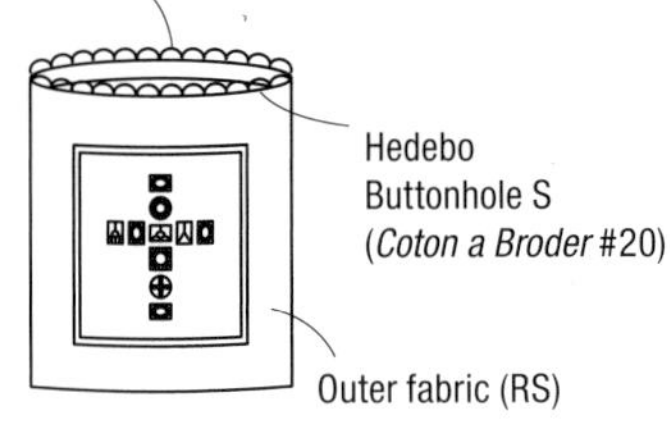
Buttonhole Scallop
(Coton a Broder #16), 24 scallops
Hedebo
Buttonhole S
(Coton a Broder #20)
Outer fabric (RS)

Turn right side out, work Hededo buttonhole stitches to make buttonhole scallops. Make 24 scallops.

3

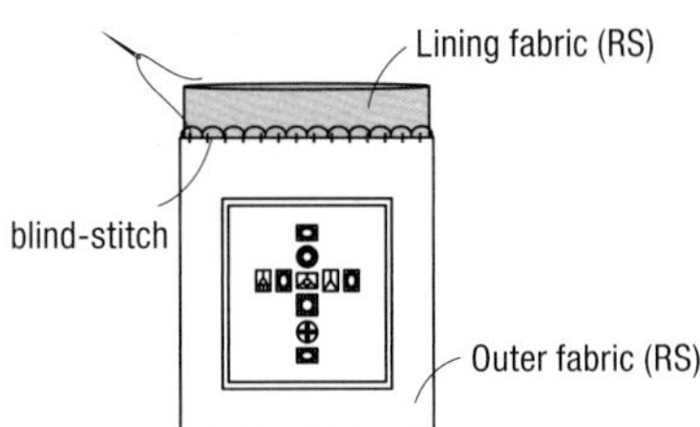
Lining fabric (RS)
blind-stitch
Outer fabric (RS)

Insert lining into outer fabric; blind-stitch top edge.

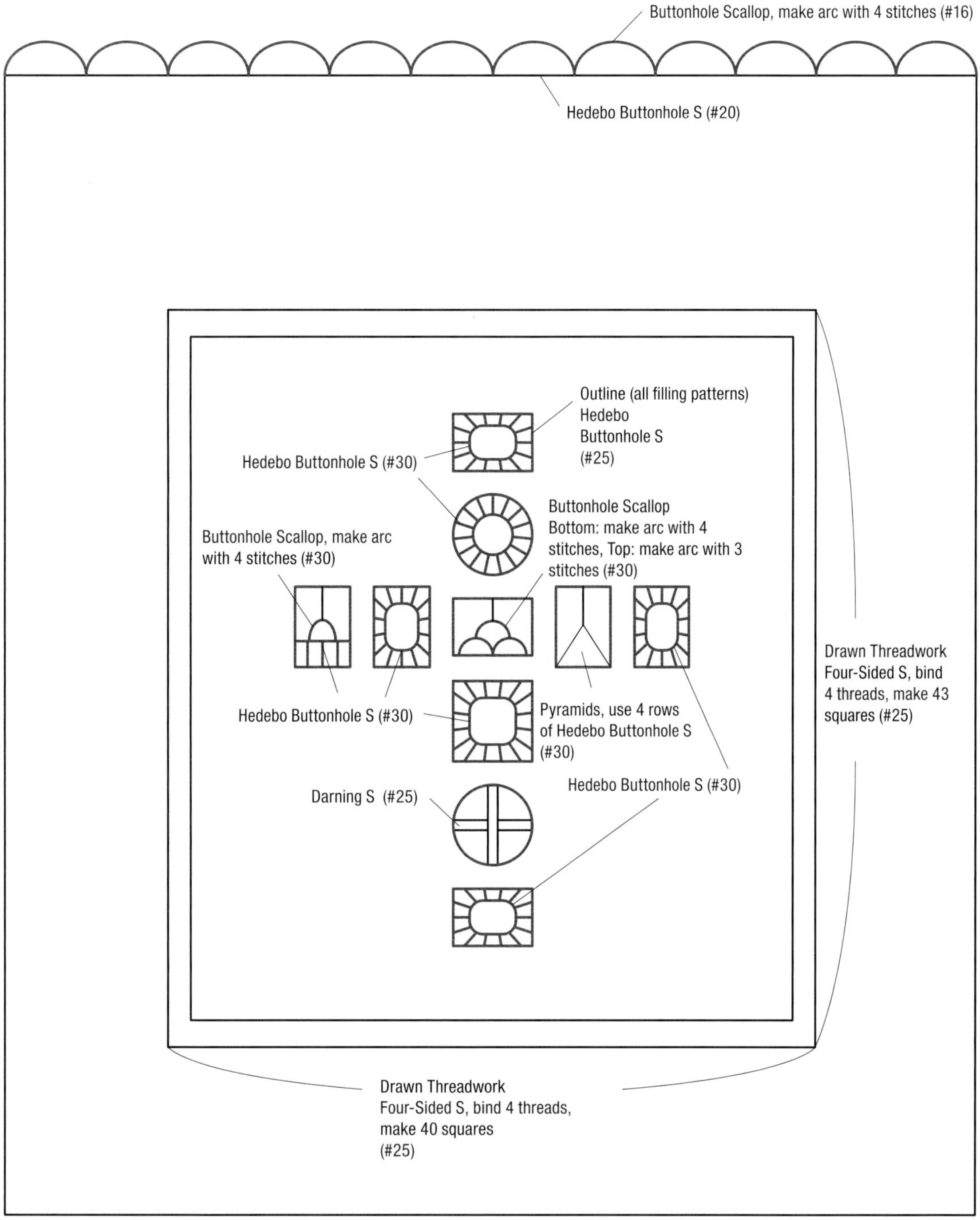

Buttonhole Scallop, make arc with 4 stitches (#16)

Hedebo Buttonhole S (#20)

Outline (all filling patterns)
Hedebo
Buttonhole S
(#25)

Hedebo Buttonhole S (#30)

Buttonhole Scallop
Bottom: make arc with 4
stitches, Top: make arc with 3
stitches (#30)

Buttonhole Scallop, make arc
with 4 stitches (#30)

Drawn Threadwork
Four-Sided S, bind
4 threads, make 43
squares (#25)

Hedebo Buttonhole S (#30)

Pyramids, use 4 rows
of Hedebo Buttonhole S
(#30)

Darning S (#25)

Hedebo Buttonhole S (#30)

Drawn Threadwork
Four-Sided S, bind 4 threads,
make 40 squares
(#25)

20. / page 44 Place Mats and Coasters

Materials A: Outer Fabric (light-blue tight-weave linen) 55 × 35cm / 21⅝" × 13¾"
Backing Fabric (White) 55 × 35cm / 21⅝" × 13¾"
DMC *Coton a Broder* BLANC #20, 25
B: Outer Fabric (white tight-weave linen) 55 × 35cm / 21⅝" × 13¾"
Backing Fabric (Unbleached cotton) 55 × 35cm / 21⅝" × 13¾"
DMC *Coton a Broder* BLANC #20, 25

Finished Size place mat—30 × 40 cm / 11¾" × 15¾", coaster—10 × 10 cm / 4" × 4"

Steps

1. Embroider on outer fabric.
2. Sew right side in.
3. Turn right side out.

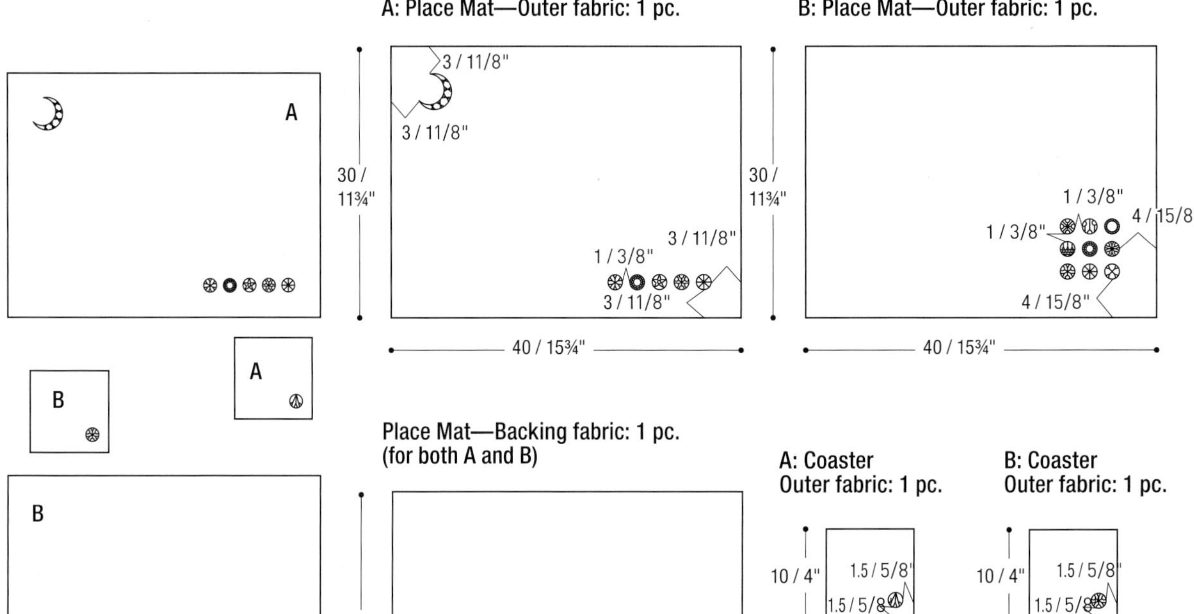

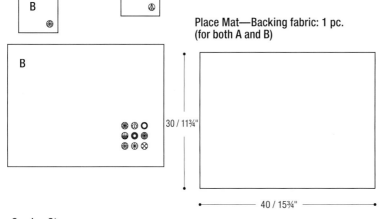

A: Place Mat—Outer fabric: 1 pc.
B: Place Mat—Outer fabric: 1 pc.
A
3 / 11/8"
3 / 11/8"
30 / 11¾"
1 / 3/8"
3 / 11/8"
3 / 11/8"
40 / 15¾"
1 / 3/8"
1 / 3/8"
4 / 15/8"
4 / 15/8"
A
B
B
Place Mat—Backing fabric: 1 pc. (for both A and B)
A: Coaster Outer fabric: 1 pc.
B: Coaster Outer fabric: 1 pc.
10 / 4"
1.5 / 5/8"
30 / 11¾"
Coaster—Backing fabric: 1 pc.

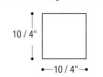

Sewing Steps

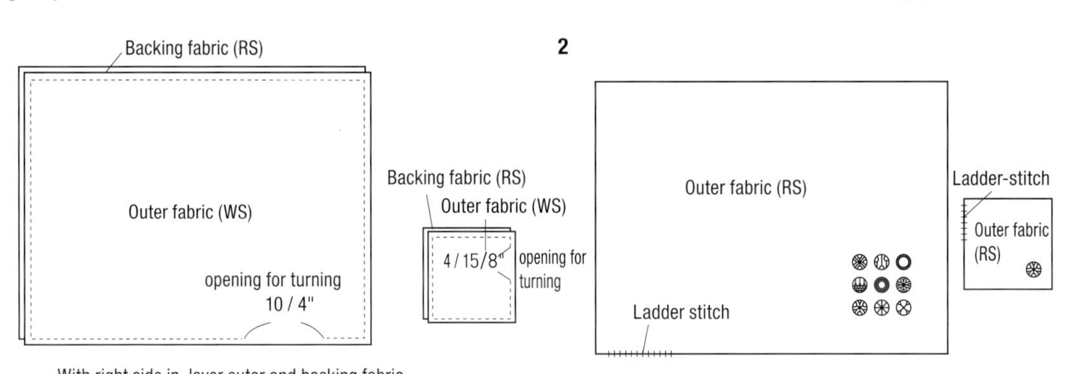

1
Backing fabric (RS)
Outer fabric (WS)
opening for turning
10 / 4"
Backing fabric (RS)
Outer fabric (WS)
4 / 15/8"
opening for turning
2
Outer fabric (RS)
Ladder-stitch
Outer fabric (RS)
Ladder stitch

With right side in, layer outer and backing fabric. Sew sides, while leaving opening for turning.

Turn right side out; adjust corners. Close opening for turning.

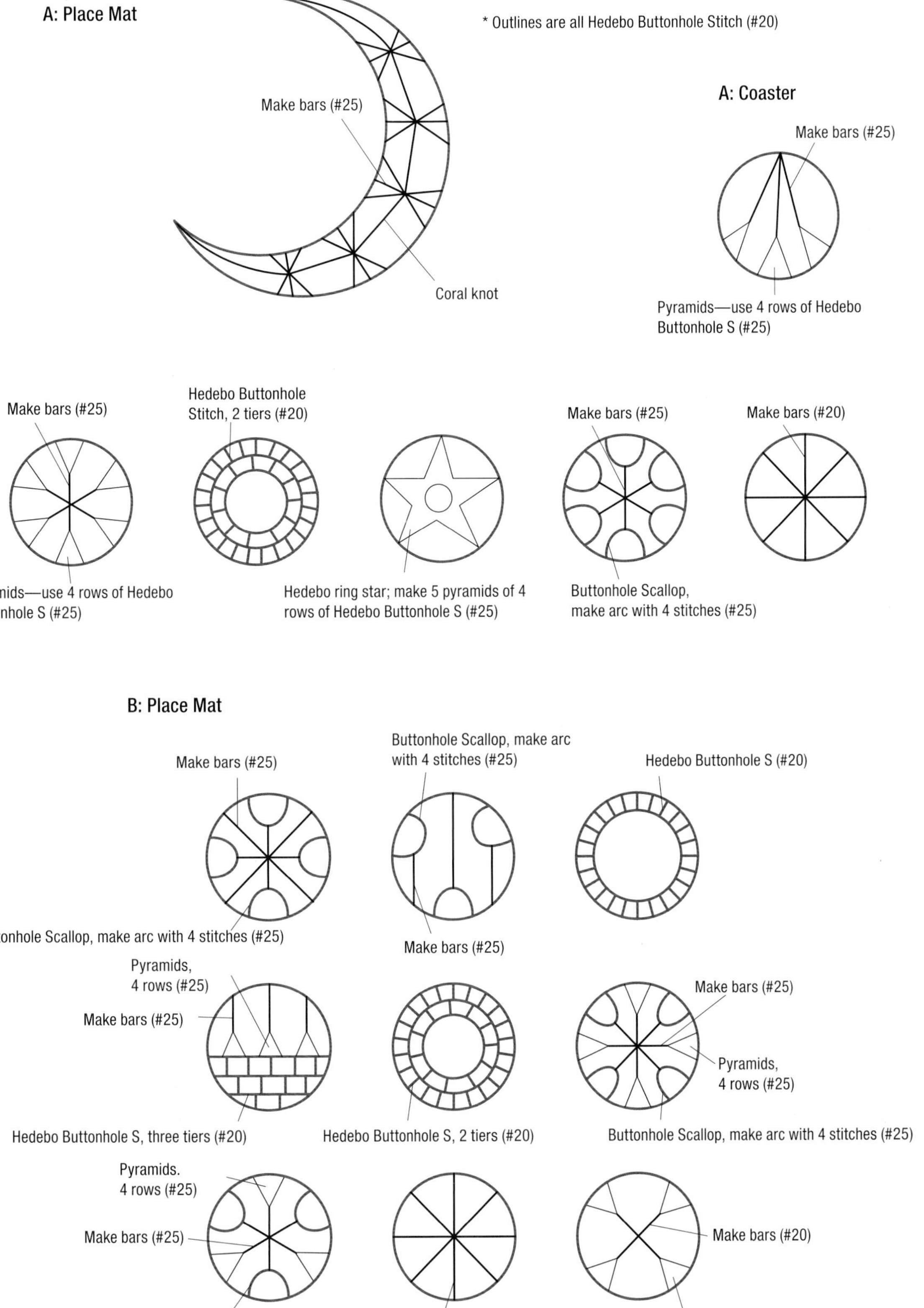
A: Place Mat
* Outlines are all Hedebo Buttonhole Stitch (#20)
Make bars (#25)
Coral knot
A: Coaster
Make bars (#25)
Pyramids—use 4 rows of Hedebo Buttonhole S (#25)
Make bars (#25)
Hedebo Buttonhole Stitch, 2 tiers (#20)
Make bars (#25)
Make bars (#20)
Pyramids—use 4 rows of Hedebo Buttonhole S (#25)
Hedebo ring star; make 5 pyramids of 4 rows of Hedebo Buttonhole S (#25)
Buttonhole Scallop, make arc with 4 stitches (#25)
B: Place Mat
Make bars (#25)
Buttonhole Scallop, make arc with 4 stitches (#25)
Hedebo Buttonhole S (#20)
Buttonhole Scallop, make arc with 4 stitches (#25)
Make bars (#25)
Pyramids, 4 rows (#25)
Make bars (#25)
Make bars (#25)
Pyramids, 4 rows (#25)
Hedebo Buttonhole S, three tiers (#20)
Hedebo Buttonhole S, 2 tiers (#20)
Buttonhole Scallop, make arc with 4 stitches (#25)
Pyramids. 4 rows (#25)
Make bars (#25)
Make bars (#20)
Buttonhole Scallop, make arc with 4 stitches (#25)
Make bars (#20)
Pyramids, 4 rows (#20)
B: Coaster

Stitches 1, 2 / pages 52, 53 Drawn Threadwork

Materials Fabric (white plain-weave linen, 12 threads per cm for both warp and weft / 30 TPI for both warp and weft)
Coton a Broder BLANC #16, 20, 25
DMC No. 25 Embroidery Floss BLANC

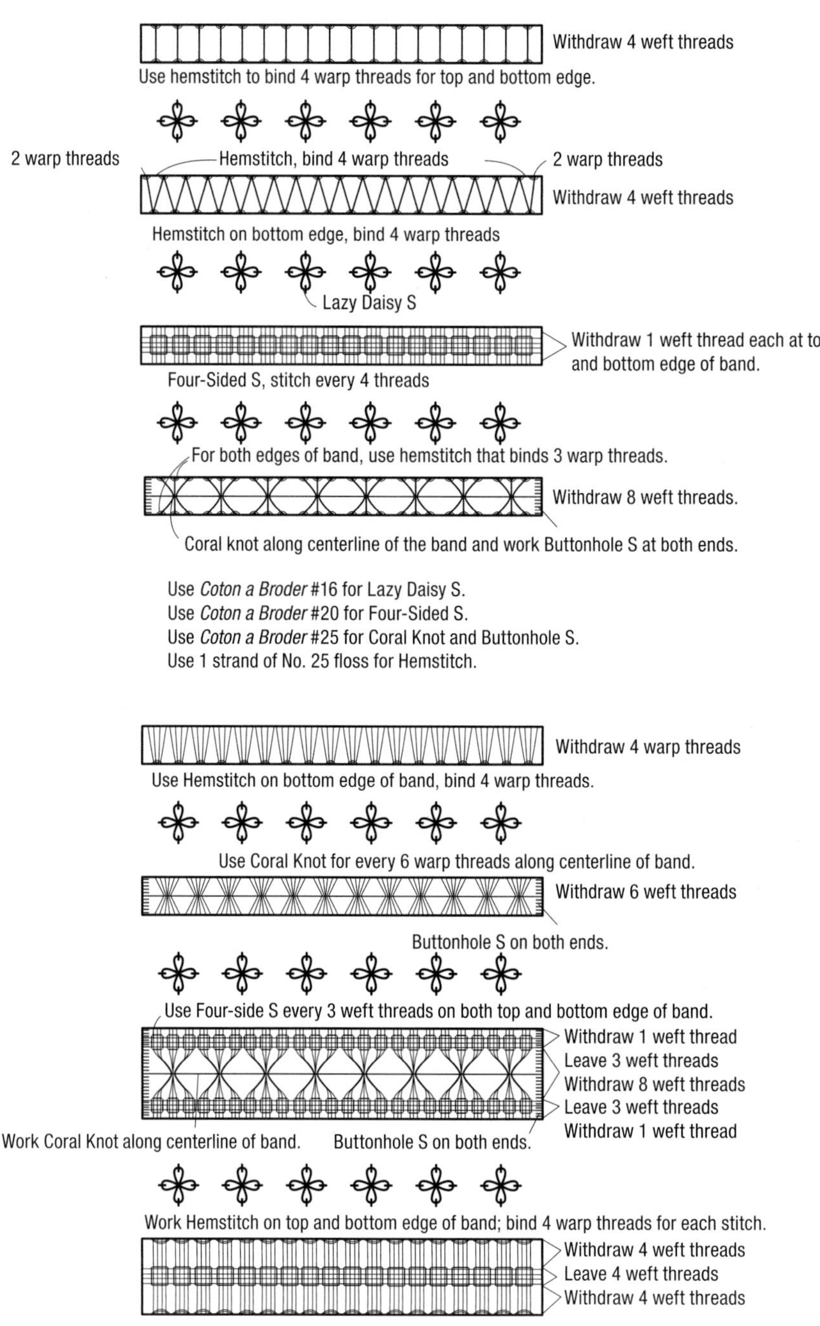

Withdraw 4 weft threads
Use hemstitch to bind 4 warp threads for top and bottom edge.
2 warp threads
Hemstitch, bind 4 warp threads
2 warp threads
Withdraw 4 weft threads
Hemstitch on bottom edge, bind 4 warp threads
Lazy Daisy S
Withdraw 1 weft thread each at top and bottom edge of band.
Four-Sided S, stitch every 4 threads
For both edges of band, use hemstitch that binds 3 warp threads.
Withdraw 8 weft threads.
Coral knot along centerline of the band and work Buttonhole S at both ends.
Use *Coton a Broder* #16 for Lazy Daisy S.
Use *Coton a Broder* #20 for Four-Sided S.
Use *Coton a Broder* #25 for Coral Knot and Buttonhole S.
Use 1 strand of No. 25 floss for Hemstitch.
Withdraw 4 warp threads
Use Hemstitch on bottom edge of band, bind 4 warp threads.
Use Coral Knot for every 6 warp threads along centerline of band.
Withdraw 6 weft threads
Buttonhole S on both ends.
Use Four-side S every 3 weft threads on both top and bottom edge of band.
Withdraw 1 weft thread
Leave 3 weft threads
Withdraw 8 weft threads
Leave 3 weft threads
Withdraw 1 weft thread
Work Coral Knot along centerline of band.
Buttonhole S on both ends.
Work Hemstitch on top and bottom edge of band; bind 4 warp threads for each stitch.
Withdraw 4 weft threads
Leave 4 weft threads
Withdraw 4 weft threads
Work Four-Side S along centerline of band. Stitch 4 threads.

21. / page 54 Dalecarlian Horse Hoop

Materials Outer Fabric (white plain-weave linen, 12 threads per cm for both warp and weft / 30 TPI for both warp and weft) 25 × 25cm / 9⅞" × 9⅞"
Backing Fabric (white plain-weave linen, 12 threads per cm for both warp and weft / 30 TPI for both warp and weft) 25 × 25cm / 9⅞" × 9⅞"
One embroidery hoop interior dimensions 17 × 17cm / 6¾" × 6¾"
DMC *Coton a Broder* BLANC #16, 20, 25
DMC No. 25 Embroidery Floss BLANC

Finished Size interior dimensions 17 × 17cm / 6¾" × 6¾"

Steps

1. Embroider on outer fabric.
2. Mount on embroidery hoop and treat fabric edges at backside.

Outer fabric: 1 pc.

no seam allowance

25 / 97/8"

4 / 15/8"

4 / 15/8"

Embroidery hoop size

25 / 97/8"

Backing fabric: 1 pc.

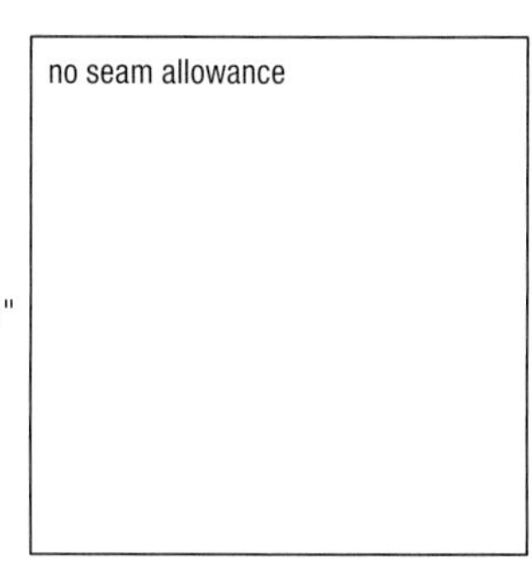

no seam allowance
25 / 97/8"
25 / 97/8"

Sewing Steps

Embroidery hoop

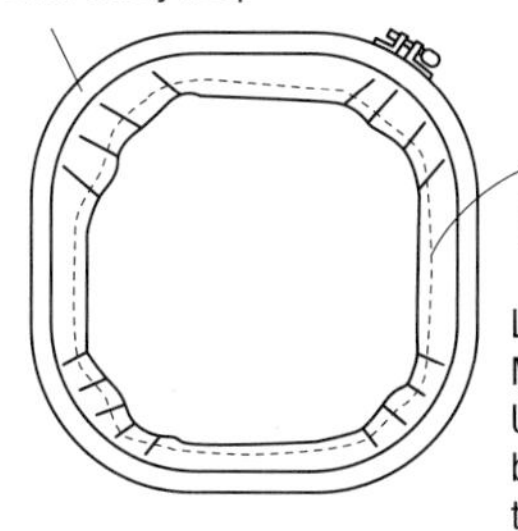

Lay backing fabric under outer fabric.
Mount on embroidery hoop.
Use running stitch on edge of fabric at backside of embroidery hoop. Pull thread to tighten edge.

Bind 4 warp threads along top edge of band.
On bottom edge, bind 2 first warp threads then 4 wrap threads all the way until the last 2. Bind last 2 wrap threads.
Zig-zag hemstitch (No. 25 floss, 1 strand)

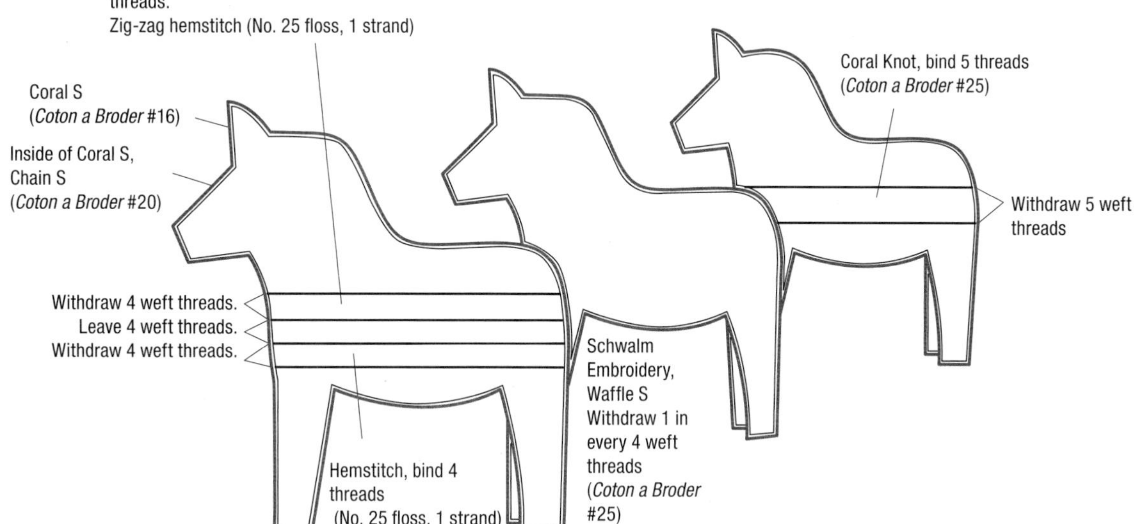

Coral S
(*Coton a Broder* #16)
Inside of Coral S,
Chain S
(*Coton a Broder* #20)
Withdraw 4 weft threads.
Leave 4 weft threads.
Withdraw 4 weft threads.
Hemstitch, bind 4 threads
(No. 25 floss, 1 strand)
Schwalm Embroidery, Waffle S
Withdraw 1 in every 4 weft threads
(*Coton a Broder* #25)
Coral Knot, bind 5 threads
(*Coton a Broder* #25)
Withdraw 5 weft threads

22. / page 55 Ribbon & Ribbon Brooch

Materials Ribbon: 120 cm / 47¼" long, 2.5 cm / 1" wide white linen tape
DMC *Coton a Broder* BLANC #25
DMC No. 25 Embroidery Floss BLANC
Brooch (white): 20 cm / 7⅞" long, 2.5 cm / 1" wide white linen tape
15 cm / 5⅞" long, 2 cm / ¾" wide velvet ribbon (brown)
10 cm / 4" long, 1.2 cm / ½" wide velvet ribbon (brown)
One 2 cm / ¾" wide brooch pin
DMC No. 25 Embroidery Floss BLANC
Brooch (light blue): 20 cm / 7⅞" long, 2.5 cm / 1" wide linen tape (light blue)
25 cm / 9⅞" long, 2 cm / ¾" wide velvet ribbon (gray)
One 2.5 cm / 1" wide brooch pin
DMC *Coton a Broder* BLANC #25
Brooch (brown): 20 cm / 7⅞" long, 1.5 cm / ⅝" wide linen tape (brown)
One 2 cm / ¾" wide brooch pin
Anchor No. 25 embroidery floss 392

Finished Size Ribbon 120 cm / 47¼"
Ribbon Brooch (white) 5.5 cm / 2⅛"
Ribbon Brooch (light blue) 7 cm / 2¾"
Ribbon Brooch (brown) 5 cm / 2"

Steps

1. Embroider.
2. Fold down both ends of ribbon and insert velvet ribbon inside. Sew side and warp middle with velvet/linen tape.
3. Install brooch pin at back.

Ribbon

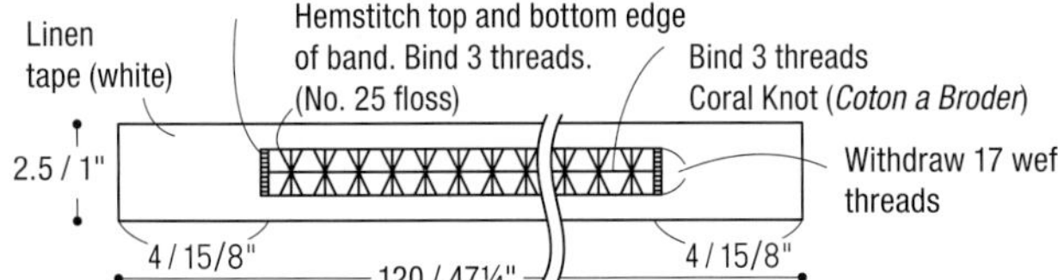
Buttonhole S (*Coton a Broder*)
Linen tape (white)
Hemstitch top and bottom edge of band. Bind 3 threads. (No. 25 floss)
Bind 3 threads
Coral Knot (*Coton a Broder*)
2.5 / 1"
Withdraw 17 weft threads
4 / 15/8"
120 / 47¼"
4 / 15/8"

Brooch (white)

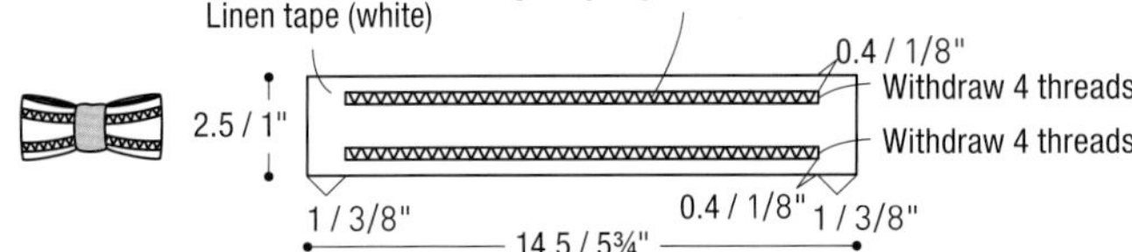
Top edge: bind 4 threads, Bottom edge: Zig-zag Hemstitch
Linen tape (white)
0.4 / 1/8"
Withdraw 4 threads
Withdraw 4 threads
2.5 / 1"
1 / 3/8"
0.4 / 1/8"
1 / 3/8"
14.5 / 5¾"

Brooch (light blue)

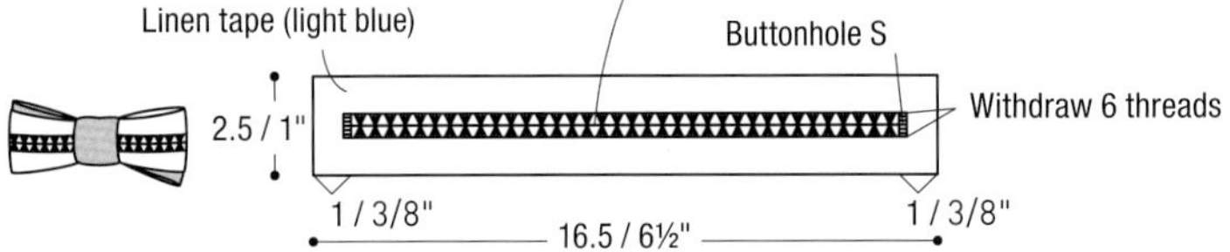
Coral Knot, bind 4 threads
Linen tape (light blue)
Buttonhole S
Withdraw 6 threads
2.5 / 1"
1 / 3/8"
16.5 / 6½"
1 / 3/8"

Brooch (brown)

Linen tape (brown)
Hemstitch on both top and bottom edge of band, bind three threads
1.5 / 5/8"
Withdraw 4 threads
1 / 3/8"
12.5 / 5"
1 / 3/8"

Linen tape (brown)
Hemstitch on both top and bottom edge of band; bind 3 threads
1.5 / 5/8"
Withdraw 4 threads
1 / 3/8"
6 / 23/8"
1 / 3/8"* For middle part

Making Ribbon Brooch (applies to all sizes)

1

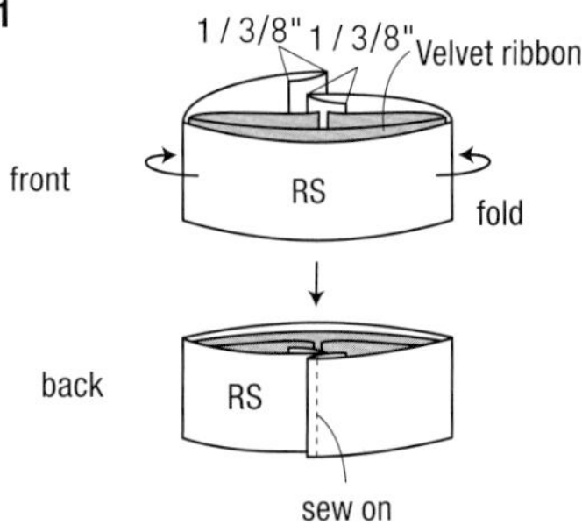
1 / 3/8"
1 / 3/8"
Velvet ribbon
front
RS
fold
back
RS
sew on

Fold embroidered linen tape as in figure above.
Sew both ends together so tape doesn't come apart.
Put velvet ribbon inside of linen tape as desired.

2

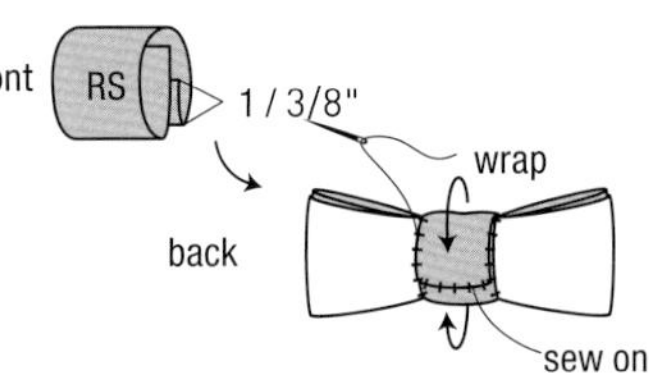
front
RS
1 / 3/8"
wrap
back
sew on

Wrap velvet/ linen tape at center. Sew.

3

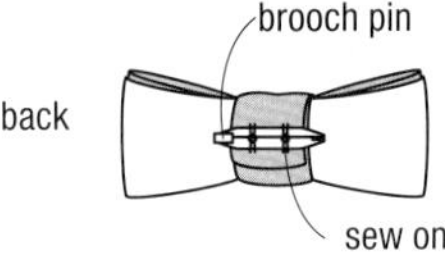
brooch pin
back
sew on

Install brooch pin.
Adjust shape of ribbon.

25. / page 61 Glasses Case

Materials Felt (white) 45 × 10 cm / 17¾" × 4"
DMC Pearl Cotton BLANC #8
Appleton Crewel Wool 991, 991B
Medium yarn, natural color
One 1.2 cm / ½" diameter button

Finished Size 8 × 18cm / 3⅛" × 7⅛"

Steps

1. Embroider design.
2. Layer felt pieces, right side in, and sew.
3. Use buttonhole scallops. Attach button.

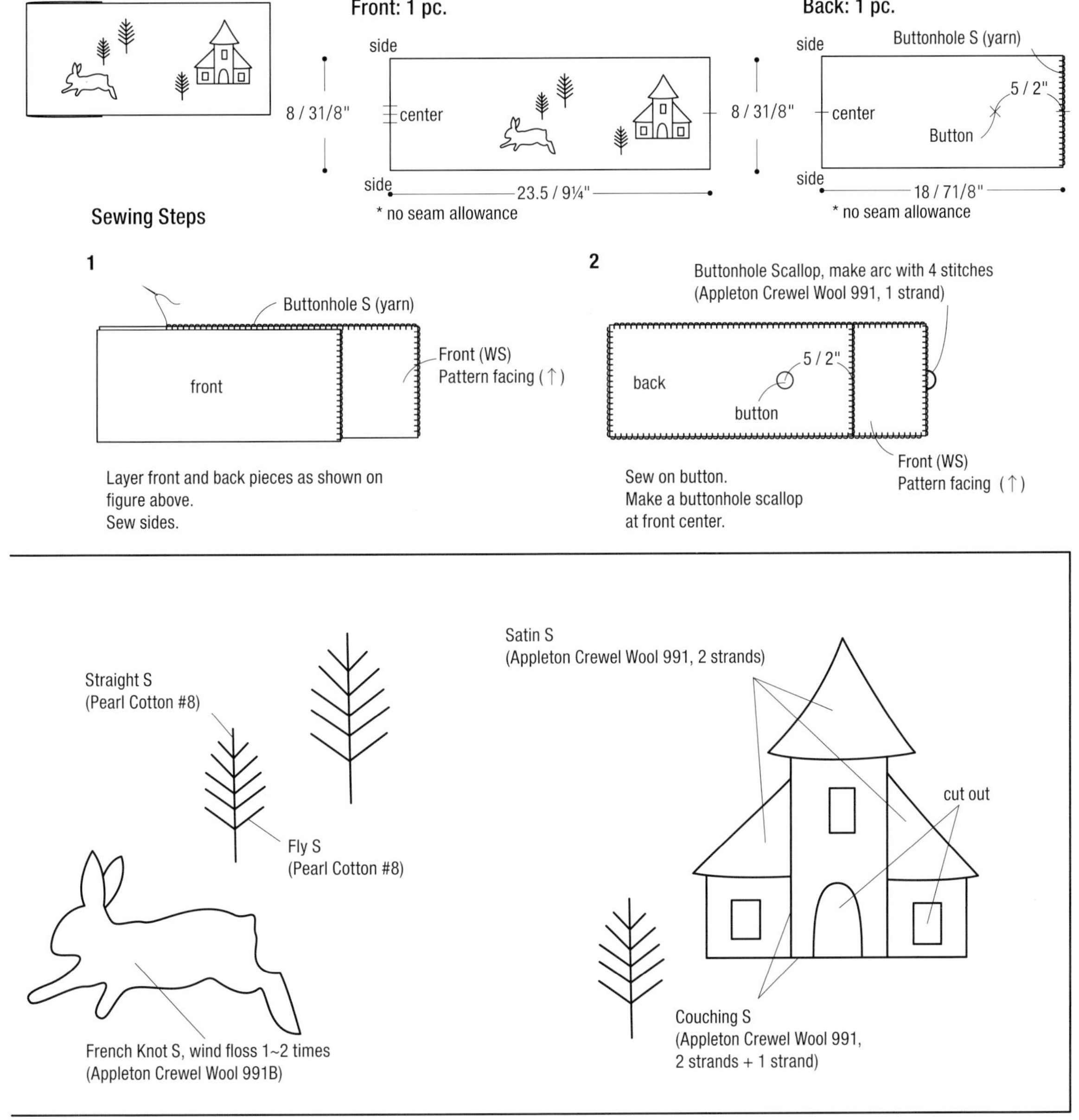

Front: 1 pc.
side
8 / 31/8"
center
side
23.5 / 9¼"
* no seam allowance
Back: 1 pc.
side
Buttonhole S (yarn)
5 / 2"
8 / 31/8"
center
Button
side
18 / 71/8"
* no seam allowance
Sewing Steps
1
Buttonhole S (yarn)
front
Front (WS)
Pattern facing (↑)
Layer front and back pieces as shown on figure above.
Sew sides.
2
Buttonhole Scallop, make arc with 4 stitches
(Appleton Crewel Wool 991, 1 strand)
5 / 2"
back
button
Front (WS)
Pattern facing (↑)
Sew on button.
Make a buttonhole scallop at front center.
Straight S
(Pearl Cotton #8)
Fly S
(Pearl Cotton #8)
French Knot S, wind floss 1~2 times
(Appleton Crewel Wool 991B)
Satin S
(Appleton Crewel Wool 991, 2 strands)
cut out
Couching S
(Appleton Crewel Wool 991,
2 strands + 1 strand)

23. / page 59 Brooch

Materials

Large: Felt (white) 5 × 5 cm / 2" × 2"
Felt (light gray) 5 × 5 cm / 2" × 2"
Brooch Base Felt (gray) 15 × 10cm / 5⅞" × 4"
One 2 cm / ¾" wide brooch pin
DMC *Coton a Broder* BLANC #25
Appleton Crewel Wool 991

Medium: Felt (white) 5 × 5cm / 2" × 2"
Brooch Base Felt (gray) 15 × 10cm / 5⅞" × 4"
Appleton Crewel Wool 991
One 1 cm / ⅜" diameter pin badge

Small: Felt (light gray) 5 × 5cm / 2" × 2"
Brooch Base Felt (gray) 10 × 5cm / 4" × 2"
Appleton Crewel Wool 991
One 1 cm / ⅜" diameter pin badge

Finished Size Large 5.7×5.2cm / 2¼" ×2",
Middle 1.9 cm / ¾" diameter, Small 1.7 cm / ⅝"

Steps

1. Embroider on felt.
2. Glue to base.
3. Glue on another base and install pin.

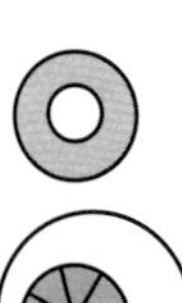

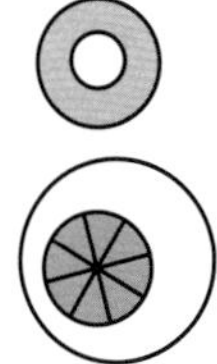

Large motif a: 1 pc. **Large motif b: 1 pc.** **Large motif c: 1 pc.**

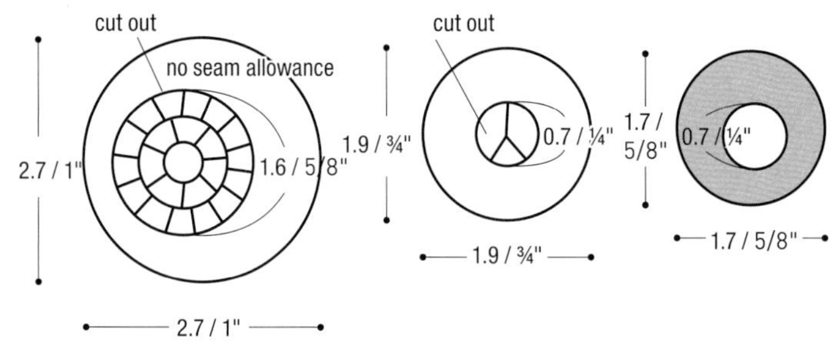
cut out
no seam allowance
2.7 / 1"
1.6 / 5/8"
2.7 / 1"
cut out
1.9 / ¾"
0.7 / ¼"
1.9 / ¾"
1.7 / 5/8"
0.7 / ¼"
1.7 / 5/8"

Large base: 2 pcs.

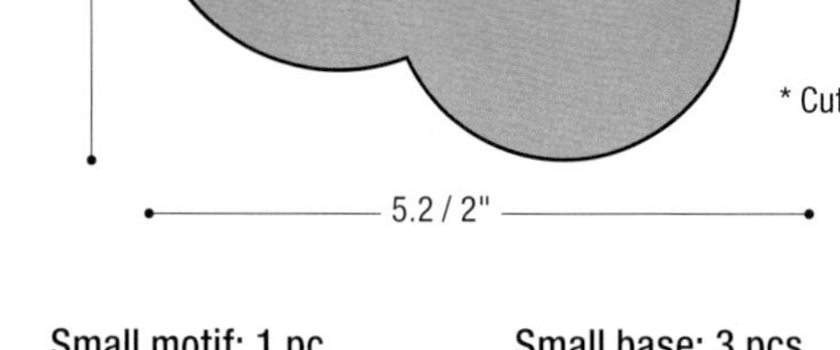
5.7 / 2¼"
5.2 / 2"

* Cut larger than needed; trim later.

Medium motif: 1 pc.

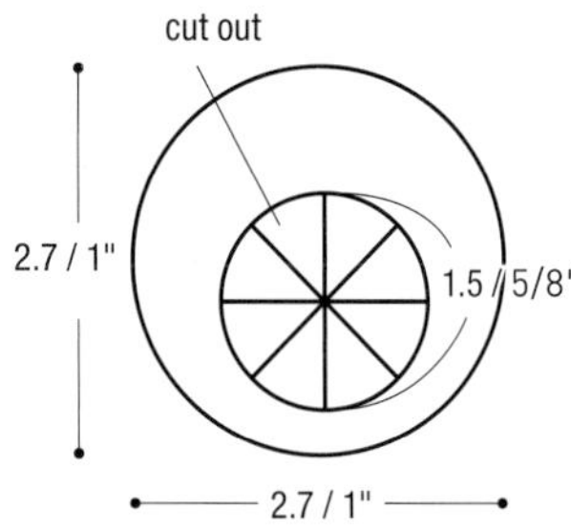
cut out
2.7 / 1"
1.5 / 5/8"
2.7 / 1"

Medium base: 2 pcs.

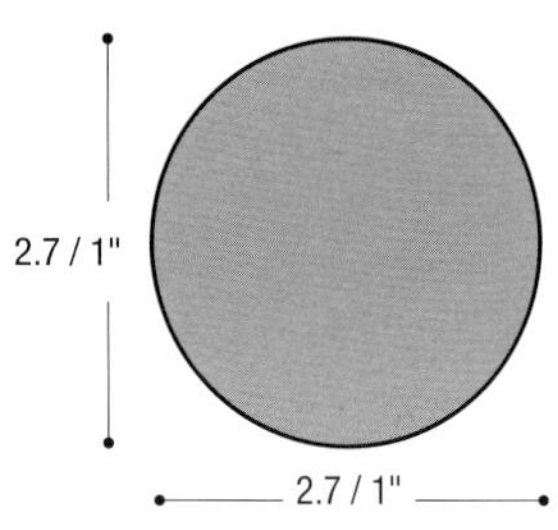
2.7 / 1"
2.7 / 1"

* Cut larger than needed; trim later.

Small motif: 1 pc. **Small base: 3 pcs.**

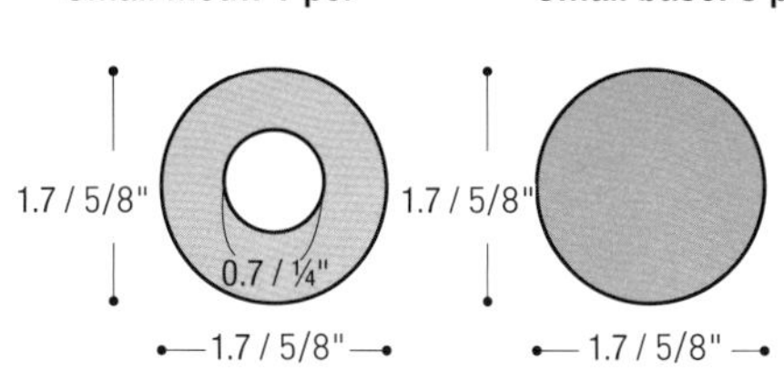
1.7 / 5/8"
0.7 / ¼"
1.7 / 5/8"
1.7 / 5/8"
1.7 / 5/8"

* Cut larger than needed, trim later.

Steps for Assembling

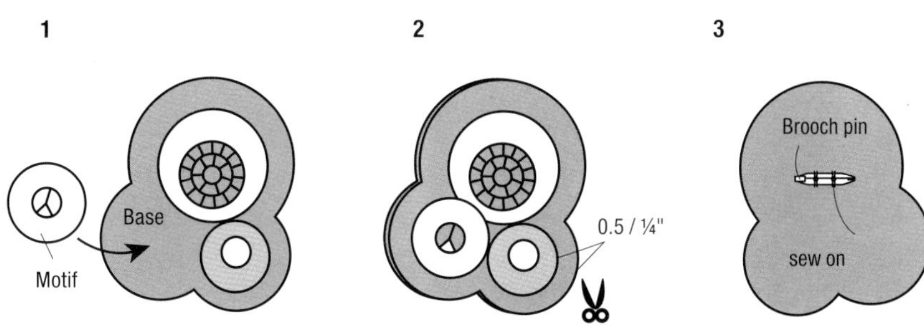
1
2
3
Base
Motif
0.5 / ¼"
Brooch pin
sew on

Glue motif on base.

Glue on other base.
Trim around outer edge.

Sew brooch pin at back.

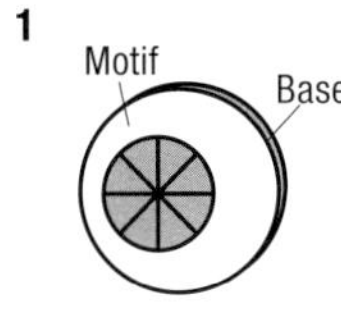
1
Motif
Base

Glue motif on base.

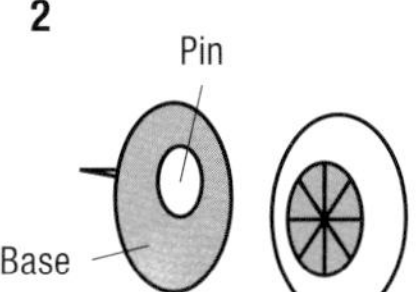
2
Pin
Base

Pierce pin through other base.
Glue on base.
Trim around edge.

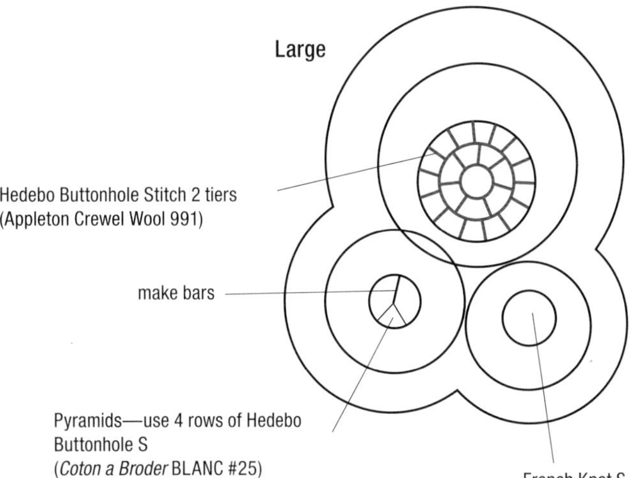
Large
Hedebo Buttonhole Stitch 2 tiers
(Appleton Crewel Wool 991)
make bars
Pyramids—use 4 rows of Hedebo
Buttonhole S
(*Coton a Broder* BLANC #25)
French Knot S, wind floss twice
(Appleton Crewel Wool 991)

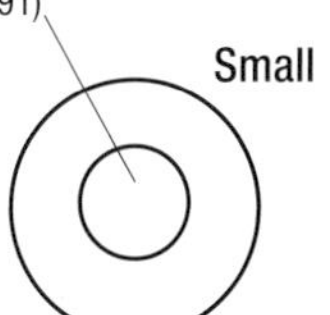
French Knot S, wind floss twice
(Appleton Crewel Wool 991)
Small

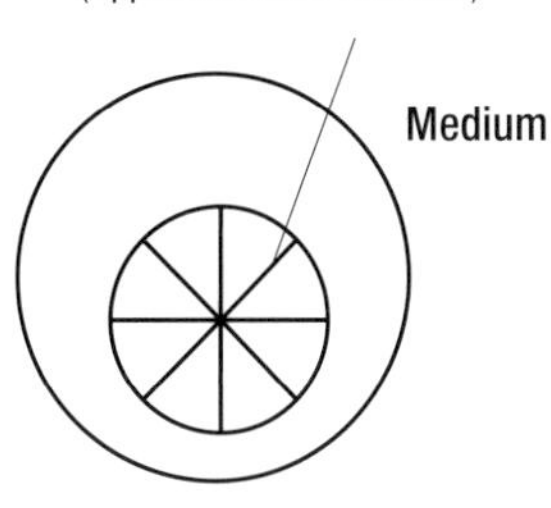
make bars
(Appleton Crewel Wool 991)
Medium

24. / page 60 Cushion Cover

Materials Felt (white) 70 × 35 cm / 27½" × 13¾"
DMC Pearl Cotton BLANC #8
Appleton Crewel Wool 991, 991B
Medium-weight yarn, natural color
One 30 × 30cm / 11¾" × 11¾" cushion insert

Finished Size 30 × 30cm / 11¾" × 11¾"

Steps

1. Embroider motifs.
2. Layer front and back, right side out; sew sides.
3. Place cushion insert.

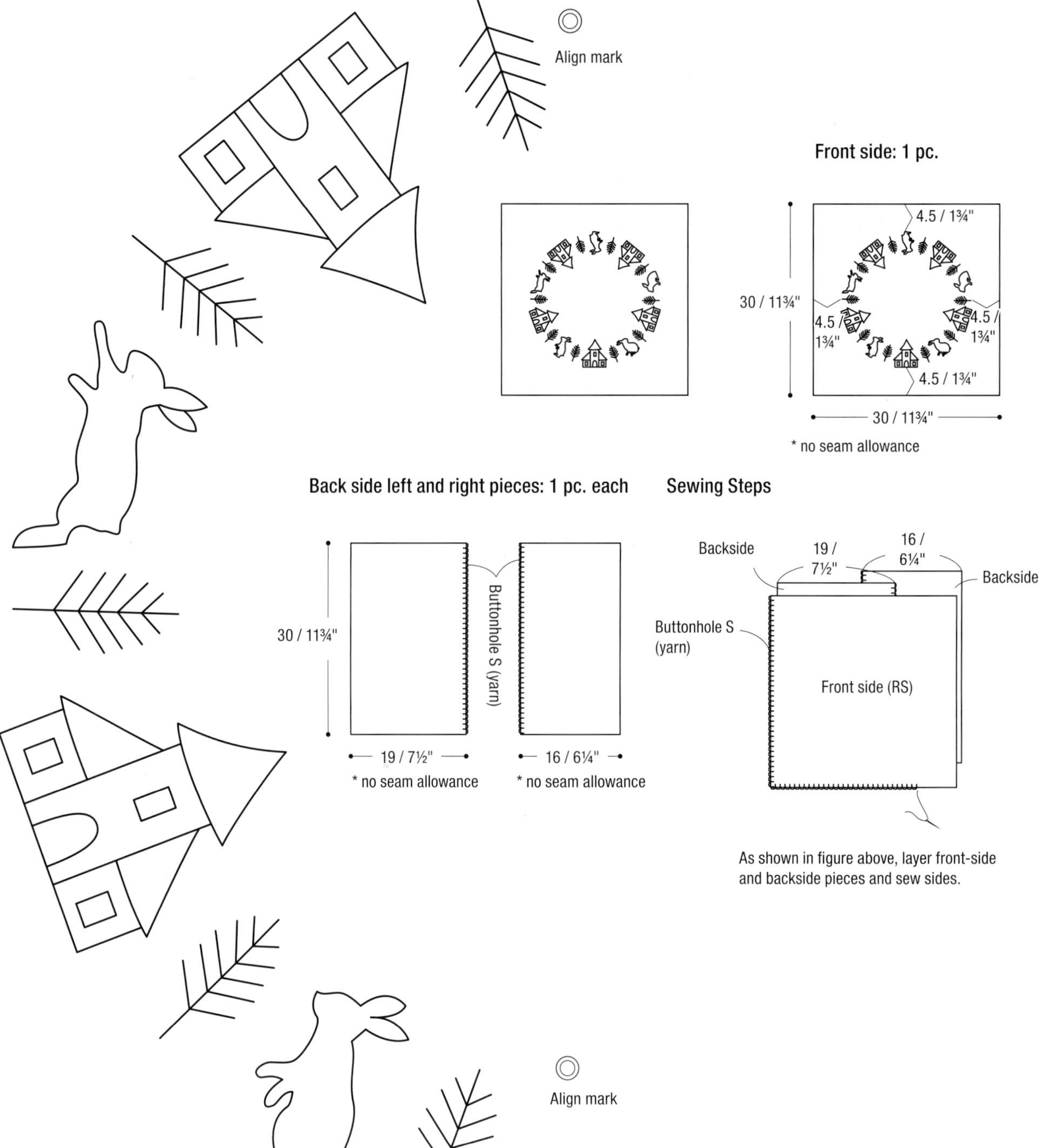

Align mark
Front side: 1 pc.
4.5 / 1¾"
30 / 11¾"
4.5 / 1¾"
4.5 / 1¾"
4.5 / 1¾"
30 / 11¾"
* no seam allowance
Back side left and right pieces: 1 pc. each
30 / 11¾"
Buttonhole S (yarn)
19 / 7½"
* no seam allowance
16 / 6¼"
* no seam allowance
Sewing Steps
Backside
19 / 7½"
16 / 6¼"
Backside
Buttonhole S (yarn)
Front side (RS)
As shown in figure above, layer front-side and backside pieces and sew sides.
Align mark

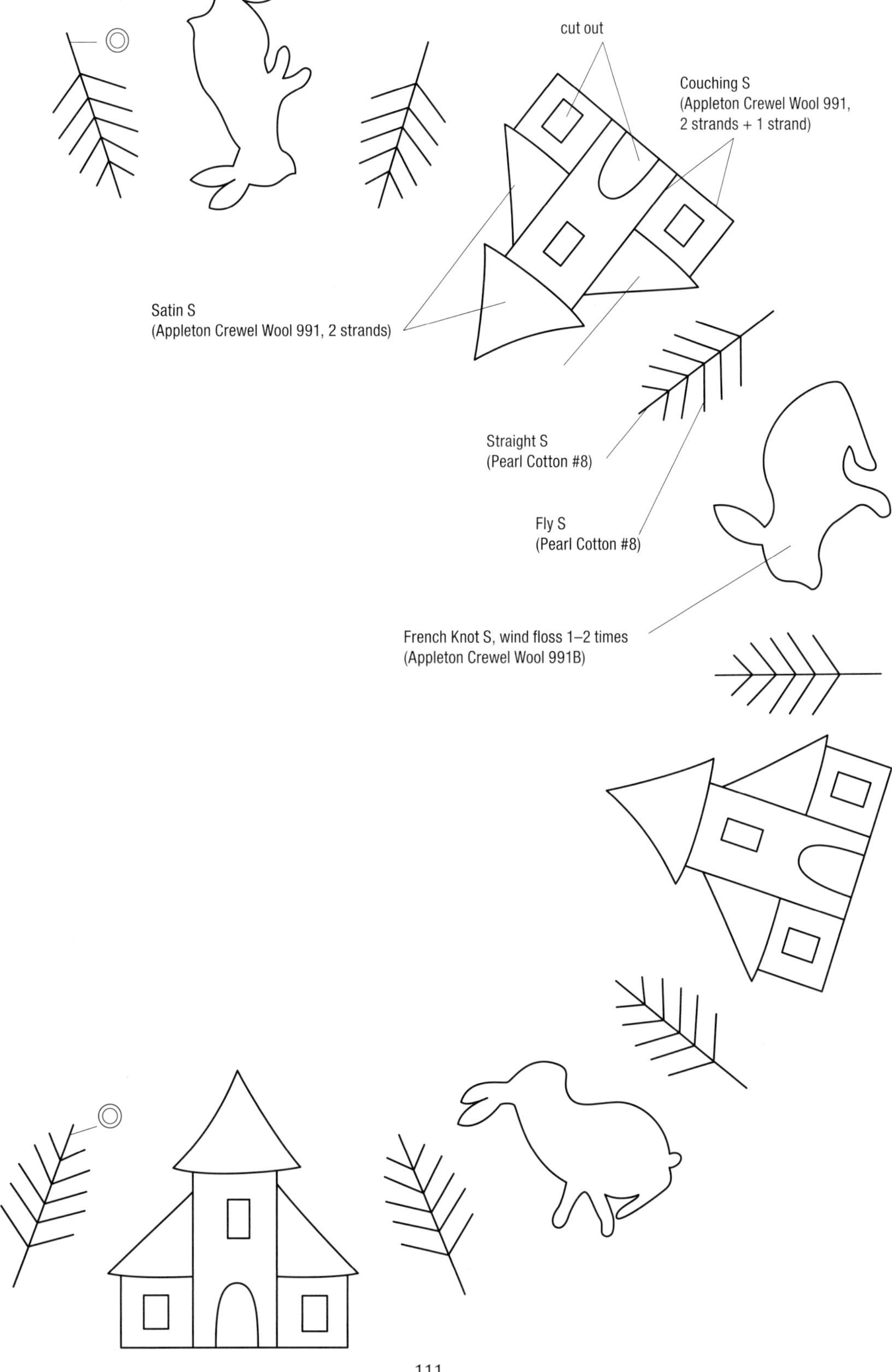
cut out
Couching S
(Appleton Crewel Wool 991,
2 strands + 1 strand)
Satin S
(Appleton Crewel Wool 991, 2 strands)
Straight S
(Pearl Cotton #8)
Fly S
(Pearl Cotton #8)
French Knot S, wind floss 1–2 times
(Appleton Crewel Wool 991B)

Seiko Nakano offers whitework classes (Warau-Embroidery) in Tokyo, Japan, and focuses her students on both mastery and fun. As a needlework artist, she exhibits her work and also curates embroidery exhibits. Her work is featured in needlework catalogs and craft magazines. She lives in Tokyo, Japan.
www.warau-embroidery.com
@warau_embroidery

Other Schiffer Books on Related Subjects:

Blooming Paper: How to Handcraft Paper Flowers and Botanicals, Laura Reed, ISBN 978-0-7643-6208-8
Inspiration Kantha: Creative Stitchery and Quilting with Asia's Ancient Technique, Anna Hergert, ISBN 978-0-7643-5357-4
Organic Embroidery, Meredith Woolnough, ISBN 978-0-7643-5613-1

Library of Congress Control Number: 2022944014

ISBN: 978-0-7643-6423-5

Printed in China

Published by Schiffer Publishing, Ltd.
4880 Lower Valley Road
Atglen, PA 19310
Phone: (610) 593-1777; Fax: (610) 593-2002
Email: Info@schifferbooks.com
Web: www.schifferbooks.com

For our complete selection of fine books on this and related subjects, please visit our website at www.schifferbooks.com. You may also write for a free catalog.

Schiffer Publishing's titles are available at special discounts for bulk purchases for sales promotions or premiums. Special editions, including personalized covers, corporate imprints, and excerpts, can be created in large quantities for special needs. For more information, contact the publisher.

We are always looking for people to write books on new and related subjects. If you have an idea for a book, please contact us at proposals@schifferbooks.com.

Whitework Embroidery
by Seiko Nakano

First designed and published in Japan in 2020 by Graphic-sha Publishing Co., Ltd.
English edition published in the United States of America in 2023 by Schiffer Publishing, Ltd.
English translation rights arranged with Graphic-sha Publishing Co, Ltd., through Japan UNI Agency, Inc., Tokyo

Original edition creative staff

Photos:	Keiichiro Muraguchi
Book design:	Mihoko Amano
Styling:	Akiko Suzuki
Drawing:	Keiko Mishima
Tracing:	Kyodo Kogeisha
Editing:	Ayako Enaka (Graphic-sha Publishing)

Material Cooperation: Echizenya, DMC

English edition creative staff

English translation:	Kevin Wilson
English edition layout:	Shinichi Ishioka
Foreign edition production and management:	Takako Motoki (Graphic-sha Publishing)